The Afterlife of America's War in Vietnam

The Afterlife
of America's War
in Vietnam

*Changing Visions
in Politics and on Screen*

GORDON ARNOLD

McFarland & Company, Inc., Publishers
Jefferson, North Carolina, and London

Library of Congress Cataloguing-in-Publication Data

Arnold, Gordon.
    The afterlife of America's war in Vietnam: changing visions in
politics and on screen / Gordon Arnold.
        p.   cm.
    Includes bibliographical references and index.

    ISBN-13: 978-0-7864-2761-1
    ISBN-10: 0-7864-2761-2 (softcover : 50# alkaline paper) ∞

    1. Vietnam War, 1961–1975—United States.   2. Vietnam War,
1961–1975—Influence.   3. Vietnam War, 1961–1975—Mass media
and the war.   4. United States—Politics and government—20th
century.   5. Mass media—United States—History—20th century.
I. Title.
DS558.A76   2006
959.704'31—dc22   2006018733

British Library cataloguing data are available

On the cover: Lyndon Johnson (center), Dean Rusk (left)
and Secretary of Defense Robert McNamara (right)
Lyndon Baines Johnson Library; background Sylvester Stallone
in *Rambo: First Blood Part II* (Photofest)

Manufactured in the United States of America

McFarland & Company, Inc., Publishers
  Box 611, Jefferson, North Carolina 28640
    www.mcfarlandpub.com

Acknowledgments

Many people were instrumental in the preparation of this book. I particularly thank my students in a course on the Vietnam War that I have taught for many years at Montserrat College of Art. Throughout the years, they have asked many interesting questions and made useful observations. In conversations with them, I have become more fully aware of how each generation shapes its own memories of the past and how it makes its own connections between memories and present experience.

A sabbatical leave provided by Montserrat College of Art was instrumental in bringing this project to a conclusion, and I thank all of the fine people there who made that possible.

I am grateful for the assistance of many librarians and archivists throughout this project. At Montserrat College of Art, Cheri Coe, Library Director, and Lisa Batchelder, Library Associate, were particularly helpful. The reference departments and interlibrary loan staffs at the Wellesley Free Library, Boston Public Library, Northborough Public Library, and Westborough Public Library, all in Massachusetts, also were helpful in tracking down various items. I also received valuable assistance from staff members at the Gerald R. Ford Library, Jimmy Carter Library, Ronald Reagan Library, and George Bush Library.

Additional thanks go to the staff at Photofest in New York City and also to John E. Arnold, for assistance with the photographic illustrations, to Ted I. K. Youn for bringing important facets of the literature on media frames to my attention, and to Montserrat colleagues, especially Robert W. Roy and Ethan Berry, for many useful conversations that have helped my understanding of American cultural life.

Finally, I thank my family, Kimberlee Arnold, Gregory Arnold, and Jeffrey Arnold, who were helpful in many ways and made it possible for me to complete the manuscript.

Table of Contents

Preface

This book aims to provide a brief overview of the Vietnam War's appearance and influence in American politics, motion pictures, and television in the three decades following 1975. Over that time, the topic of the war surfaced regularly and was powerfully portrayed. Yet, the resulting picture was often selective and limited, as politicians, news organizations, film directors, and television producers framed the war for their particular purposes.

Shifting perceptions of the Vietnam War are of more than academic interest. Memory of the war has helped shape many subsequent events. Influence of the conflict can be found in wide-ranging contexts. It can be seen in the Iranian hostage crisis, the Iran-Contra affair, the Persian Gulf War, and the War on Terror, to name only a few. Its influence has been profound.

The memory of the war has also played an important part in shaping America's perception of itself in a changing world. As incarnations of the war have appeared in the political landscape, the conflict was also represented in a multitude of films and television productions. In such productions as *Apocalypse Now, Rambo, China Beach,* and *We Were Soldiers,* screen versions of the war provided audiences with widely varying interpretations of the conflict. Combined with the invocations of the conflict in political contexts, the result was a stew of mixed messages that remain difficult to sort out.

To explore questions relating to this phenomenon, this book aims to re-establish some of the original contexts and chronology in which various manifestations of the war's memory have appeared. Several themes recur repeatedly. We find, for example, the war resurfacing in questions about the plight of Prisoners of War and Missing-in-Action soldiers, about whether the war should have been undertaken at all, about a "Vietnam Syndrome" affecting the use of American military power in the post–Vietnam world, and about the honor and character of those who served and did not serve in the military. On occasion, some of these themes have seemed to run their course, only to reappear in new situations. Indeed, few episodes in American history have inflamed passions and prompted controversy for such a long time.

The book aims to provide a straightforward discussion of these changing perceptions and representations of the war. This volume does not seek to advance a "corrected" version of how the Vietnam War should be remembered, leaving such conclusions for readers to make themselves. Instead, using a conceptual framework rooted more in sociological and media-studies frameworks than most other works on the topic, the book accepts as a starting point that there are different interpretations for the same events. The book's purpose, therefore, is not to judge which uses of the war's memory are correct or incorrect, but to look broadly at these different uses in order to provide readers with ways to think about the topic.

Relationship to Previous Studies

A mammoth outpouring of books address the Vietnam War in its many aspects. Only a relative few of these directly consider the history of the war as an iconic and emblematic force after the fact. Of the books that have looked at how the war has been invoked after its conclusion, few take a broad chronological look at the topic or treat the political, motion picture, and television incarnations with equal emphasis. More often, the best of such works emphasize certain aspects at the expense of others.

Of those books examining the after-effects of the war in the United States, particularly in relation to war-related political issues, books such as Arnold Isaac's *Vietnam Shadows* (1997), Mark Taylor's *The Vietnam War in History, Literature and Film* (2003), and D. Michael Shafer's edited volume *The Legacy: The Vietnam War in the American Imagination* (1990) stand out for their clear and valuable discussions on many aspects of the topic. Each contains cogent discussions of how various aspects of the war have been publicly recollected, and they contain interesting discussions of the war's influence in certain facets of American politics. The war's influence as part of a wider context is considered in Marita Sturken's *Tangled Memories: The Vietnam War, The AIDS Epidemic, and the Politics of Remembering* (1997), which also brought new insights into the ways in which the war's memory has been shaped and transformed. These works tend to selectively focus on either directly war-related issues (e.g., the POW controversy or what has been called the "Vietnam syndrome") or as treatises on the conceptual foundations which structure public recollections of the war. They are less aimed at providing readers with an overview of the broader topic over time.

The war as a theme in screen media has also been the topic of several informative books. Among the most useful of these are Jeremy M. Devine's *Vietnam at 24 Frames a Second* (1995; 1999), Linda Dittmar and Gene Michaud's edited book *From Hanoi to Hollywood* (1990), and Michael Anderegg's edited volume *Inventing Vietnam: The War in Film and Television* (1991). These are also valuable works, which focus on analyses of films and television programs that have Vietnam War themes. Although efforts are made to place discussions in historical context, contemporaneous political developments are not the major foci of these works. And though such works contain insightful analyses of the motion picture and television programs that have been produced about the war, they tend to pay less attention to contexts in which these productions were produced and originally viewed.

In general, works such as these make valuable contributions to our understanding of the continuing place of the Vietnam War in American life. They differ quite significantly in emphasis, conception and intended audience from this book, which is interested in a more explicit exploration of the ebbs and flows of attention to various elements of the Vietnam War in a developing chronology.

Background to the Book

The book is the result of a long process of information-gathering and research. In relation to courses I was teaching, beginning in the early 1990s I started collecting material that related to the portrayal of the war in film and television and in contemporary news accounts. In subsequent years, as world events unfolded and as the influence of the war remained pronounced, an early version of this project began to take shape, suggesting a broad outline that is largely retained in this book. The time that followed involved extensive searches through multiple indexing sources of print- and broadcast media and in gathering news accounts, political statements, media reviews, and other materials that collectively form the record upon which the book is based. By the end of the project, thousands of pages of such material were examined and organized, compared against each other, and against other analyses of the topic as appearing book, journal and journalistic sources.

1

Ambiguous Memories

The Vietnam War ended long ago, but in many ways it lives on. Since the fall of Saigon in 1975, U.S. society has seen numerous changes and unexpected events that, at times, seemed poised to eclipse the memories of what Americans often simply called "Vietnam." But throughout the years, that war has resurfaced in American social and political life, summoned from the past by a wide array of circumstances and complexities of the present. Whether through large scale political events—the Soviet misadventure in Afghanistan, the Gulf War, the 2004 presidential campaign, to name a few— or smaller, more personal and intimate reminders, it is no exaggeration to observe that the Vietnam War has retained a prominent place in the American experience, even as the conflict itself recedes into history.

Decades may have passed, but the war remains an enigmatic and bewildering episode for the American people. Clearly, the passage of time has not generated consensus, and the simple mention of the war stirs strong sentiment. The long shadow cast by those tumultuous events in Southeast Asia evokes differing responses as its memory is continually reconstructed and invoked in a wide variety of differing circumstances. So potent is this memory that political leaders still take great pains to avoid anything that could possibly be labeled "another Vietnam." The war endures as a powerful presence in American culture.

Indeed, the Vietnam War is hard to forget. It was a comprehensively documented period in American history, and many descriptions and images of it remain in wide circulation. As the "first televised war," a vast output of moving images and photographs captured the starkness and ugliness of war in a visceral form. Much of this material, however, suggests a picture that contrasts sharply with the ideals of American society.

What, for example, are the enduring images of the Vietnam War? Asked the same question about the Second World War, many Americans might cite the famous image of the American flag being raised over Iwo Jima or a photograph from the Allied invasion of Normandy. But the memory of the Vietnam War evokes a very different type of imagery: the photograph of a Vietnamese girl running down the street after her clothing was burned off by Napalm; or perhaps the image of a Vietnamese officer holding a gun to the head of a detained Vietnamese citizen; or the haunting picture of a fallen student protester at Kent State University. Such responses point to the anguish that the memory of the Vietnam War still holds for the American public.

The American memory of the Vietnam War is multi-faceted and contested. A war that caused widespread domestic turmoil and discontent as it transpired, it retains a remarkable capacity to raise conflicting and ambiguous feelings. It is clear that the conflict has not lost its power to influence our perceptions, even in a new century.

Unlike many other wars, to Americans it seemed as though the war in Vietnam did not so much reach a final climax as fade away. (It surely did not seem so to the Vietnamese, since the war continued in a brutal fashion after Americans disengaged.) Well before 1975, direct American military involvement ended in the culmination of a slow process that Richard Nixon called the "Vietnamization" of the war. Soon after the end of American fighting in Vietnam, the Watergate scandal and subsequent resignation of the president revealed the disenchantment of a society largely unconvinced that government had the capacity to deal with its problems.

To some extent, the undignified end of the Nixon presidency, and Gerald Ford's later pardon of his disgraced predecessor, redirected some of the conflicting feelings about the Vietnam War away from broad considerations of the war itself and toward the former president. Added to that, the economic picture in the U.S. soured in the years immediately following the war. Gerald Ford urged Americans to wear buttons bearing the word "WIN," but now the war in question was economic, and "WIN" was the call to "Whip Inflation Now." By the last half of the 1970s, Americans often put the war out of their thoughts, as much of the United States turned inward in a process accelerated by a series of national diversions and the rise of what was then called the "me generation."

It was not that memory of the conflict was far from view. As the U.S. struggled to move beyond many of the divisive aspects of the war, reminders were everywhere. For example, the long duration of the war had affected a generation and their families, and tens of thousands of veterans returned home to communities throughout the country. The Vietnam War veterans, however, were not greeted with the heroes' welcome that was bestowed upon G.I.s at the end of World War II a generation earlier. Instead, the public's feelings were mixed. To some Americans, Vietnam veterans were

For American troops, the Vietnam War was complicated by an unfamiliar culture, as well as an unfamiliar and often unrecognizable enemy. In this photograph, American Marines question a captured Vietnamese youth during a combat mission. Photograph: National Archives and Records Administration.

painful reminders of a war that ended badly. The nation struggled to decide how, if at all, it should acknowledge the Vietnam veterans. They were too numerous and visible to completely forget, but they often were ignored in many ways nonetheless.

Decades later, the Vietnam War is still part of the picture in American life, but making sense of it can be difficult. The generation of Americans that fought in and about the Vietnam War has been joined by new generations for whom the Vietnam War has always been history. But since remembrance of America's War in Vietnam has not settled into a dominant, coherent narrative, it remains controversial. There are many questions, but often little agreement about answers. Was the war a matter of honor or of madness? Was the United States defeated, or did it defeat itself? And what did it all mean? The many differences of interpretation about the U.S. experience in Vietnam remain evident, and for the generations who have grown up since 1975, a confusing picture has emerged.

The legacy of the Vietnam War may be ambiguous, but that is not because there has been a lack of attempts to shape the ways in which the war should be remembered over the years. Just as it was the object of ideological debate as it happened, since that time it has often been represented and interpreted through political lenses of the day. Though the world changed, even major, more recent events, such as the collapse of the Soviet empire or the terrorist attacks of September 11, 2001, have not succeeded in pushing the Vietnam War far from public view. It remains a powerful, though disputed, symbolic presence in American consciousness. Unresolved, the picture remains as cloudy as ever.

Wars, like other large-scale public events, demand meaning. This process of finding and attaching meaning to historical events is inherently a political process. Depending upon which meaning is successfully attached to an event, a course of action may appear either justified or unjustified.[1] Throughout the years, political leaders and the mass media have promoted multiple, often conflicting, ways of thinking about the war. Examinations of the Vietnam conflict itself, and of the domestic American controversies about what the Vietnam policy should have been, routinely focus on the very different interpretations of the same actions. This lack of consensus about what meanings to attach to the events in Vietnam lies in striking contrast to the Second World War, about which there has been far less disagreement. Thus, the Vietnam War exhibits the power to continually resurface in the American consciousness—and for some, perhaps, conscience — often exerting influence that has helped shape the contexts of later events.

Some people, to be sure, have steadfastly maintained that the Vietnam War obviously holds certain meanings for the U.S., but others, just as steadfastly, have concluded that it has always meant something else. The war has been a remarkably amorphous, ambiguous presence in the American imagination, and memory of it has been marked by continual transformations. Over the years, there has been little, if any, abatement in level of dispute about how to interpret the conflict. Not only is the picture we have of the Vietnam War different now from when it was happening; it is different now from a few years ago. Moreover, it must be noted that it has never been true that Vietnam meant just one thing in American society, but rather that it has meant very different things to different people.

If the past were important only as purely academic matters, these might be topics of idle speculation for most people. The power of the war's memory is strong, however, and its invocation in numerous political contexts has helped shape and mold perceptions of those contexts and has influenced subsequent events. The Vietnam War's persistent presence in American politics and culture since 1975 therefore suggests that the story of shifting perceptions and representations of the war is important in its own right. One can especially see these changing perceptions and representations in the considerable interplay between mass-media portrayals of the conflict

The heroic image of the American flag being raised over Iwo Jima is one of the most enduring images from World War II. Photograph: National Park Service.

The Vietnam War sparked widespread protests throughout the United States. This photograph shows war protesters in the 1967 March on the Pentagon. Photograph: Lyndon Baines Johnson Library.

and the unfolding political contexts in which the memory of the war has been invoked.

Conceptual framework. In a process at once political and sociological, the American war in Vietnam — like other traumatic public events— has been the subject of multiple interpretations. To think about ways in which the Vietnam War has reappeared over the years for the American public, we look to its appearance in the mass media, which so powerfully shape our awareness of the world beyond our immediate experience. It has long been recognized, for example, that the mass media play a significant role both in focusing attention toward (or sometimes away from) issues and in presenting interpretative contexts about these issues.[2]

Embedded in the ways that issues are presented — in the language, imagery and contexts used — are assumptions about society's values and about social and political life generally.[3] These assumptions find expression in media accounts and representations of issues and of people associated with issues, in which some people are cast as heroes, others as villains.[4] Though often such portrayals radically oversimplify the complexities of persons and events, the simplifying process serves to make such complexities more comprehensible by sifting out many of the ambiguities and indeterminacies that more accurately reflect real people and real issues and events.

If we look at a number of media accounts of persons, issues and events, we begin to see that the ways in which these are "framed" by the media for public consumption.[5] In the general sense, such a frame can be understood as a cognitive mechanism that enables "its user to locate, perceive, identify, and label a seemingly infinite number of concrete occurrences defined in its terms."[6] Thus, a frame is a "central organizing idea or story line that provides meaning to an unfolding strip of events, weaving a connection among them."[7] In this way, frames help provide meaning and political order in a world of confusing complexity.[8]

These ideas are reminiscent of observations made by scholars of mass media, journalism and public opinion. In a discussion about media accounts of political events, for example, J.R. Zeller makes the important observation that:

> political information carried in elite discourse is ... never pure. It is, rather, an attempt by various types of elite actors to create a depiction of reality that is sufficiently simple and vivid that ordinary people can grasp it....[9]

Thus, media frames help "subjects to determine the personal relevance of the issue, to provide linkage among issues, and to formulate arguments from which opinions could be drawn."[10]

In the modern, media-saturated environment, political messages emanate from a wide variety of sources. Political elites have access to a stage unlike that of ordinary citizens, but that stage is shared with others and mediated by the vast array of electronic and print media, only some of which are traditional news organizations. In this realm, news organizations have no particular monopoly in conveying messages that have the result of influencing our perceptions of political and social life and the historical past. Frequently, news media organizations are embedded in corporate settings that are shared with entertainment media. (Consider, for example, the cases of Time Warner or the News Corporation.) When reviewing the ways in which events such as the Vietnam War have appeared in the media, there is a need to expand beyond the boundaries of traditional news accounts to consider those other media messages, which compete with, and arguably subsume on occasion, those produced by the news media.[11]

Indeed, the way the Vietnam War has persisted in the public imagination is not quite like that of other social or political issues in our society. Unlike other social controversies (the issue of abortion, for example) in which the issue remains in the here and now, the Vietnam episode in American life would seem to have been concluded in the mid–1970s. Yet, despite the many years since American disengagement in that conflict, the controversy continues, retaining a powerful place in the American imagination and influencing later actions. How is this so?

As we see in the following chapters, once the war was over, the contest over meaning was reoriented. No longer was it necessary to persuade the American public to accept one interpretation over another for the purposes of justifying or condemning U.S. foreign policy in Vietnam. Americans were out, and Saigon would soon become Ho Chi Minh City. Little or nothing of the present remained to be justified.

It might seem, then, that the contest over the meaning of the Vietnam War entered a phase that was strictly about arriving at that consensus of meaning that had been so elusive during the war. This would seem to imply that the contest over meaning was backwards looking, about clarifying how the Vietnam War would enter into the American Saga. This, indeed, is part of the story. Such consensus never fully developed, however, and the Vietnam War has repeatedly been inserted into the political world that followed it.

The enduring place that the Vietnam War held in the American public consciousness for four decades is about more than that, however. Rather than an "academic" discussion about events in the rear view mirror, the changing interpretations and reconstructed memories of the Vietnam War themselves have served multiple purposes. The Vietnam War has been used to bolster arguments for and arguments against a variety of subsequent policies. The reconstructed memories of the war have been attached to an array of events, policies and controversies, some of which would seem, on the surface, to have little to do with what happened in Southeast Asia more than a generation ago.

This book aims to develop an understanding of the reappearances of the Vietnam War in American public life and the shifting shape and perceptions about the war in these reappearances. Special attention is directed to the contexts and uses of the Vietnam War as a recurring subject and to the conceptualizations and re-conceptualizations inherent as the subject has resurfaced. Following the waxing and waning of public attention to the Vietnam War in the years that followed it, we see how this conflict has been used as a potent, though not agreed upon, symbol that has been repeatedly re-contextualized as it has been attached to a host of subsequent events and conditions.

Method of the Book

To develop an understanding of the reincarnations, of the shifting shape and perceptions about the war, then, we especially look to the contexts and uses of the Vietnam War as a recurring subject and to the differing conceptualizations and re-conceptualizations of it. Interrelated strands of public discourse and media attention can help us develop a portrait of the Vietnam War's afterlife in the social and political world. These strands are: first, the interrelated records of rhetoric from political elites and the news media; and second, the record of entertainment-oriented mass media, with emphasis on film and television.

Political news. We look to the news portrayals of the Vietnam War in American politics since 1975 in order to consider the specific ways that the war has been put to use in political rhetoric of American leaders. What circumstances cause political leaders to raise the memory of Vietnam? What symbols have been used to epitomize the Vietnam War in these after-the-fact discussions? How has the rhetoric of political elites reflected perceptions about both that conflict and America's "Vietnam years"?

The declarations of political elites, however, are embedded within the reporting and dissemination of the news media. Few citizens hear more than a few, if any, unmediated political messages from the nation's leaders. The politicians may choose what to say, but the media choose which messages will receive attention. The widespread use of "sound bites," and the written equivalents of such, demonstrates that the news media have a wide latitude in selecting how much of such utterances to report and which aspects will be disseminated. Thus, an investigation of the rhetoric of political elites is inevitably intertwined with journalistic accounts of it.

Occasionally, however, the news media sometimes have raised the subject of the Vietnam War on their own, without prodding by political elites. The war is a powerful, pre-existing storyline, and certain occurrences—such as anniversaries, international developments, and persons with war-related experiences coming to public attention—lead the news media to revisit the subject. In addition, over the years new revelations about certain aspects of the war have led print- and broadcast journalists to refocus on it.

Thus, when looking at news media accounts, attention is called to occurrences and contexts that have employed the memory of the war. In print and in broadcast and other electronic media, the subject of the Vietnam War has arisen on many occasions and in many contexts. But what were those contexts? How has news media evocation of the Vietnam War unfolded over the years? And how has the war been represented in various usages?

To address these questions, one can look to the record of print and broadcast media. In preparing this study, a wide range of such sources was consulted. Yet, despite the enormous number of broadcast and print news media, a much smaller number of these usually play a dominant role in set-ting the news agenda that Americans encounter. Newspapers such as *The New York Times* and *The Washington Post* call attention to certain events and themes for readers throughout the country, often influencing what sto-ries and issues other news media choose to follow. Similarly, the major American weekly news magazines, *Time, Newsweek,* and *U.S. News and World Report* play a significant part in shaping perceptions about what con-stitutes the important news stories of the day.

In broadcast media, it has been the network news organizations, joined in more recent decades by cable news operations, which play a major role in directing attention to specific issues and events. Until the 1980s, the tra-ditional broadcast networks—CBS, NBC and ABC—were enormously influential. Later, they shared their influence with the likes of cable net-works, especially CNN and subsequently by FOX News.

Although these major, nationally influential news outlets do not com-pletely establish the news agenda, their influence has been disproportion-ately large for their small numbers. Accordingly, although sources extending well beyond these sources were examined for this study, these dominant news outlets receive major attention in the following chapters.

Screen entertainment media. The other central strand we follow lies in the ways that the Vietnam War has been evoked and represented in screen entertainment mass-media. Though other aspects of the entertainment media have played a part, these have not generally been successful in reach-ing as wide an audience as the arguably more passive screen media. Indeed, of all media, film and television have had the most substantial penetration into American culture in the period following the Vietnam War. Possessing entertainment, commercial and sometimes artistic aims, such productions can vividly call to mind certain conceptualizations of past events. Some aspects of history are emphasized, others forgotten. Sometimes their fictional accounts are taken as a type of truth-telling, causing an intensely emotional response to traumatic events of the past. At other times, creative license is taken so far as to almost completely distort what is known of the past, not so much altering it as manufacturing in its place a fictional substitute.[12]

The emotional power of screen media can be intense. Highly fiction-alized interpretations of historical events can provoke an emotional response that is as strong, or stronger, than a more historically accurate portrayal. Sometimes, viewers may prefer a film known to be a highly fictionalized account to a more historically accurate one. Considering such issues, what shape have those portrayals of the Vietnam War taken? How have they influenced the ongoing process of constructing and reconstruct-ing our shared memories of that time?

In screen entertainment productions, especially film, there has been an enormous output of works dealing in some way with the Vietnam War theme. This book does not aim to exhaustively list and discuss each of these works, nor does it attempt to provide a full-blown critical analysis of the works that are discussed. Instead, the purposes here are more specific: to identify those productions that have been most widely disseminated and influential in American culture; and to briefly examine how certain themes in the various productions have related to ongoing reconstruction of the Vietnam War in American memory.

Some of the works discussed have been widely admired by film critics; others have been dismissed, or sometimes even ridiculed. There is no clear relationship between the aesthetic quality of a screen production and its social influence. Indeed, some of the most popular productions, which might even cause reviewers to cringe, have exerted a powerful influence in mass culture. For the purposes of this book, then, it is the productions that receive the most attention and that have made a significant impact with the public that are examined for their important part in establishing or perpetuating certain themes about the war.

Weaving news and entertainment representations together. When these strands are combined, a complicated picture emerges, prompting reflections about how news representations of the war and screen entertainment versions of it have intersected. It soon becomes evident that symbol and myth can become enmeshed in public representations of the historical past.

In the case of the Vietnam War, different evocations of the war have led to the choice of very different symbols to represent it. The selectivity of these choices emphasizes some aspects of the war and minimizes attention to others. These often have glossed over the very ambiguities and problems that characterized America's experience of the war as it happened. And so in seeking to understand the various ways in which the Vietnam War has been represented and remembered, it is useful not only to attend to the symbols chosen, but also to those not chosen. Sometimes, certain aspects of the war that are regarded as troubling do not explicitly appear in reconstructed versions of the war. At other times, such aspects receive almost all of the attention. Assumptions about race, class, gender and culture, moreover, can be found embedded within the simplified words and imagery evoked to represent the war since 1975 by political leaders and by news and entertainment media.

Chronological Signposts

The following chapters explore the ways in which the Vietnam War has been remembered and invoked in American screen media and politics since the conflict's final months. Before looking at this story in more detail, however, it is useful to consider some of the most important themes and events that have developed in this period. These can be found in a preliminary picture of the overall chronology of events, as appears below.

Turning away in the late 1970s. In the next chapter, we begin with the time of American disengagement in Vietnam and the fall of Saigon and with the years that immediately followed. Interestingly, by 1973, much of American society already regarded Vietnam as past history, even though the war was not over. The period between U.S. withdrawal and the defeat of the Republic of Vietnam produced a number of events that accelerated American psychological disengagement with a war that had been its fixation for a decade. Gerald Ford became the only person ever to assume the presidency who had not been elected president or vice president, and he overtly attempted to prod Americans beyond the internal conflicts of the preceding years. Ford took at least two major actions in that direction: he pardoned his predecessor, Richard Nixon, and he granted amnesty (with some conditions) to men who had evaded the draft or deserted the military. Such actions were met with both satisfaction and outrage, but they were clear evidence of a society struggling to free itself at last from the "quagmire" of Vietnam, as it was so often called.

Indeed, in the immediate aftermath of the war, American society quickly turned its attention away from Southeast Asia, almost as if in a communal state of denial. The long years of pain and conflict had worn down the nation, and there was no obvious "victory" to help ease the pain. Tens of thousands of deaths and war-related injuries, fractured families on opposing sides of the Vietnam issue, and enormous strains on existing social and political institutions had taken a heavy toll on the willingness of Americans to retain a focus on a faraway place in Southeast Asia that it understood little better after the war than before it.[13] The rise of the so-called "me generation" was perhaps only one reaction to the trauma only recently ended.

The Vietnam War was still recent and clearly not forgotten, but it was an episode lurking in the background, often avoided as an explicit topic. It was, as the popular saying goes, the elephant in the living room that everyone sees but no one talks about. Surely politicians, commentators and the mass media were reluctant to push the subject too much to the foreground and were unsure about what to say about it anyway.

Perhaps symbolic of the lingering confusion was the way in which Francis Ford Coppola's epic film, *Apocalypse Now*, was greeted in 1979. His surreal, in some ways almost lyrical, depiction of the Vietnam War offended many. Pro-war and anti-war viewers alike failed to see their perceptions of

Vietnam reflected in the film. In some ways that film was like the Vietnam War itself, not familiar, not fitting the grand narrative patterns that were expected and desired. In any case, the appearance of motion pictures with Vietnam War themes—along with literary works on the same topic, such as Tim O'Brien's *Going After Cacciato* and James Webb's *Field of Fire*—marked a tentative new beginning and a willingness to re-engage public conversation about the war that many felt had shaped a generation, for good or bad.

Vietnam memories and "morning in America." In chapter three, we examine how the Vietnam War was presented and discussed in the early 1980s and era of neo-conservatism. The election of Ronald Reagan in 1980 was symbolic of a turning point in American social and political life.

At the dawn of Reagan's "morning in America," conservatives looked out at recent events in the U.S. and used their newly reclaimed power to present their views on the state of the nation. From the bully-pulpit of the presidency, Ronald Reagan was not embarrassed to voice his opinions about what the Vietnam War meant in his vision of America. Nor was he reluctant to argue that if the war had ended badly, this was because the American military had its hands tied behind its back during the conflict. Indeed, the legacy of the Vietnam War was evident throughout the Reagan years, as American armed forces were revitalized and as the United States confronted the U.S.S.R., which became weakened by it own "Vietnam," as commentators labeled the Soviet Union's disastrous exploits in Afghanistan. Closer to home in the Western Hemisphere, U.S. policies in Central America—particularly regarding Nicaragua and El Salvador—came to evoke the legacy of the Vietnam War despite the administration's efforts to the contrary.

In the early 1980s, moreover, Americans came to increasingly reconsider the matter of American military personnel who had served in Vietnam. The issue of recovering soldiers missing in action (MIA) and continuing legal actions about Agent Orange lawsuits meant that the memory of Vietnam was never far from newspapers, news magazines and television news. The 1982 unveiling of the Maya Lin's Vietnam War Memorial further reinvigorated public discussion. As Lin stated, "Many earlier war memorials were propagandized statements about the victor, the issues, the politics, and not about the people who served and died. I felt a memorial should be honest about the reality of war and be for the people who gave their lives."[14] Lively debate followed. Though it was soon regarded as a deeply moving remembrance, at first appearance the stark, non-literal simplicity of the memorial—markedly different from the traditional design of public monuments to which the public was accustomed—caused controversy, heightening public memory.

Another high-profile treatment of the Vietnam experience, again sparking disagreement, was the 1983 appearance of the public television series, *Vietnam: A Television History*. As with the Memorial, very differing reactions greeted this widely discussed television event. It was seen as a fair-minded by some and as left-wing propaganda by others. The series, which would be used in class rooms for decades, was successful in reaching a civic-minded class of people who, correctly or not, looked to "educational" television for elucidation of world affairs. It provided its own interpretation of the events, largely through a lens consistent with that of writer Stanley Karnow, who was widely admired as an expert on the war. Still, *Vietnam: A Television History* provoked numerous media responses.[15] The group Accuracy in Media (AIM), known for its blistering critiques of what its members viewed as the very liberal media, took the lead in denouncing the series.

Reagan, Rambo and Vietnam. By the campaign season of what would be Reagan's second term, public awareness of the Vietnam War was further fueled by an increasing number of motion pictures and television shows dealing with the Vietnam War in various aspects, as is shown in chapter four. The popular 1984 film *Missing in Action,* for example, played upon the public's continued interest in the MIA issue and suspicions that official declarations about the status of MIA soldiers might not tell the whole story. The most attention-getting of the era's filmic treatments of the Vietnam issue, however, were the Rambo films, featuring the popular action-film star, Sylvester Stallone. In the second of the Rambo films, released in 1985, Stallone's Rambo character returns to Vietnam, a lone American soldier whose mission can be seen as a metaphorical attempt to avenge the indignities of the historical American experience in Vietnam.[16] Symbolic of the transformation in the ways in which the Vietnam War would be recalled, the Rambo films, like others of its time, were described as "films that endorsed the myth of political betrayal in Vietnam."[17] (Interestingly, at about this same time former president Richard Nixon issued his book *No More Vietnams*,[18] which also contributed to the public re-envisioning of the war, in this case by one of its protagonists.)

Added to such films, television viewers received steady exposure to Vietnam veterans, whose image was now reconstituted in a modern, independently heroic mold. Previously, these military veterans had been relegated to the sidelines or else depicted in unflattering ways. In the 1980s, the television media often presented Vietnam veterans as rugged heroes, capable of overcoming the burdens that their Vietnam experiences had heaped upon them.

Ironically, Reagan's second term was threatened by the Iran-Contra scandal, a political crisis resulting in the Congressional hearings that attracted more attention than any such hearings since the Watergate hearings of more than a decade earlier. Again, the specter of Vietnam loomed in the background, as the public came to see the convoluted machinations that had ultimately led to clandestine U. S. involvement in another guerilla war in a place that seemed out-of-the-way to most Americans. In the chapter we also explore, then, how the nation's still painful memories of Vietnam influenced the ways in which the Iran-Contra episode was both reported to and interpreted by the American public.

Vietnam in the era of the Gulf War. In many respects, the Reagan legacy continued into the presidency of George H. W. Bush. The sting and immediacy of the Vietnam War, still felt when Ronald Reagan first assumed office, had diminished. Now, other world events demanded public attention, the most notable of which was the final collapse of the Soviet Union, a development popularly attributed to Reagan's years of struggle and personal diplomacy with what he called the "evil empire." President Bush oversaw what was perceived as a dramatic realignment in the world of international affairs. In this "new world order," as he called it, it may have seemed as if Vietnam was a relic of the past, chained in public memory as it was to a clearly bygone era.

Yet, as chapter five shows, the Persian Gulf War of 1991 immediately brought the memory of Vietnam back to public attention. Although the U.S. had engaged in several small "wars," could it now show that it was capable of overcoming the Vietnam legacy, finally demonstrating to the world and itself that the "Vietnam syndrome," as Reagan had phrased it earlier, was now indeed dead? Moreover, in the time between the Vietnam War and Persian Gulf War, both the news media and their audiences had developed heightened levels of sophistication in making sense of news reporting. The news media, whose reputation had declined since the public confidence it enjoyed during the Watergate era, had the twin difficulties of garnering audience attention and of reporting the war in the new contexts that had emerged in the post–Reagan era. The Pentagon had long ago learned its lesson, and now media access to the battlefields was tightly controlled. In addition, the Pentagon had devised military tactics to fight the war, as much as possible, from arm's length. Still, the resulting comparisons to the Vietnam-era may have been inevitable.

There is no doubt that the meaning that was taken from the war in the Persian Gulf was highly dependent upon the historical backdrop that the Vietnam War provided. The use of Vietnam as part of a prelude to then-current events can be found, for example, in President Bush's 1992 State of the Union Address, in which he declared:

> The cold war didn't end; it was won. And I think of those who won it, in places like Korea and Vietnam. And some of them didn't come back. Back then, they were heroes, but this year they were victors.... The world saw not only their special valor but their special style, their rambunctious, optimistic bravery, their do-or-die unity....[19]

Another phenomenon of the 1990s had a strong connection to the Americans' reconstructed memories of the Vietnam War and its surrounding circumstances. The increased cynicism of that era, which had been growing for some time, found popular expression in a fondness for conspiracy theories about a wide range of topics. Surely, the assassination of John Kennedy had provoked such ideas among some people decades earlier, but by the 1990s these were increasingly mainstream ideas. Reinforced by regular appearance in fictional media, this perspective affected political discourse as well as private opinion.

Typifying this response was the 1991 film *JFK*, directed by Oliver Stone, a Vietnam veteran who had become a powerful figure in Hollywood. In that pseudo-historical film, a supposed rift in the government and military had motivated the assassination and led to a massive cover-up. Preposterous as the claims may have seemed, and despite the lack of any serious corroborating evidence to support the general thesis, many viewers seemed to accept the premises of the film as essentially factual. A published account cites the example of one law school graduate who stated "Of course that's what happened. We knew that. Why is this such big news?"[20]

The Vietnam War subject continued to appear throughout the popular media. Many of these occurrences were perceived as more reasonable, or at least less contentious, than the approach taken by Stone. One can look to the example Tim O'Brien's whose novel *The Things They Carried* was highly regarded and seen as a moving response to the war some 25 years after it had ended. Also, several new series, including *China Beach*, brought Vietnam back to prime-time network television. *China Beach* notably focused on the experience of American women in the war zone. Seldom had the fact that numerous women had served in Vietnam been acknowledged in any meaningful way at all. Here, viewers they were seen on the center stage, although it is questionable how far their portrayal strayed from the presuppositions and conventions that often characterized the portrayal of women in televised series.

The Clinton years. As discussed in chapter six, during the presidency of Bill Clinton, the United States entered a phase of transition in which the so-called "Vietnam generation" marched to the center of the political stage. As suggested above, the barrage of films, televisions shows, books, and video games of the preceding years had worked to influence the perceptions of the Vietnam War. Moreover, by this time a post–Vietnam generation had itself come of age in America, not touched by the war because of its immediacy to them (since the events were over before many of them were born), but still curious, and sometimes perplexed, by the effect that the war had on their parents' lives. For this new generation, the seeming oddity of grandfathers recounting their experiences in World War II contrasted quite vividly with the reluctance, sometimes refusal, of fathers and uncles to discuss their wartime experience in Vietnam at all. Indeed, the fiftieth anniversary in 1995 of the end of the Second World War and the subsequent valorization of the young Americans of that era as "the greatest generation," as a popular book phrased it, carried the not-so-subtle message that the Vietnam generation had fallen far short of the mark, failing to meet the standards passed down to them.

As early as the campaign of 1992, the Vietnam-era military service records of the candidates were matters of media interest. The incumbent, George Bush, could quite accurately point to his record as a combat pilot during World War II, even if the Vietnam-era record of his running mate, Dan Quayle, seemed more questionable to those who put weight in such matters. For his part, Bill Clinton had spent the Vietnam years in college, and though his running mate, Al Gore, was a Vietnam veteran, somehow his service as a military journalist, though honorable, was not quite the stuff of military heroes. (The contrast between the older and newer generations remained pronounced in the 1996 campaign, in which one of the last of the World War II-generation leaders with a distinguished war record, Kansas Senator Bob Dole, challenged Clinton for the White House.)

Clinton, as his wife records, "carried with him into the White House the unresolved feelings of our country about that [Vietnam] war."[21] Still, the first Clinton term saw a number of developments between the U.S. and its old enemy, Vietnam, which by this time was one of the few remaining communist states. The United States trade embargo against Vietnam ended in 1994, and the following year, against the wishes of many conservatives, the U.S. finally normalized relations with Vietnam and extended full diplomatic recognition. Later, despite the numerous distractions and atmosphere of scandal that hampered Clinton's second term, his administration continued working on this issue, and by 2000 the U.S. and Vietnam had reached a trade agreement. Finally, as the end of his presidency drew near, Bill Clinton became the first president to set foot in Vietnam since the end of the war, with the hope of bringing a measure of closure to the complex, strained relationship that the two countries had endured since mid-century.

Of the various world crises coinciding with the Clinton presidency, the American experience in Vietnam still influenced the contexts in which the startling violence in places such as Kosovo and Somalia would be interpreted.

The mayhem in the disintegrating Yugoslavia provoked mixed feelings in Americans, who were unsure of the extent to which the U.S. should commit military force, if at all, though NATO eventually took the lead in that conflict. Elsewhere, the televised pictures of a slain U.S. soldier being dragged through the streets in Somalia provoked feelings of outrage and humiliation in a way perhaps unseen, at least to this extent, since the Vietnam era.

Legacies of the Vietnam War, then, continued to play a prominent role in American civic life during much of the 1990s. One aspect of this was the twentieth anniversary of the end of the fighting in Vietnam, which prompted the media to take another look at the war. At about the same time, books such as Robert McNamara's *In Retrospect: The Tragedy and Lessons of Vietnam* were released, which further provoked debate. Overall, the escalating polarization in American politics during that era created a milieu in which there was little hope that a consensus about the American experience in Vietnam would emerge.

Remembering Vietnam in the new millennium. During the relative calm that characterized the early months of George W. Bush's first term as president, a Vietnam War-related controversy involving former Senator Bob Kerrey abruptly surfaced. Allegations that he had been involved in misdeeds during the war briefly reignited old, conflicted feelings. The revelations brought renewed interest to unpleasant aspects of the war, prompting a writer for *Time* magazine to observe that "the ambiguity of his experience reminds us that good men did terrible things in Vietnam, making us examine what it means when honor is peeled away from war."[22] Indeed, like other topics in American politics, the views and recollections of the Vietnam War in many ways hardened during the 1990s, as it was reinterpreted though the new ideological contexts of that time.

To Americans, the world seemed to change on September 11, 2001. In the period following the terror attacks of that date, however, the memory of the Vietnam War returned forcefully to center stage. Chapter seven examines the re-emergence of the Vietnam War in political life in light of the post–September 11 world.

It would have been possible, in theory, to interpret the 2001 terrorist attacks either as heinous international crimes or as acts of war. Thus, the American response could have been molded by the logic of international criminal justice or the logic of war. To many Americans— and, most importantly, to George W. Bush — there was little question that these were acts of war. The subsequent War on Terrorism was described as a wholly new and different kind of war than the more traditional wars between states. Nonetheless, as it progressed, facets of it would eventually draw comparisons to conflicts of the past, most notably Vietnam.

Particular attention is directed toward two general areas in this regard. First is the matter of comparisons between the Iraqi phase of the War on Terror and the Vietnam War. These were prominently raised during 2004 and extensively appeared in news media. Second is the question of the Vietnam-era military service records of George W. Bush and his Democratic challenger, the Vietnam combat veteran John Kerry, also a topic sparking great media interest. Both types of questions relied upon certain assumptions about the Vietnam War that had developed over time and the many different ways in which Vietnam had been framed in public discourse over the decades. The interests of the electronic and print media were activated not only by the vividness of the comparisons to Vietnam War-era politics, but also by the looming presidential election, the first since the tragic events of September 11, 2001.

Conclusions. The book's last chapter looks back at major themes from the previous chapters' chronological analysis. In considering the mediated memories and understandings of the Vietnam War as a major public controversy, it is revealed that although the war has remained a powerful symbol in American political and cultural life, invocations of it have been incomplete. Though definitive answers lie beyond the limits of this book, an examination of media constructions and public understandings of the Vietnam War, as one historical episode, provide interesting clues about where we might look in the future, as more recent national crises take their places in the pantheon of American memory.

2

The Other End
of the Tunnel

In January 1973, in the midst of what seemed to be the last throes of the Vietnam War, the nation mourned the death of Lyndon Johnson. He had departed from the White House under the cloud of the war four years earlier, passing responsibility for it to Richard Nixon. Yet, Johnson had been one of the war's chief protagonists, and his death seemed to be a milestone as the nation neared the end of one of the longest and most painful episodes in its history.

By this time, American troops were already disengaging from the conflict in the slow process that the Nixon administration called the Vietnamization of the war. Only days after Johnson's death, the U.S. and Democratic Republic of Vietnam (North Vietnam) finally signed peace accords in Paris, effectively ending American involvement in combat. (Some American troops remained with a mission to provide U.S. installations with protection.) The peace agreement was negotiated by the U.S., which was looking for something it could regard as an honorable exit, and by the communist regime in North Vietnam. Notably absent in the negotiating was South Vietnam. That country's president, Nguyen Van Thieu, objected to the deal, but the Nixon administration pressured him to accept it. He had little choice but to acquiesce, since the U.S. was determined to bring its participation to an end.

Well before 1973, the American public had tired of the long war. Now, with the cessation of active U.S. military participation in it, the administration terminated the military draft. This ended a significant source of divisiveness in American society. Although underlying disagreements about the war were not resolved by the end of American combat participation, it seemed that much of American society was ready to leave the Vietnam War in the past. In the next two years, a number of events sometimes accelerated

Lyndon Johnson (center) was determined not to be the first United States president to lose a war. As victory remained elusive and protests increased, the war came to consume his presidency. Shown with Johnson in this 1968 photograph are Secretary of State Dean Rusk (left) and Secretary of Defense Robert McNamara (right). Photograph: Lyndon Baines Johnson Library.

American psychological disengagement with a war that had been its fixation for a decade. The final end of the war two years later was the denouement that American society accepted, even if it left few wholly satisfied.

Soon after the peace accords were announced, American soldiers in Vietnam (with the few exceptions noted) were withdrawn, but it was not then clear what ultimately would happen to South Vietnam. Henry Kissinger believed that the accord's agreement-in-principle to a reunified Vietnam indicated that it would only be a matter of time until the demise of South Vietnam. Other American officials hoped that somehow such an outcome would at least be delayed.

The conditions of the peace accords left the Republic of South Vietnam mostly on its own. South Vietnamese leaders felt abandoned by the U.S., but they struggled to endure. As would soon become clear, however, warfare in Vietnam was temporarily suspended, not over. Fighting would resume without the Americans, and it would continue to inflict pain on the Vietnamese people for two more years, until April 1975, when the Saigon government would finally succumb.

Along with the withdrawal of American forces, Hanoi released the American soldiers who were being held as prisoners of war (POW). This, at least, was the official description of North Vietnam's actions, and it was greeted in the United States with a strong sense of relief. As later became clear, however, even this development was not so clear cut. In the years that followed, the assertion that North Vietnam had not returned all of the POWs would emerge as a powerful part of the war's lasting memory in the United States.

Still, at the time the return of the POWs seemed to imply that the war, at last, was ending for Americans. The television networks reinforced this interpretation, paying little attention to the fact that the situation between North and South Vietnam was not yet resolved. Thus, on April 29, 1973, American networks broadcast special news programs with titles such as "Vietnam: A War That is Finished," "7382 Days in Vietnam," and "Vietnam: Lessons Learned, Prices Paid."[1]

The war had been a highly complex episode that was often difficult to understand, and the period between the departure of American troops and the end of the Saigon government presented additional ambiguities. Having embraced the war as an essentially American affair, many Americans seemed content to think that the war was finished when U.S. military personnel departed Vietnam in the spring of 1973. In the U.S., there had been little enthusiasm for more war for some time, even among those who originally had wished to achieve a traditional military victory. The problem had been how to end the war and at what costs. Finally, it seemed that the United States had made its way, literally and metaphorically, out of the forest.

As attention drifted and the topic of the war seemed to disappear from the public arena, the nation began to feel after-effects of the war. The influence of the war could be seen throughout society, in the lives of the many American veterans of the war, in the sagging national economy, and in a widespread — though not universal — mistrust of government. These and other themes, which in future years would have an important effect on the interpretation of the war, began to take shape. In the nebulous period of the war's last months, then, changing perceptions and priorities asserted themselves as the process of reconstructing the war in political and media culture got underway.

Over the years of U.S. participation in the war, the American people had witnessed a dizzying array of societal and political changes. The Vietnam War, and the strong emotional responses to it, had played a part in these changes, but the effects of change extended beyond the war issue. The Civil Rights and women's movements, for example, had transformed many conventions in American life. As a result, the American society that witnessed

After succeeding Lyndon Johnson in the White House, Richard Nixon also found the war to be a difficult issue. This photograph shows Nixon during an April 1970 press conference on Vietnam and Cambodia. Photograph: National Archives and Records Administration.

the end game of the Vietnam War had many differences from the society that had originally embarked upon war in Southeast Asia years earlier. One effect that had emerged by the mid–1970s was a sense of cynicism that had seeped into many aspects of American life.

Watergate takes center stage. As American participation in the war was ending, the Watergate scandal emerged as a major national spectacle. Already, American attention to events in Southeast Asia was drifting, and the new scandal helped to further redirect the nation's attention. Even during the height of the war, there had been little that would compare with the intense media gaze precipitated by the Watergate affair. It is difficult to understand the immediate American response to its diminishing role in Vietnam without considering the pervasive impact of that scandal, in which Nixon's presidential legacy, the end of the war, and attitudes about American politics became intertwined.

The implication of the president in the politically motivated Watergate burglary, and its subsequent cover-up, profoundly rocked the nation. Mistrust in government and other major institutions in American society had been building for some time. The Vietnam War had played a major role in this, of course, as there were lingering suspicions about many aspects of the war.[2] With the Watergate scandal, the already-shaky confidence in government eroded still further.

In May of 1973, just as the American military presence in Vietnam ended, a Senate committee convened to investigate Watergate and Nixon's possible involvement in it. The television networks sensed an importance to these proceedings and provided extensive live coverage of the hearings.

In an era when the three television networks, NBC, CBS, and ABC, dominated television with little competition (other than from a relatively few number of public and independent broadcast stations), this coverage had a large impact on the viewing public. The testimony of key administration officials slowly revealed an increasingly incriminating picture of the president and his inner circle. As one writer noted, the hearings soon approached the level of a "bigger media circus than anyone imagined."[3] The intensity of the coverage in both broadcast and print news media was remarkable, focusing public attention on this single topic in a way that was quite unusual. In this context, the conflict in Vietnam largely fell from prominence.

Well into the autumn of 1973, media attention to and public awareness of Watergate showed few signs of abating. The firing of special prosecutor Archibald Cox at Nixon's behest, in October 1973, was regarded with special importance. This episode was soon widely known as the "Saturday Night Massacre." (In light of the fact that the incident often called the My Lai Massacre was still strongly embedded in public memory, the use of the "massacre" term was an interesting rhetorical twist.) As support for the president continued to weaken, calls for Nixon's resignation grew.[4]

Throughout this time, Nixon's attempts to divert the trajectory of the Watergate scandal away from his administration were repeatedly thwarted. Weeks of turmoil and uncertainty turned into months. Nixon's approval ratings plummeted. In Washington, Nixon became increasingly isolated, which was a situation that the glare of the news media made very apparent. Whether seeing accumulating evidence of misdeeds or simply not wishing to be tainted by association, many of Nixon's former supporters abandoned him. As Senator James Buckley observed, the Watergate affair reached a level that amounted to "a crisis of the regime."[5]

The magnitude of Watergate in American political culture at this time can hardly be under-estimated, but prior Vietnam War controversies (such as the incursion into Cambodia) had helped create the environment that in which Watergate was reported and interpreted. Indeed, the perceived animosity between the Nixon administration and the news media had incubated almost since the month Nixon took office. The complexities of the administration's

Vietnam policies provided many opportunities for the press and the president to stare warily at one another.

Now, the Watergate episode grew to epic proportions, undermining public confidence in government to historic levels. The focus on Watergate became almost a national obsession, often eclipsing other events of the day. In this climate, the slowly ending war in Vietnam received much less public notice than might otherwise have been the case. Indeed, the intensity of the spotlight on Watergate left little room for any widespread rumination of the Vietnam War in the public sphere.

Articles of impeachment went to a vote in the summer of 1974. Although two of these articles, relating to the secret bombing of Cambodia, were defeated, other articles were approved by a wide margin. These cited obstruction of justice, abusing powers of office and violating Congressional subpoenas. Finally, Nixon concluded that a subsequent impeachment trial might have an unpleasant outcome for him. Soon after, therefore, in August 1974, he resigned the presidency and left the White House in disgrace. After this traumatic series of events, the public and the media seemed to have less appetite for focusing attention on the past anguish of the Vietnam War, which had been overshadowed, at least for the moment, by Watergate.

Since the elected vice president, Spiro T. Agnew, had already been forced from office in another scandal involving bribery charges, the office of the president then fell to Gerald R. Ford, who had been appointed as Agnew's successor. As the nation's first president who was not elected as either president or vice-president, Ford had no mandate of his own. He took office in circumstances that seemed to accord him less stature than elected presidents enjoyed.

Upon assuming the presidency, Ford nonetheless recognized that the Watergate scandal (which he called "our long national nightmare") and the Vietnam War were still deeply felt wounds in the national consciousness, and he set out to do something about it.[6] Ford's desire to move the nation beyond these controversies motivated him to make two important decisions. At first, anyway, these decisions were not completely successful in generating the intended healing effects. Instead, they created new disagreements.

Nixon pardon. First, in response to Watergate, Ford granted a presidential pardon to Nixon for any crimes or misdemeanors that Nixon may have committed while in office. In his autobiography, Ford recalled an aide's characterization of Watergate as a national addiction that would "go on and on unless someone says that we, as a nation, must go cold turkey."[7] Regardless of the motivation, the decision was greeted coldly by much of the country.

The storm of controversy surrounding the Nixon pardon did not help Ford's political standing. Among other things, his politically weakened state limited his ability to successfully pursue policies for the benefit of South Vietnam, which was continuing its struggle with the North Vietnamese and which the administration still hoped would retain its independence.[8]

The cease fire of 1973 had not been welcomed by President Thieu, who thought the U.S. was abandoning its long-standing commitments. With the departure of American troops, the South Vietnamese found it difficult to maintain its position upon the resumption of wide-scale fighting in early 1974. For the Saigon government, the situation grew increasingly dire. Back in the United States, some notice was made in nightly network newscasts and newspapers, but now that American lives were not at risk the sense of urgency was largely absent.[9] As the war resumed for what would be its final months, it became, for Americans, foreign news.

Ford's efforts to secure from Congress $722 million in military aid to South Vietnam, for example, were rebuffed. The intentions of Congress with respect to Vietnam had by that time been made clear. It had specifically curbed the president's ability to use appropriated funds for ground or air military actions in Vietnam, Cambodia and Laos. Ford was not in a position to challenge the legislature on these matters.

Conditional amnesty. In a second decision, Ford sought a response to the devastating effects that the Vietnam War had on the American public. As he later wrote, "There was a revulsion among the American people against the Vietnam War, the lives lost, the television pictures, the seemingly inconclusive nature of it."[10] Aiming to put the bitter debate about the Vietnam War in the past, then, Ford offered conditional amnesty to draft resisters and military deserters. Although it may have been well intentioned, the president's offer ignited a new controversy, prompting criticism from many of the war's opponents and supporters.

The background to Ford's eventual decision to offer conditional amnesty had been developing for some time, as questions about matters of military service continued to be difficult to navigate. A major source of discord was the status of those who had refused induction and those who had deserted from the military. There was strong difference of opinion as to what course of action was most appropriate in dealing with these young men.

Some months earlier, as the war was winding down, a group called the Vietnam Veterans Against the War began calling for the Nixon administration to offer amnesty to those who had refused service in the war.[11] (Several years earlier, this group had risen to prominence in a highly publicized protest at the Capitol. In that event, news cameras recorded participants casting away their military medals as part of their statement against the war.) Nixon vehemently opposed the idea, and especially rejected the thought of giving amnesty to deserters. Though clearly conflicted about the war, at this time the public largely seemed to side with the Nixon's view. A poll conducted by Louis Harris and Associates in March of 1973, for example, showed that 67 percent of the public opposed the idea of giving amnesty to young men who took flight from the U.S. to avoid in the military draft during the war.[12]

After inheriting the presidency, Ford reached a different conclusion. He reasoned that pardons or amnesty would help to reduce the divisiveness that the war had caused throughout American society. Since he had experienced the backlash precipitated by his earlier pardon of Richard Nixon, he realized that a decision to offer amnesty to draft avoiders or military deserters would be controversial. Nonetheless, in a September 1974 announcement, the administration offered conditional amnesty to the approximately 50,000 draft resisters (or draft dodgers, as many called them) and military deserters of the Vietnam-era. Under Ford's controversial policy, draft resisters and deserters were given the opportunity to "earn" amnesty, which would allow them to "return to society." Amnesty was contingent, in part, on pledging of allegiance to the United States and on providing public service. (Deserters, for example, were required to provide two years of years to their respective branch of the military.)[13]

As Ford anticipated, the decision was criticized both by those on the left, who saw it as too strict, and those on the right, who were outraged that such an offer would be made at all. Yet, the president saw the move as intimately related to the nation's healing. He later said, "It upset me deeply that people were so down on their country," and he believed that something needed to be done to get past it.[14] The policy may have been unsatisfactory to many, but it was evidence of the president's desire to provide some measure of closure to a contentious issue that had resulted from the war.

A changing situation. Ford still hoped that South Vietnam would remain independent, at least for the near future, but the administration was hardly keen to revive extensive public attention to Vietnam. In fact, later observers concluded that Ford's rhetoric on the Vietnam War at this time manifested a sense of forgetting and silence.[15] (This assessment, however, should be tempered with an appreciation for the many domestic issues that surfaced in the mid–1970s, especially relating to the poor economic climate.) For the most part, Ford focused on other pressing matters.

By early 1975, the continuing warfare in Vietnam escalated as the North Vietnamese began what would be their final push to the south. Throughout the first months of that year, the American news media noted the increased fighting. Public attention was again directed to the region, but it was no longer the nation's main concern. Without the participation of the American military the previous sense of urgency, which earlier news accounts demonstrated, was largely absent.

War and the Military in Society and the Media

As American participation in the war came to an end, many questions remained unresolved. Perhaps the most prominent of these questions revolved around the U.S. military — specifically around the young men who did, and did not, serve in it during the war. The public's attitude on these matters was complex. To some extent, it seemed that many members of society had ignored American soldiers as they returned home from the war; a smaller number of citizens had insulted and abused these veterans. By the mid–1970s, however, the plight of returning veterans and POWs was gaining more explicit interest among politicians, the news media, and the public.

Then there were those young men who had refused to serve. As public reaction to Ford's offer of conditional amnesty to this latter group revealed, there was still widespread disagreement about how to treat the young men who had evaded the military draft or who had deserted.

More generally, the U.S. armed forces had become to some extent a divisive symbol. It seemed to embody the ideals of patriotism for many of those who had supported the war and its aims, but it had become a symbol of what was wrong with America in the eyes of many war opponents.

As had been the case earlier in television's young history, during the 1960s the networks aired several successful television series with military themes. Some were dramas, such as the popular series *Combat!* (which appeared from 1962–1967) and *Twelve O'clock High* (1964–1967), both of which were set during World War II. Not unlike movie versions of the Second World War, which had been produced regularly since 1940s, these weekly television dramas largely reproduced standard patriotic themes. Heroic deeds, personal sacrifice, and valor were the main fare. Reflecting the common attitudes of the World War II era, moreover, authority was seldom questioned. There was little doubt that the protagonists of the various series were serving a just and righteous national cause.

Television also produced comedy series with military themes in the 1960s. Although series combining military and humorous themes may seem to have been a more unusual proposition than military-oriented dramas— especially during the contentious war years— such comedies were relatively common and often quite popular. The series *Hogan's Heroes* (1965–1971), for example, followed the unlikely comic exploits of Allied soldiers in a German prisoner of war camp during the World War II. Another series — a spin-off of the popular comedy *The Andy Griffith Show* — was *Gomer Pyle, U.S.M.C.* (1964–1969), which was set in a contemporary stateside Marine base. Amazingly, casual viewers of *Gomer Pyle* might scarcely have known that the U.S. was at war, as the hapless title character tried to make good as a new recruit in the Marine Corps.

For the most part, the underlying narratives of these and other comedy series of the 1960s with military themes also did not question or challenge the underlying rightness and legitimacy of military or governmental institutions. The usual source of humor in these series was found instead in the characters, who appeared to be misfits within the system, and in the presentation of absurd situations, which were far removed from reality and that were played for comic effect. Viewers of these series, then, were not given the idea that the series were ridiculing or mocking the military itself. Rather, such shows seemed to suggest that the military was simply another setting or context that served as a pretext for the comic adventures of a show's characters.

Of course, most of American television's entertainment programming did not involve military themes and did not even remotely acknowledge that the nation was at war. There is little to suggest that American audiences wanted it any other way. Indeed, throughout the Vietnam War American television viewers never lost their appetite for shallow television programming that perhaps allowed them to forget about the realities of their lives. It was, after all, an era when the quaint CBS comedy *The Beverly Hillbillies* was a great ratings success, even if the show's intentionally unsophisticated and decidedly rural flavor would eventually seem an embarrassment to the network.

Against the backdrop of major social upheaval of the late 1960s, however, television series that reflected more of American society's troubles and controversies began to appear. By the late 1960s and early 1970s, these more politically adventurous shows started to make their mark. On CBS, *The Smothers Brothers Comedy Hour*, which premiered in 1967, probably seemed an unlikely source of politically oriented programming. The two conservatively attired brothers, Tommy and Dick Smothers, at first seemed to be pleasant hosts whose seemingly apolitical comedy and song act centered on their decades-old sibling rivalry. (The running joke in the series was captured in the often repeated line, "Mom always liked you best.") Appearances were deceptive, however. As the show progressed it increasingly included very topical material that was clearly critical of the war and the Nixon administration. Increasingly frustrated by the program's forays into politically charged material, CBS cancelled the show in 1970.

Another socially adventurous program was the very successful NBC sketch-comedy *Rowan & Martin's Laugh In*, which aired from 1968 to 1973. It suggested an irreverent world in tune with a somewhat sanitized version of 1960s counter-culture. (Apparently wishing to broaden his appeal, Richard Nixon made a cameo appearance in an episode during the 1968 presidential campaign.) If it did not overtly endorse the counter-culture, it nonetheless called attention to some counter-cultural ideas that some-times offended traditional sensibilities. The series seemed to find humor in the ideas of non-conformity, calling to mind the younger generation's atti-tudes about such things as sexual revolution, recreational drug use, and, at least implicitly, anti-war inclinations. This is not to say that the series was overtly political, but it was clearly an indication of network television's new willingness to look at fresh subject matter.

By the early 1970s, then, it was clear that television programmers were growing more comfortable with the idea of scheduling series that addressed socially divisive issues of the day more directly. Audiences not only accepted some of these series; at times they enthusiastically flocked to them. For five years beginning in the 1971–1972 television season, for example, the prime-time television program with the highest season ratings was the CBS series *All in the Family*, a comedy from television producer Norman Lear.[16] Skew-ering bigotry and ignorance in American society as epitomized in the lead character of Archie Bunker, the topical and highly controversial show mir-rored the growing cynicism in some segments of American society. The contentious world that the Vietnam War and the turbulent 1960s had cre-ated, and that Watergate had perpetuated, was in full view. The conserva-tive, working-class Bunker character was shown in high contrast to his liberal and stereotypically long-haired son-in-law. *All in the Family* focused on the clash of ideas and of generations, which by then was recognized as a pervasive feature of American society. The veneer of politeness and aver-sion to politically sensitive subjects, usually hallmarks of network televi-sion, were cast aside.

The politics of the Vietnam War appeared more prominently, if indi-rectly, the following year. In September 1972, the CBS network began air-ing the comedic series *M*A*S*H*, which was based on director Robert Altman's 1970 anti-war film of the same name. The series was very success-ful for the network, and it remained on its prime-time schedule until 1983.

Like earlier television military comedies, the main characters in *M*A*S*H* seemed to be misfits, brought together while serving in a mobile army surgical hospital during the Korean War. The series was ostensibly about these misfits—an insubordinate surgeon, an alcoholic commanding officer, and a cross-dressing corporal, among others. The show was set in the past, but the allegorical relationship between the Korean Conflict that was depicted in the series and the contemporary Vietnam War was hardly subtle. It was clear in the series that the underlying credibility, wisdom and legitimacy of the military and, by extension, the government, were being called into question. At times, these institutions were explicitly ridiculed.

Tellingly, the main character (the frequently insubordinate surgeon, "Hawkeye" Pierce) was presented as the most reasonable and humane of the group. By contrast, his main nemeses in the series, two officers who were straight-laced and by-the-book, often were portrayed as little more than buffoons. The series was very popular, and though this does not necessarily mean that audiences supported its implicit themes, it does reveal that large numbers of Americans were willing to hear these messages repeatedly.[17]

Elsewhere on American television, characters who were veterans of the Vietnam War made appearances in various dramatic series on the networks' schedules in the early 1970s. In the 1974 season, for example, Vietnam War veteran characters could be found in various episodes of such popular crime series as *Columbo, Cannon,* and *Hawaii Five-0.* Significantly, and portending of later screen productions, the veteran characters were portrayed in a negative light. This may have reflected Hollywood's, and perhaps the nation's, ambivalence and misconceptions (and some people suggest also guilt) about the war and those who served in it.[18]

Television, the dominant medium of the era, had thus produced entertainment programming that in some ways evolved along with the changing attitudes of many Americans. It is true that entertainment series that deeply challenged long-cherished ideas about the righteousness of the nation and its institutions were never in the majority. By this time, however, some television series did venture, sometimes gingerly, into implicit commentary about the moral questions of the day, of which the Vietnam War was a prime example.

The Fall of Saigon and Its Aftermath

Television news, like print news, had played an obvious part in reflecting, and probably helping to change, public thinking about the Vietnam War. Since the return of American POWs and the disengagement of American ground forces from the war in 1973, however, other matters, particularly Watergate, had largely captured the news media's attention. In the spring of 1975, the news media returned its focus to the fate of the region where 58,000 Americans had lost their lives.

In April 1975, it became evident that the Saigon government was about to capitulate. President Thieu resigned and fled to Taiwan. By April 23, with the demise of Saigon all but certain, Gerald Ford remarked that the war was "finished." Two days later, Thieu's vice president handed power over to South Vietnamese General Duong Van Minh. (Ironically, twelve years earlier, Gen. Minh was a leader of the coup that deposed President Ngo Dinh Diem.)

On the evening of April 29, 1975, viewers of American network newscasts witnessed the spectacle of frenzied evacuation efforts in Saigon. Reports showed U.S. troops working to airlift remaining American personnel and hordes of their South Vietnamese allies to the safety of aircraft carriers off the Vietnamese shore. The televised images, including the chaotic picture of U.S. Marines trying to maintain order as surging Vietnamese crowds clamored for access to the hastily arranged airlift, were sobering. The long conflict was finally ending, but there was little rejoicing in the United States. President Gerald Ford later noted, "It was the saddest hour of my life in the White House ... watching those last Americans being finally evacuated from Vietnam."[19] By the following day, the ambassador himself was airlifted to safety and the last of the Marine contingent followed. Two U. S. Marines died in the final hours. These were the final combat deaths of American troops in a divisive and anguishing war.

The end had come swiftly for South Vietnam's government. Only a day after the Americans hastily began their evacuation on April 29, General Minh completed the surrender to the communists. Accompanying the cascading series of events that ended with the surrender was extensive coverage of the events by the news media. Though they had all but declared the war over in 1973 when Americans largely left the stage, it was clear that a truer ending was imminent.

American society had been turning its attention away from Southeast Asia by the demise of the Saigon government. With the 1975 evacuation of the American embassy in the South Vietnamese capital, the U.S. said farewell to a Vietnam War of the present. From that moment on, America's war in Vietnam was a struggle with the past and what that past meant. The long years of pain and conflict had worn down the nation. Not only was there no obvious victory to help ease the pain; to most Americans it seemed that the U.S. had lost a war for the first time in its history.

Events in Cambodia. Meanwhile, the Communist forces in Cambodia, the Khmer Rouge, had already overrun the capital city of Phnom Penh on April 17, marking the beginning of what would become a humanitarian tragedy of immense proportions. Much, if not most, of the American public was now weary of continuing warfare and strife in Southeast Asia, however.

South Vietnamese President Nguyen Van Thieu (shown here in 1968) considered his country to be a strong ally of the United States. He was disappointed when the U.S. and communist North Vietnam negotiated a peace settlement, announced in January 1973, which led to the withdrawal of American forces. Photograph: Lyndon Baines Johnson Library.

The demise of allied governments in South Vietnam and Cambodia within the same month no longer implied dire international consequences that had been predicted by the Domino Theory decades earlier. War in Southeast Asia had continued for so long that a generation had passed since those arguments had first been made, and the Cold War climate in which the Domino Theory arose had markedly changed.

American responses. In the United States, the effects of the far-away war were keenly felt close to home, even if many Americans wished otherwise. The cost in American lives was well known, at over 58,000 deaths and more than 150,000 injured (some sources put the injured figure at double this number). The deeply polarizing war issue had fractured families and communities and placed enormous strains on existing social and political institutions. Moreover, the effects of the war on the economy had yet to be fully felt. Though difficult to pin down exactly, the cost in dollars for the U.S. was at least roughly calculable, with common estimates running from about $110 billion to $140 billion for the period from 1964 onward. Many of the less tangible costs of the war, however, had a price that was far more diffi-

After inheriting the White House upon Nixon's resignation, Gerald Ford stood watch as the Republic of Vietnam (South Vietnam) fell. This photograph shows Ford (right) consulting with Secretary of State Henry Kissinger (left) and Vice President Nelson Rockefeller (center) about the evacuation of the American embassy in Saigon in April 1975. Source: Gerald R. Ford Library.

cult to assess, even at the time of the 1973 peace accords. The long-term toll that the war would take on American society was not immediately clear.

It was already evident that Americans generally took away from the war-years experience a vision of past events that was mostly concerned with Americans. The number of U.S. war casualties was often repeated, but if the record of media attention is any indication, Americans did not seem to pay much attention to the toll in Vietnamese lives. Indeed, American society expressed little inclination to continue dwelling on the fate of a faraway country in Southeast Asia.

Malaise of the 1970s. There was, indeed, much else on which to focus. The American economy of the era was far from sound. In his first term, Nixon had instituted mandatory wage and price control in efforts to stem inflation. Only two years later, in 1973, the Yom Kippur War crisis led to the oil embargo, and the resulting shortage of petroleum created a significant energy crisis. The sudden and precipitous drop in foreign oil available for American import led to long lines at gas pumps, rationing schemes, and dramatically increasing prices. The oil crisis did not end until 1974, by which time significant economic damage was already done.

In other parts of the economy, American consumers faced significant increases for other goods, as well. Food prices, like prices generally, rose significantly during the early 1970s, one consequence of which was a widespread boycott of beef by American households. Indeed, infla-tion was a persistent problem throughout the 1970s, rising to double-digit rates by the end of the troubled decade. A major recession affected nearly all parts of the society by 1976. The deficit rose to a massive 66 billion dollars. The economic situation of the decade presented a very differ-ent picture from the decade of the 1960s, which had an average annual inflation rate of only 2.3 percent and an average unemployment rate of 4.7 percent. In compar-ison, the averages for the decade of the 1970s were 7.1 percent for inflation — which, as noted, was much worse at the end of that decade than the beginning — and an average unemployment rate of 6.5 percent.[20]

As inflation rose, so did unemployment. Thus, a worsening economic picture during the final years of the war became even more severe after its conclusion. The stagnant economic growth, coupled with dramatically accelerating inflation was a significant source of stress. The bleak economy weighed heavily in the minds of political leaders and the public.

After the exhausting, and in many ways perplexing, experience in Viet-nam and the region, then, Americans seemed ready to focus on other things. The Vietnam War was still recent and could not be completely ignored. Often, however, it seemed to be an episode lurking in the background; it was a topic to be avoided in conversation. With the war finally over and with its ambiguous ending, from the American perspective, politicians, commentators and the mass media seemed reluctant to push the subject too much to the foreground and seemed unsure about what to say about it anyway.

The Mayaguez incident. Less than two weeks after the defeat of South Vietnam, another crisis erupted in Southeast Asia. On May 12, 1975, Cambodian communist forces captured an American merchant ship named *Mayaguez.* This created a high-profile international problem for the Ford administration and presented a major news story to the Ameri-can press.

Members of Congress had differing views about how much and how swiftly the United States should react. The specter of Vietnam was fresh on the minds of leaders and the public, and it was realized that the episode could be seen as a measuring stick for U.S. stature and resolve in the wake of its recent setback in Southeast Asia. Given the delicacy of the circum-stances, however, many observers were concerned about what the response should be. News commentator Eric Severeid was not alone when he urged caution in U.S. reaction to the incident on the *CBS Evening News.*[21]

The *Mayaguez* story dominated the headlines and the network news for the next few days, but the crisis abruptly ended on May 15, when it was announced that the ship and its crew had been rescued by American military forces. The entire episode was brief, but because of its timing and context, it was widely interpreted as a test of the United States' position in the post–Vietnam world. The immediate results, however, were inconclusive. Although it could not have been known at the time, the *Mayaguez* incident would be only the first of many subsequent international circumstances in which the U.S. would find itself confronting the ghosts of its Vietnam experience.

Cultural Reflections in the Mass Media

For a time after the fall of Saigon, the Vietnam War was seldom seen in American screen entertainment productions. Indeed, the viewing interests of the public seemed to have changed. In the year after the end of the war, *All in the Family* lost its top spot in the season's ratings. It was replaced by the escapist series *Happy Days*, a comedy series that retold the era of the late 1950s in a sanitized and almost completely apolitical way. In the following two years the equally (if not more) escapist series *Lavern & Shirley*, a farce about two young women of the same era, was the nation's most-watched television series.

During the early summer of 1976, television audiences were presented with many news and feature stories about the Bi-Centennial anniversary of the United States. The occasion of the two-hundredth anniversary provided a stage on which all of American history could be paraded. Directing attention to the American story as a whole did not remove the troubling perception of national failure in Vietnam. By extending the reconsideration of important events deep into the past, however, a process was established in which the Vietnam War could be seen as only one episode in the grand narrative. In this long view, the lost war could be seen as potentially less central than it may have seemed just a few years earlier. The place of the Vietnam War in public was thus somewhat reduced as the presidential campaigns entered their high season.

In the motion picture realm, Hollywood films of the era sometimes continued to reflect some of the underlying political themes of the day, sometimes overtly and sometimes indirectly. Martin Scorsese's 1976 film *Taxi Driver* presented the story of a Vietnam War veteran named Travis Bickle (powerfully portrayed by Robert De Niro) who had returned to American society as a psychologically impaired misfit. In a complicated plot that involves electoral politics, attempted assassination, and the lurid world of prostitution, Scorsese shows Bickle's unsuccessful efforts to adjust to post-military life after the war and his outbursts of violent and anti-social behavior. Although the character's military experiences are mentioned infrequently and are clearly in the background to events in his civilian life, the film vividly drew viewers' attention to the powerful theme of the Vietnam War veteran as a disturbed outcast.[22]

The same year, American politics were an essential element in the film version of *All the President's Men,* a Hollywood treatment of the Watergate affair. Director Alan J. Pakula's film portrayed famed *Washington Post* reporters Bob Woodward and Carl Bernstein in a nearly heroic manner and highlighted the intrigue involved as the reporters slowly unraveled the scandal. The film featured A-list actors Dustin Hoffman and Robert Redford in lead roles and was widely admired by movie critics. In telling the story of how the Watergate episode came to be revealed, of course, a rather negative picture of the government, or at least the Nixon administration, was almost inevitable. This theme obviously contrasted sharply with traditional conceptions of American myth, even if there was little in the film that was unfamiliar to audiences. Still, the film arguably reinforced a cynicism about government that had been building during the preceding decade.

For the most part, however, Hollywood preferred themes that were less controversial. The surprise blockbuster film of that year, for example, was *Rocky,* a film about a down-on-his-luck boxer with a relatively benign winning-against-the-odds theme. On the surface, *Rocky* seems to be a film completely unrelated to such works as *Taxi Driver* or *All the President's Men,* but all three films commented upon American ideals in some way. Unlike the dysfunctions of American society and politics on display in the other films, however, in *Rocky* the American story is deeply affirmed. Bruised and seemingly defeated, Rocky overcomes all obstacles and goes on to victory. The film was a mythic interpretation of the American experience, and audiences responded enthusiastically. Many of the themes of the film would reemerge later not only in sequels to *Rocky,* but in the *Rambo* films that featured its star and creator, Sylvester Stallone.

Presidential Campaign of 1976

The end result in Vietnam may have been unsatisfactory for many Americans, but they did not seem to hold Ford accountable for the perceived failure. Just before Saigon's demise, much of the public had been critical of Ford' actions on this issue. [23] A survey commissioned by *Time* magazine a month later, however, showed nearly 70 percent of those surveyed did not blame him for events in Vietnam and Southeast Asia.[24] Consequently, the war in Vietnam, which had been a central part of recent presidential contests, was not a major factor in the 1976 presidential campaign. Instead, domestic politics and the serious economic situation drew much attention.

Although the now-finished war played a relatively minor role in the 1976 presidential politics, it was not completely absent in the campaign. Ford and his opponent, Jimmy Carter, were keenly aware of the lingering effects of the war on the American public. In the campaign, both seemed determined to move the nation beyond the pain of its recent war experiences.

In the debates between the two candidates, for example, some discussion of the Vietnam War emerged. The issue may not have played a pivotal role in the election's outcome, but its appearance did help establish themes about the war and its effects that would be important in the future. In the first of three debates, the economy ranked high in the questioning of the candidates, but war-related themes continued to receive attention. One point of contention was centered on the still-unresolved attitudes about draft resisters and deserters. On this topic, Ford was questioned about his amnesty program and Carter about his proposal for pardons.

Ford explained:

> The amnesty program that I recommended in Chicago in September of 1974 would give to all draft evaders and military deserters the opportunity to earn their good record back. About fourteen to fifteen thousand did take advantage of that program....
> Mr. Carter has indicated that he would give a blanket pardon to all draft evaders. I do not agree with that point of view.... I think we gave them a good opportunity. I don't think we should go any further.

In his response, Carter drew a comparison between Ford's full pardon of Nixon and the program, which had many more conditions, that was offered to the resisters and deserters. He further explained:

> I think it's ... very difficult for President Ford to explain the difference between the pardon of President Nixon and ... his attitude toward those who violated the draft laws. As a matter of fact ... I don't advocate amnesty; I advocate pardon ... Amnesty means that ... what you did was right. Pardon means that what you did, whether it's right or wrong, you're forgiven for it. And I do advocate a pardon for draft evaders.

In the second debate, on October 6, the Vietnam War was again not the main issue, but it nonetheless appeared in different contexts. Carter, for example, linked the war to the Ford administration's policies relating to recent events in Angola. He asserted that Ford had "tried to start a new Vietnam in Angola, and it was only the outcry of the American people and the Congress when their secret deal was discovered that prevented our involvement in that conflagration which was taking place there."

The issue of American soldiers missing in action was also debated in relation to Vietnam's bid for membership in the United Nations. On this matter, Ford said, "As long as Vietnam, North Vietnam, does not give us a full and complete accounting of our missing in action, I will never go along with the admission of Vietnam to the United Nations."

Carter used this as an opportunity to criticize the administration's progress on the MIA issue. His blunt comments sounded themes that in later years would continue to resurface as Americans looked back at the war. According to Carter:

> One of the most embarrassing failures of the Ford administration ... is his refusal to appoint a presidential commission to go to Vietnam, to go to Laos, to go to Cambodia and try to trade for the release of information about those who are missing in action in those wars.... I would never normalize relationships with Vietnam, nor permit them to join the United Nations until they've taken this action.... We need to have an active and aggressive action on the part of the president, the leader of his country, to seek out every possible way to get that information which has kept the MIA families in despair and doubt, and Mr. Ford has just not done it.

More generally, it can be seen that as the election drew closer, the Vietnam War was being framed differently and more narrowly in public discourse. Discussion edged away from the earlier, policy-centered discourse that focused on it as a series of events with an unsatisfactory ending and the first large-scale defeat of the U.S. military. In that discussion, there was— and would be later — disagreement about whether the war was a great mistake from the beginning or whether the perceived failure was because American forces had too many restraints and did not receive sufficient support from Congress, the media or the public. (Reagan would later make this argument.)

The manner in which the war was discussed during the debates, however, shows that by 1976 the war was being discussed not only with apologies, but as an apology itself. The war — and also Watergate —could be found at the root of a public malaise. It was, in a way, both an explanation and a scapegoat. As Ford explained in the final debate on October 23, "I believe that the American people have been turned off in this election ... by the revelations of Watergate ... [and] because of the problems that came out of our involvement in Vietnam." Still, he added, "What counts is, that the United States celebrated its two-hundredth birthday on July Fourth. As a result of that wonderful experience all over the United States, there is a new spirit in America. The American people are healed, are working together.... We are at peace. Not a single young American is fighting or dying on any foreign soil tonight."

The theme of healing the nation, which Carter would also later embrace, was at this time a central part of reflections on the painful experiences of the recent past, in which, as Ford demonstrated above, Vietnam and Watergate were bound together. The wounds were still fresh, however, and the assertion that the nation had healed appears to have been wishful thinking at this time.

A sense of alienation, which the candidates themselves perceived in the electorate, was clearly visible on election day. Only 53 percent of eligible voters cast ballots, continuing a downward trend in voter participation in presidential elections that began some years earlier.[25] Carter narrowly won the popular vote (with just over 50 percent of the votes, to Ford's 48 percent) but easily won in the electoral college. It is impossible to know exactly how much voters wished to move away from the Ford administration's proximity to the war and Watergate, but surely the troubled memories of those events could not have helped Ford's efforts to remain in the White House.

Vietnam War Themes in the Carter Years

James Earl Carter began his presidency at a difficult time. Indeed, when later recounting his explanation for winning the election, he included, among "the most significant factors ... the disillusionment of the American people following the national defeat suffered in Vietnam [and] the Watergate scandals...."[26] Immediately upon assuming office, he instituted his pardon program for draft resisters.

Once in office, Carter continued to sense a need for the nation to move beyond the bitter memories of the war. In the coming months, the war's legacy emerged in several ways, some predictable, others less so. Perhaps the most prominent war-related issue that was coming to increased public attention was the fate of missing-in-action soldiers (MIAs).

The MIA issue had already become an emergent theme in public consciousness, and as months (and later, years) passed, the hope that more American soldiers would yet be returned alive was slow to fade. Prior to Carter's term, when the government of newly reunited Vietnam began to express interest in gaining membership in the United Nations, American officials began a campaign linking their acquiescence on this matter to Vietnam providing more information about those still missing. A Vietnamese petition for U.N. membership in 1976 was thwarted by the U.S., which was unhappy with progress on the issue. The U.S. also made clear that any hope of normal diplomatic relations between the Democratic Republic of Vietnam and Washington hinged upon a more acceptable accounting of the MIA soldiers.

In February 1977, Carter sent emissaries to discuss the MIA issue with

Jimmy Carter, shown here in a press conference in February 1977, faced a number of difficulties during his term, the most notable of which was the Iran hostage crisis that erupted after the overthrow of the pro–American Shah of Iran. Photograph Jimmy Carter Library.

Hanoi officials, and in the following month the Vietnamese invited the U.S. to talks about these issues in Paris. By May, the administration and Vietnam made progress on the issue, and the U.S. announced it would no longer stand in the way of Vietnam's bid for U.N. membership. In return, Vietnam agreed to increase its efforts to account for the missing.

Accordingly, Vietnam's second try for U.N. membership was approved on September 20, 1977. The vote to accept Vietnam into the United Nations attracted some media attention, although the heyday of American interest in the fate of that country appeared to have passed.[27] In a broader sense, reporting of these events in the American news media had focused some attention on MIA issue, but it was a long way from resolution. Discussions aimed to bring about progress in normalizing relations between Vietnam and the U.S. would continue for years to come, as would American suspicions about the fate of the MIAs.

The "boat people." The end of the war had sent a wave of refugees from Vietnam in search of a new life. Although it could be argued that this exodus should have been expected, to a remarkable degree this result seems not much anticipated by most observers and the public.This after-effect received attention throughout the Carter years. Often traveling by sea, the refugees had been labeled the "boat people" very shortly after the demise of the Saigon government. Their plight was obvious, but how to best deal with the situation was less so.

News stories about Vietnamese refugees appeared throughout the late 1970s and into the following decade. Many of these were simply descriptive, "factual" accounts, citing how many refuges were involved, what their means of transport had been, and what their status was once they arrived at a foreign destination. As reports indicated, the refugees were not always welcomed when the arrived at their various destinations, either in the U.S. or elsewhere. As some nations balked at accepting the many refugees who found their way to their borders, the U.S. sometimes tried to accommodate more itself.

As the issue persisted, the language used in news accounts of the boat people sometimes called attention to their plight in a way that paralleled the traditional telling of the American story. For example, the headline to a 1979 story in *The New York Times* read "Boat People Brave Adversity to Seek New Lives in U.S."[28]

Many refugees, however, sought a new life closer to their homeland. The continuing troubles of refugees attempting to put ashore in Malaysia gained particular notice. The major news media continued reporting the issue, occasionally addressing the matter in opinion pieces. In one example from 1978, for example, a piece in *The New York Times* commented on "America's Duty to the Boat People," stating that, "The photographs of Vietnamese refugees jammed on the decks of unseaworthy craft as Malay peasants block their way to shore continue to tear at the conscience."[29]

Unfortunately, the sometimes tragic circumstances did not abate. In one incident, which was reported the following year, the Malaysian government indicated that 70,000 encamped Vietnamese refugees would be expelled and further, that refugees attempting to put ashore in the future would be shot.[30] As these and other less dramatic episodes revealed, the boat people were often victimized in a number of ways.

As a result of the flight from Vietnam and other parts of Indochina, the U.S. did see a rise in the number of new immigrants from that region. Although the flight was a troubling situation, it is doubtful that the majority of the American public ever considered the refugee issue to be as important as issues that more directly involved the United States.

Developments in Cambodia. American interest in the fate of Cambodia and its people seemed to have lessened considerably after that government fell to the Khmer Rouge revolutionary forces in 1975. Since that time, the situation in that country was dramatically worsening. As the world later realized, a tragedy of immense proportions was unfolding, in which well over a million Cambodians died as the direct result of Khmer Rouge actions. It was not until late in the decade that disturbing hints of tragedy began to be noticed in the American media.[31]

In early 1979, the American government was instead concerned that Vietnam had invaded Cambodia and also that several weeks later China had invaded Vietnam. This development involved a complex set of relations among Vietnam, Cambodia, China and the U.S.S.R. The situation was confusing, and though it drew official notice, to the American public it seemed remote from direct national interests. These events were dutifully reported in the American media but seemed to make little lasting impression on the public.

The Agent Orange issue. Another major issue that brought back memories of Vietnam was more unexpected, and for thousands of affected veterans and their families, much more frightening. This was the mounting fear that the defoliant commonly known as Agent Orange was causing negative health effects in American soldiers who had been exposed to the chemical in Vietnam. The powerful herbicide Agent Orange had been widely used by the U.S. military during the war; more than 10 million gallons of it were sprayed in Vietnam between 1965 and 1970.[32]

Among soldiers who had come into contact with it, suspicions about ill-effects from exposure to Agent Orange had been developing for several years. The public was only beginning to learn of the issue, however, and in terms of wide public awareness, the issue emerged slowly. At first, claims of negative health effects were dismissed by the U.S. government. Nonetheless, some veterans pushed the issue, and the Agent Orange question began to attract notice.

As late as November 1979, the government continued to insist that there was not a problem. By then, hundreds of veterans had filed claims with the Veterans Administration in which Agent Orange was listed as the cause of some malady. The agency found no cases it deemed related to Agent Orange. Others were not so sure. A former Veterans Administration doctor, for example, claimed that Agent Orange might be the cause of "the so-called Vietnam veteran's syndrome — characterized by withdrawal, hostility and paranoia."[33]

In November 1979, a federal judge permitted Vietnam veterans to go forward with a lawsuit against five companies that had been involved in the production of Agent Orange. Days later, the issue received still more public attention when a Government Accounting Office report contradicted previous Pentagon claims regarding U.S. military personnel and exposure to the chemical. The legal course of the Agent Orange issue would extend into the following decade.

From its outset, the Agent Orange issue was clearly an important matter for those directly affected. In a larger sense, the Agent Orange and MIA issues became important elements in public rhetoric about what the U.S. "owed" to its veterans. Moreover, both issues helped foster a climate in which government conspiracies could seem plausible. It was evident, after all, that the original denials and claims of the government in the Agent Orange case, at least, did not stand up to scrutiny. The issues would persist for some time.

The Entertainment Media Revisit the War

In the later 1970s, the American public remained concerned with economic and domestic matters and at times found diversion in the fantasies of popular culture. Among the most popular films of that time, for example, were *Star Wars* (1977) and *Saturday Night Fever* (1977), both of which were far removed from society's controversies of only a few years earlier.

In looking at events of the recent past, it seems that by 1978 most Americans had concluded that the Vietnam War had been a mistake. A national poll conducted for the Chicago Council on Foreign Relations, for example, revealed that 72 percent of respondents saw it as an not only an error, but also morally incorrect.[34] By this time, however, several Hollywood projects about the Vietnam War were ready for release, and the public seemed at least somewhat curious about what they would say.

It was in this environment that director Michael Cimino's film *The Deer Hunter* premiered in December of 1978. It marked a new willingness for Hollywood to look more closely at the war years and its aftermath. Interestingly, however, Cimino's film seemed unconcerned in the question of whether or not the war was justified. As Cimino explained, "My film has nothing to do with whether the war should or should not have been."[35] Indeed, it was his view that "Vietnam is not the only war in the history of the world where there have been atrocities. There have been and there probably will be far worse. Vietnam was not the apocalypse...."[36]

Despite the director's intentions, some viewers were unaccustomed to thinking about the war without thinking about it bigger questions. *New York Times* film critic Vincent Canby, for example, concluded that some aspects of *The Deer Hunter* were "terrifying." His concerns were prompted by the observation that in the film "Not once does anyone question the war or his participation in it."[37]

Cimino saw the subject differently, however. His focus was not on war policy, but on the effects that the war had on American soldiers. He explained,

"During the years of controversy over the war, the people who fought the war ... were disparaged and isolated by the press. But they were common people who had an uncommon amount of courage."[38] It was later said that the ordinary characters exemplify "a working class who are viewed as both the war's heroes and its victims" with the resulting film being "so sympathetic that it allows the late 1970s audience to feel somewhat relieved of its uneasiness and distress" about the ambiguities of the war.[39] Regardless of whether the film actually had such an effect on audiences, the theme of Vietnam veterans as victims was already becoming a major part of thinking about the war.

It was probably the intense storyline, which follows the post-war story of three friends who had been POWs during the war, and the visceral nature of the filmmaking in *The Deer Hunter* that most captured public attention. According to the film's narrative, the intensity of their wartime experiences haunted these men after the war. The sequence of the film that audiences found most shocking was the depiction of the friends being forced by their Vietcong captors to play Russian roulette with each other. The intensity with which this segment was directed and the magnitude of the violence were, according to Canby, "savage" and "as explicitly bloody as anything you're likely to see in a commercial film;" he found these aspects of the film "deeply troubling."[40]

The Russian roulette sequences implied that random chance and luck had replaced meaningful purpose, perhaps not only in the experience of the three friends, but also as a factor in the greater war itself. This point was similar to Cimino's stated view and to much of what had been said in the U.S. during the war. In a similar line of thinking, some later writers have suggested that this film, among others, had the effect of "dialectical disorientation," [41] a phenomenon in which the traditional mythologies of war, especially as understood in the U.S., are undermined. The result, according to this argument, is that audiences were left with a heightened sense of the ambiguities the war.

The Deer Hunter and another 1978 film dealing with the theme of returning Vietnam veterans, *Coming Home*, were both nominated for Academy Awards. Between them, they won most of the major awards in the February 1979 ceremony. Awards for Best Picture, Best Director and Best Supporting Actor (Christopher Walken) were bestowed on *The Deer Hunter*. Awards for Best Actor (Jon Voight) and Best Actress (Jane Fonda, the polarizing actress whose anti-war activities had led her to be called "Hanoi Jane" by her detractors) went to *Coming Home*. As this highly visible recognition of the subject indicated, the Vietnam War had found a place with American motion-picture audiences. It seemed that the war had returned as a topic for everyday conversation as the result.

Apocalypse Now. The appearance of *The Deer Hunter* had been antic- ipated. The film received entertainment press coverage in production, and it was heavily promoted upon its release. Another "Vietnam" film was per- haps even more eagerly awaited, however, though it was not be ready for release until the summer of 1979. That film, which captured the imagina- tion of film industry watchers, was *Apocalypse Now,* from the director Fran- cis Ford Coppola, whose acclaimed *Godfather* films had made him a major player in Hollywood.

After many well-publicized production setbacks, *Apocalypse Now* was released at first in a few major cities in August 1979, and then nationally later in the autumn. In important ways, it was a different type of film than the Vietnam-veteran-centered films that had swept the awards of the Motion Picture Academy earlier that year. Rather than looking back at the war through the effect that it had on returning veterans, Coppola's film was set in the midst of the war, showing a wide array of increasingly surreal scenes that depicted war (or that war, anyway) as madness.

The film followed the story of a young soldier, Capt. Benjamin Willard (played by Martin Sheen), who is given the mission of assassinating a seem- ingly insane American Colonel who had taken up a position in a remote, jungle region. As the soldier is escorted up the river to carry out his mis- sion, a series of disjointed scenes are presented. The cumulative visual effect was quite unlike the narrative of a traditional war film. These increasingly surreal scenes were sometimes horrifying and sometimes bizarre. It was not always obvious how to interpret them.

To many viewers at the time, the final section of the film was partic- ularly unsatisfying. In this segment, Willard finds and confronts the object of his mission, Col. Kurtz (played by Marlon Brando). The confrontation between the main characters did not seem to be anchored in any reality, and it was especially not recognizable as a picture of the way things actu- ally happened in Vietnam. It depicted so much a dream, or perhaps a night- mare, that it disturbed many viewers, whose expectations were clearly something other than what Coppola had envisioned.

In fact, Coppola had used the Joseph Conrad novella *The Heart of Dark- ness,* set on a different continent in an earlier era, as his model for much of the plot. Some aspects of Conrad's work that were incorporated into the film struck viewers as perplexing. The end result was by no means a straight- forward war story. For such reasons, the film initially received mixed reviews from critics and audiences.

Critic Vincent Canby, for example, noted that during the parts of the film focusing on the Vietnam War itself, *Apocalypse Now* was a "stunning work."[42] Like many other film writers, he was less sure what to make of the

Francis Ford Coppola's vision of the Vietnam War, which appeared in his *Apocalypse Now,* made a lasting statement about the war, but at first it seemed too abstract for many viewers. In this photograph, Martin Sheen is shown in the role of Capt. Benjamin Willard. Photograph: Photofest.

concluding sequences. Indeed, audiences did not seem quite sure about how they should interpret the film. After the wide release of the film in the U.S., a Harris poll conducted for the Veterans Administration found that 40 percent of those in the sample who had seen the film thought that the portrayal of veterans who fought in Vietnam was favorable, whereas 44 percent thought it to be unfavorable.[43]

Overall, whatever Coppola had achieved with *Apocalypse Now,* it was not cathartic for American audiences, and it did little to promote a consensus in thinking about the war. Such expectations, of course, would have been unrealistic. Yet, some aspects of *Apocalypse Now* did touch on themes about the war that were coalescing in the broader society. The film's hallucinatory vignettes could be interpreted as a comment on the war in general, suggesting an element of madness to that war.

In addition, the portrayal of American soldiers in the film may have reinforced negative ideas about American combat troops. Like other works at the time, the account of the war in the film contrasted sharply with traditional

American narratives about war.[44] The U.S. soldiers in *Apocalypse Now* seem disconnected from authentic purpose. In a visually and aurally stunning section of the film, for example, the commander (Robert Duval) of a group of American helicopters unleashes a massive assault on a peasant village for the purposes of making it possible for a young solider to display his surfing abilities. For the most part, in fact, American soldiers in the film exhibit a wide array of discomforting, maladaptive responses to their stressful situations. Suggestions of random violence, drug and alcohol abuse, and psychological disorientation are scattered throughout the film. Many of these characteristics exhibited traits that were akin to those seen in portrayals of the Vietnam veteran's syndrome that the public had heard about in the mass media. From the film's account of the war, the appearance of the dysfunctional Vietnam veteran may not have seemed surprising.

Apocalypse Now garnered a substantial reputation among film-goers. The superb cinematography certainly helped, as did Coppola's considerable reputation. As a result, the messages of ambiguity and madness in the film remained widely accessible for years after its release. The film continued to receive attention in following decades, emerging in film history textbooks, in cable television broadcasts, and in home video formats. Coppola's conception of the war was not, however, one that would be repeated often in future productions.

Developing Themes

Thus, by the end of 1979 several strands of political and media messages were in place that indicated an emerging shift in the place of the Vietnam War in public memory. The MIA and Agent Orange issues implied that the government, at times, might not have had the best interests of its soldiers in mind during or after the war. These issues also brought attention to the many veterans who had received scant attention during the war years, and the nation struggled to reconcile its conflicted attitudes about how to treat them.

Moreover, the way in which these issues were framed placed a heavy emphasis on the negative consequences of the war for American participants, with much less attention directed to the ill effects of the war on the people of Vietnam itself. This was a further step in the Americanization of the memory of the war, in which American conceptions of the conflict continued to drift away from the past and present situations in Vietnam.

Oddly, in some ways the Vietnamese people themselves continued to play an ever-decreasing part in American thinking about the war. Even the word "Vietnam" was coming to be used less as a place with its own unique people and culture and more as a label Americans might apply to international situations gone awry or to policy blunders.

The entertainment media reinforced such views of the war. Whether the continuing portrayal of the absurdities and ironic cruelties of war and bureaucracy in the *M*A*S*H* television series, or the cruel pointlessness of the dehumanizing Russian roulette in *The Deer Hunter*, or the madness and unfathomable surreal nature of *Apocalypse Now*, Americans were always the main characters. The Vietnamese (or their Korean surrogates in *M*A*S*H*) were but supporting players.

In fact, according to this way of thinking it seemed that the South Vietnamese did not even "lose" their own war; instead it was America's loss. Even in defeat, it seems, the Vietnamese were minor characters in the story. The centrality of the idea that the Vietnam War was a fundamentally American experience was by now firmly entrenched. As future events unfolded, the way the war was remembered and the meanings taken from it would change, but for decades to come, the American tendency to claim ownership of the war would remain largely unchallenged.[45]

New International Crises

In 1979, the U.S.S.R. invaded Afghanistan. It was not the first time the Soviets had ventured into a neighboring state, but events there would later take a path quite different from what the Soviets originally envisioned, causing westerners to see parallels between this episode and the American experience in southeast Asia a few years earlier. At first, however, the ultimate consequences of the Soviet military incursion into Afghanistan were not realized.

For the U.S. meanwhile, a serious national crisis of a different sort developed in 1979. The American-supported regime of the Shah of Iran was overthrown by Islamic fundamentalists loyal to Ayatollah Khomeini. During these events, the American embassy in Tehran was captured, and Americans were taken hostage. The rapid pace and severity of these events riveted the attention of U.S. political leaders, the media and the public. Soon, for example, ABC News began broadcasting special late-night reports focusing on the crisis, in which news anchor Ted Koppel emphasized the Americans in captivity. In the coming months and throughout the presidential campaign season, the Carter administration would work feverishly to free the hostages. The emergence of the crisis was the strongest test to that date about the after-effects of the unseemly end to America's involvement in the

Vietnam War. It was soon evident that the hostage crisis was, to some degree, an opportunity for redemption but also one that, if things were to go badly, could further damage not only U.S. stature in the world, but also confidence at home.

Undoubtedly, the ghost of the war in Vietnam lurked in the background of these events, especially for Jimmy Carter on the eve of the election year.

3

Envisioning a Noble Cause

Speaking at a February 1980 campaign event held in Nashua, New Hampshire, Ronald Reagan declared that the problem with the war in Vietnam was that it was a "war our government was afraid to let them win."[1] Reagan and four other candidates addressed many topics that evening, but it was Reagan's invocation of the Vietnam War that drew the largest and most enthusiastic response. Indeed, his words would come to characterize his view of the Vietnam War and its meaning. Reagan pronounced that never again should a "Godless Communist tyranny" be permitted to over-run a "small country."[2] The perceived threats of communism and "God-lessness" were a major part of Reagan's rhetoric as his candidacy progressed. The Soviet Union, which later he famously called an "evil empire," was his gravest concern, embodying both perils. As would become apparent in his presidential campaign and later presidency, Reagan took these views seri-ously. He consistently pushed for a stronger military and a bolstering of the place and prestige of the U.S. on the world stage.

At the New Hampshire campaign event, the continuing and deepen-ing plight of the American hostages in Iran was also a topic of discussion. Reagan thought that the Carter administration's handling of the situation was ineffective. Reagan's opinion was that "the time has long passed when we should have set a date certain for their release."[3] This comment was consistent with his view that America's standing in the world had dimin-ished at the hands of poor leadership. By very early in the campaign, it already was evident that his prescription for the nation's recovery would include a large dose of increased attention to the U.S. military, which he clearly thought was in a weakened position compared to that of the U.S.S.R. It was also becoming clear that to Reagan, the way that the pub-lic and previous leaders thought about the Vietnam War was hampering the nation's ability to assume what he saw as its rightful place of leader-ship in the world.

Ronald Reagan, often called the "Great Communicator," envisioned a bold, new America that would be unhampered by the lingering effects of what he called "Vietnam syndrome." His calls for renewed patriotism and a revamped American military resonated with many Americans. Reagan (right) is shown here with his wife, Nancy Reagan, during a 1986 speech celebrating the Centennial of the Statue of Liberty. Photograph: Ronald Reagan Presidential Library.

American perceptions of diminished power. Running for re-election, Jimmy Carter, too, was wary of a diminished American military and also of policies that would make him appear to be a weak leader or "soft" on defense. At his insistence, Selective Service (military draft) registration for young men was reintroduced in the midst of his term, though the draft itself was not revived. More generally, he also took special care to avoid the appearance of excessive rapprochement with the U.S.S.R., even as his administration worked to improve relations with the communists. In the months leading up to the election year, the Soviet support of Vietnam in its incursion into Cambodia was one difficulty that already had surfaced.

American and Soviet interests in Southeast Asia clashed again in 1979. Following the Vietnamese invasion, the new Cambodian government sought for its representative to be seated in the United Nations. Because the petitioning regime was backed by Vietnam, however, the U.S. was among the nations that opposed. American officials reasoned that if the U.S. were to agree, it would be tantamount to granting the U.N. seat to a government of usurpers.

Cambodia's U.N. bid occurred in the context of complicated political wrangling. In particular, the U.S.S.R. and China were engaged in a struggle for power and influence, in which the Cambodian question had great symbolic value. China favored seating a U.N. representative from the ousted Khmer Rouge government, while the Soviets backed representation from the newly installed Heng Samrin regime, which it and Vietnam supported. The U.S. sided with China and other regional states in this matter. As a result, in an action that in hindsight appears remarkable, the Americans cast their vote in favor or seating a representative of the Khmer Rouge.

At this time, the world outside Cambodia had not yet recognized — or been willing to acknowledge, perhaps— the full extent of the mayhem that had been inflicted on the Cambodian population by the Khmer Rouge, under its already-notorious leader, Pol Pot. Even by this date, however, there had been troubling signs of a seriously grave situation in Cambodia, and recognition of repression under the Khmer Rouge regime was widespread. As the U.N. representative from Singapore observed, the Khmer Rouge had "a very, very bad record of violations of human rights."[4] Officials in the U.S. government were also aware of serious allegations against the Khmer Rouge. (This is clear from the comments of a member of the American U.N. delegation, who pointedly said at the time of the vote that the U.S. "condemns and abhors the brutal human rights violations of the Pol Pot regime."[5])

The American government partly justified its U.N. vote in favor of seating the Khmer Rouge by focusing on the judgment that Vietnam had

acted illegally by invading Cambodia. The U.S. was already on record as vigorously opposing the Vietnamese invasion, and it had previously voted in
the U.N. General Assembly to demand a withdrawal.[6] Generally speaking,
then, it appears that the United States' past conflict with Vietnam and its
continuing rivalry with the U.S.S.R. were the most prominent concerns for
American decision-makers in the debate about which party would be
granted Cambodia's seat in the United Nations. The American vote in favor
of the Khmer Rouge was seen as intimately connected to the state of
American-Soviet relations and the Vietnam legacy. The U.N. vote was,
according to *The New York Times,* "a rebuff to the Soviet Union."[7]

This episode, though largely reflective of the struggle between the rival
states of the U.S.S.R. and the People's Republic of China on the world stage,
was surely not one that enhanced American prestige internationally. For
many people, such events, taken together with the seeming inability of the
American government to address the hostage situation in Iran or to
influence the 1979 Soviet incursion into Afghanistan, seemed to indicate
that American power and prestige were greatly diminished. The widespread
sense that American power had been seriously and somewhat successfully
challenged by the Soviets left Carter in a weakened situation politically. By
the beginning of 1980, Reagan and his advisors clearly saw it as a situation
that could be exploited in the race for the White House.

Indeed, the uncertain fate of the fifty-two hostages held in Iran continued to be a major source of anxiety into the summer months of 1980.
Even as nightly reports continued to focus on the situation, the Senate
Armed Services Committee investigated Operation Eagle Claw, the aborted
rescue attempt of a few months earlier. (The failed rescue was a serious
embarrassment to the Carter administration. In the doomed operation, a
sandstorm, malfunctioning equipment, and the collision of American aircraft were among the factors leading to the deaths of eight American servicemen.) When a Senate Armed Services Committee report on the matter
became public in June, a Republican senator charged that "major errors"
had been committed, both during planning and implementation of the rescue plan.[8] The focus on this failed episode increased attention to perceptions of weakened American military and leadership in the post–Vietnam
War world.

Reagan's view of the Vietnam War. It was in these contexts that, during the summer of 1980, Ronald Reagan argued that Americans had understood the Vietnam War incorrectly. His rhetoric on this subject had
crystallized, conveying in no uncertain terms his belief that a major revi-
sion in thinking about the war was necessary. At an August meeting of the
Veterans of Foreign Wars, he complained that a "Vietnam Syndrome" had

swept over much of the nation, making the United States fearful and immobile in world affairs. Instead of succumbing to this malaise, Reagan proposed that "it's time we recognized that ours was, in truth, a noble cause," adding that "We dishonor the memory of 50,000 young Americans who died in that cause when we give way to feelings of guilt as if we were doing something shameful."[9] Thus, by the time he had been certified as the Republican candidate for the upcoming election, Reagan had reframed the memory of the war, tying a re-envisioned version of it to what he perceived as political necessities for the U.S. in the 1980s.

The new conception of the war that was expressed by Reagan, and others who shared his view, modified and brought together previous lines of thinking. In the late 1970s, it was widely thought that the war had been a mistake. Reagan's view did acknowledge mistaken aspects, but with substantial differences in substance and emphasis. The mistakes, according to the Reagan line, were clear: First, the United States and its leadership had failed to "let" the military win the war by placing too many restrictions and offering too little support to the military; second, too many Americans failed to see that though the war had ended as a (perceived) failure, it had actually been a righteous ("noble") undertaking.

With the MIA issue still capturing public sentiment (as it would for many more years to come) and with the Agent Orange issue still making its way through the courts, a line of thinking in which government failure was a central theme in remembering the war was already in place. Perceived governmental mistakes in the MIA and Agent Orange issues and the larger errors that Reagan described were different, of course, but the earlier perceptions had planted seeds of distrust. They paved the way for Reagan's broader argument, especially in light of the disarming finesse with which he articulated this message.

It was clear that Reagan believed the government, or some of its leaders anyway, had inappropriately yielded to war critics and therefore not only failed to "let them win," but also had been instrumental in bringing about a defeat. If not quite scapegoats, they at least represented question marks. Moreover, the perceived defeat in Vietnam, having already been interpreted as a fundamentally American defeat, could be represented as an inept and morally indefensible outcome. It was implied that Americans should not accept this outcome willingly, since that would be thinking about the war the wrong way. Instead, if the public were to recall the Vietnam War in the "right" way, this would lead — with apparent inevitability — to the conclusion that it had been a good and just effort all along and that the war would have turned out better if America, and especially its leaders, had not faltered.

This way of reframing public memory about the war was especially timely for those who were concerned about the perceived diminishment of American military might since the war years. It suggested that Americans were not defeated by a foreign enemy, after all. Instead, implicit in the revised view was the idea that it was Americans who had defeated themselves, or at least had allowed themselves to be defeated. Such an interpretation could be seen as less threatening to national identity and could be presented as a situation that could be reversed through hard work, persistence and election of the right leaders. This conception of the Vietnam War, along with the lessons Reagan and his circle took from it, were to be basic building blocks in plans for a future in which peace would be achieved and maintained through military strength. As Reagan had stated, "...it must not be peace at any price. It must not be a peace of humiliation and gradual surrender."[10] The "Vietnam Syndrome," with its fears of moral ambiguity and its hand-wringing, were not, then, simply the result of the America's Vietnam War experience and loss. Instead, according to this argument, the Vietnam Syndrome and its failure of nerve and determination caused that loss, as well as precipitated the dangerous situation that Reagan saw American facing in 1980.

Election politics. Between the end of American involvement in the war in Vietnam and the 1980 presidential campaign, the mood of American voters had shifted noticeably.[11] Some attention was directed to foreign affairs in the national news media during the campaign, largely focusing on the continuing Iran hostage crisis and concerns about the Soviet incursion into Afghanistan.[12] For the most part, however, Americans worried about domestic matters. Asked which of the many problems facing the U.S. was most important, 48 percent of respondents in a Gallup survey reported economic concerns (i.e., inflation, prices, cost of living) or energy issues; only 18 percent thought the Iran hostage situation was most important, and even fewer respondents said they regarded the threat of war as the most pressing issue.[13] Despite Ronald Reagan's questioning of United States military strength and the larger matter of place of the nation in world affairs, then, the 1980 campaign largely focused on domestic issues. As a study of election editorials in leading newspapers that year revealed, foreign policy did not play as significant a role in the campaign as it had prior in the elections during the war.[14]

More generally, the electorate did not seem much more engaged in the political process than in the previous election. Voter turnout in November 1980 was under 53 percent, fractionally less than even the previous presidential election.[15] Nevertheless, Ronald Reagan's victory brought a symbolic shift in national politics, heralding a new era of conservatism in which military and foreign affairs would play a larger role.

Almost simultaneously with Reagan's inauguration in January 1981, the American hostages in Iran were freed. It may have been seen by some as the harbinger of a new start for a nation that had been beset by many problems and that had suffered from the "Vietnam Syndrome." Surely the new administration felt sufficiently emboldened that it would argue for a course of future U.S. action that was unhampered by bad memories of the war.

Changing Media Image of the Vietnam Veteran

The political rehabilitation of the Vietnam War in national memory that Reagan championed was accompanied by a cultural reorientation of it, as well. One indication of this could be found in changing perceptions of Vietnam veterans and in the increasing public willingness to acknowledge them. The new image of the veterans was an increasingly diverse picture. The older picture of veterans — vague and shadowy figures beset by problems — was replaced, to an extent, by an image with more nuances and complexities. In the new decade, representations of Vietnam veterans would take on many forms and continue to play an important part in shaping assumptions in political debates.

The "Vietnam Syndrome," which Ronald Reagan lamented, had a vaguely familiar sound, evocative of the "Vietnam veterans' syndrome" label that had been in use for several years. In both cases, these "syndromes" described malaise and dysfunction, with the obvious implication that these were conditions that needed to be made right. Just as Reagan's prescription for the Vietnam Syndrome was renewed confidence and boldness in America at home and abroad, so, too, was there a media response to the Vietnam veterans' syndrome. In many instances, Vietnam veterans had previously been depicted as angry, socially ill-at-ease, despondent, addicted, or otherwise victims. Frequently, they were represented as being unfit for life in the American mainstream. In the 1980s, that picture began to shift markedly, as more positive portrayals of the veterans began to emerge.[16]

One example of changing media depictions of Vietnam veterans could be found in the popular CBS television series *Magnum, P.I.*, which was first broadcast in the late autumn of 1980. It appearance on the heels Reagan's election victory may have been fitting. The series' interpretation of Vietnam-veteran themes had more in common with Reagan's reinterpretation of the Vietnam War than it did with most earlier media portrayals.

The program focused on its main character, Thomas Magnum, a private investigator. (The title character was played by Tom Selleck.) According to the story line, Magnum, along with two regular supporting characters, were Vietnam veterans who had served in combat together during the war.

Their wartime experiences created a strong bond that extended from the past and into the present. The Vietnam War, it seems to have been suggested, was the reason that the men still had a close association, but it was also a reason that they were still separated, to some extent, from everyday American life. In the series, for example, each of these characters held a job with some unconventional aspects. (The characters were respectively a private detective, a charter helicopter pilot, and a night club operator) Magnum and his friends therefore gave the appearance of being somewhat outside the corporate and business mainstream that much else in 1980s television culture embraced. Yet, Magnum and his associates were strong and rugged characters, cast in a conservative mold of traditional male identity and patriotism that was in keeping with the reinvigoration of conservatism of the early 1980s.[17]

Magnum's quiet (private) and heroic deeds not only brought about justice at the fringes of the "system," but also afforded him an exciting life in what was presented as an exotic Hawaiian setting. (CBS had been successful in combining this setting and a crime drama narrative before; it aired the well-known *Hawaii Five-O* series from 1968 until 1980.) Magnum's life was well beyond the mundane middle-class experience assumedly familiar to many of the series' viewers. The Magnum character's job, which officially entailed providing secu-

In popular CBS television series, *Magnum, P.I.,* actor Tom Selleck portrayed a dashing Vietnam veteran who led an exciting life as a private investigator. The series was one of the first screen versions in which the Vietnam veteran is seen as a hero. Photograph: Photofest.

rity services for an estate belonging to an absentee tycoon, gave him considerable freedom in interpreting his duties. This not only allowed him to undertake daring private investigations on the side, but also gave him access to many of the fruits and excesses of conspicuous wealth. (Magnum often drove his employer's lavishly expensive Ferrari sports car and lived in a cottage on the idyllic estate itself.)

Yet, Magnum was not tied to the lifestyle that generated affluence or to the obligations that went with it. His relatively carefree life of danger and occasional romance could be seen, perhaps, as a type of poetic justice for a character who had dutifully served his country at great personal peril during a divisive war. Bold and daring, possessing a charming personality and wit, the Magnum character was decidedly different from the troubled Vietnam veterans who had previously been presented by the entertainment media. Both the character and the actor who portrayed him soon were recognized as sex symbols in American popular culture.

This portrayal was largely consistent with a new conception of Vietnam veterans that was emerging in the entertainment media. Perhaps still not in the mainstream, still not completely free from the negative influences of the war, and at times still angry for those experiences, this new portrayal of the Vietnam veteran saw the veterans as a strong, quiet heroes. It was a significant turnabout from the dysfunctional victim found in many earlier media incarnations. Moreover, the seeming strength and wiles of these new-style veterans fit congruently with Reagan's assertion that the American soldiers could have won the war, if only they had been given the tools and permission to do so. This way of picturing the veterans, and variations of it, joined existing modes of representing the theme in television and films for the next several years.

Complications in Central America

Shifting views of Vietnam veterans, however, did not necessarily signal that the American public had a profound rethinking of what the Vietnam War meant. This became evident in the early months of the Reagan administration as new conceptions of American foreign policy were advocated in Washington.

The reinvigoration of the military was a cornerstone in Reagan's vision of renewed American strength and prestige in the world. Of the many obstacles that stood in the way, two were especially significant: the legacy of the Vietnam War and the then-present threat of the Soviet Union. Thus, changing perceptions of American soldiers who had fought in Vietnam, anger about the continuing Soviet incursion into Afghanistan, and anxieties about further adventurism by the U.S.S.R. all played a part in Reagan's efforts to gain support for rebuilding the military. After he took office, Reagan worked to overcome the Vietnam Syndrome he saw, and he showed a renewed willingness for the U.S. to intervene in situations where a Soviet threat was perceived.[18]

The fear of Soviet influence and the after-effects of the Vietnam War on the public mood would soon come together somewhat unexpectedly. Very early in Reagan's administration, it was evident that Central America would be a testing ground for the new, outward-looking — and, to some, hard-line — approach to foreign policy that the president advocated. Though it would shift in tone and scope dramatically, Reagan's policies regarding Central America were to be a major thread running through both terms of his presidency.

Nicaragua. In the months prior to the election, events in Central America caught the attention of American political leaders and policy-makers. The first trouble spot was in Nicaragua, where, for almost a half-century, the family of its then-leader, General Anastasio Somoza Debayle, had wielded power. Throughout these decades, Nicaragua had been a reliable client state of the U.S. By the late 1970s, however, conditions for civil war were brewing. Major fighting broke out by mid–1979, and the Nicaraguan government came under siege by the Sandinista National Liberation Front. The government subsequently fell to the rebels, whose leaders espoused a Marxist philosophy, weakening American influence in the region. The situation seemed to hold the potential for destabilizing much of Central America.

Once Reagan assumed office, it became very clear that the new administration linked these troubles to the international threat posed by the Soviets and their allies in Cuba and Vietnam. The administration wanted to take action, and in the early months of Reagan's presidency, the C.I.A. was directed to aid Nicaraguan opponents to the communist regime, who became known as the *contras.* A few years later, American involvement in Nicaraguan events would make headlines and create scandal, but for the time being another brewing situation in the area captured the news media's attention.

El Salvador. Instability in the region extended beyond Nicaragua. The military government in neighboring El Salvador was threatened by leftist guerillas at the time Reagan assumed office. The administration perceived an ominous, creeping communist threat. It was not a situation that the administration took lightly, as it seemed as though the forces of communism were at the doorstep of the Americas with a renewed vigor.[19] As a response, in the first months of the administration the U.S. began sending support to the Salvadoran government as part of a campaign in Washington for a strong American role in the developing situation. Almost $5 billion in aid was sent to support the Salvadoran regime over the next eight years, but it often appeared that the Reagan administration was seeking a more direct American military role in the situation.[20]

In office for barely a month, administration officials began efforts to rally support for their position regarding El Salvador.[21] The State Department revealed that it possessed captured material, unauthenticated at the time, showing that the Soviet Union was backing the rebel forces.[22] On February 17, Secretary of State Alexander Haig (who had been a commander in Vietnam and had served with the National Security Council) held a press briefing on the administration's outlook for El Salvador. At this event, Haig stated:

> A well-orchestrated international Communist campaign designed to transform the Salvadoran crisis ... to an increasingly internationalized confrontation is under way. With Cuban coordination, the Soviet bloc, Vietnam, Ethiopia and radical Arabs are furnishing at least several hundred tons of military equipment to the Salvadoran leftist insurgents. Most of this equipment, not all but most, has entered via Nicaragua....
> We consider what is happening to be part of the global Communist campaign coordinated by Havana and Moscow to support the Marxist guerillas in El Salvador.... We will not remain passive in the face of this Communist challenge.[23]

According to Haig's statements at the briefing, the administration "had not yet decided on the precise steps" it would take in response to the situation. Yet, it was clear that the administration was wary of how Congress and the public would interpret its call for an American response to the civil strife and internal conflict in a small, impoverished nation about which it knew little.

In the briefing, Haig took special care to dissociate the administration's ideas about El Salvador from the past war in Southeast Asia. "Off the record," Haig was quoted as saying in *The New York Times*, "I wish to assure you we do not intend to have another Vietnam and engage ourselves in another bloody conflict where the source rests outside the target area."[24]

Haig's denial of a comparison between El Salvador and Vietnam, however intended, was unconvincing to many observers at the time. As was clear almost immediately, interpretations of what was happening, and what was being proposed, in Central America came to be mixed with negative feelings about the Vietnam War that still were not resolved. An article in *The Washington Post*, for example, asked if the administration was "using El Salvador to battle the ghosts of Vietnam."[25] The administration soon recognized more pointedly that the nobility of American purpose in Vietnam was not the lesson Americans took from that war. Indeed, in the following months and years, comparisons between Reagan's El Salvador policy and the Vietnam War were repeatedly voiced. The administration would spend much time denying that there was a valid analogy between Reagan's policies in Central America and the American experience in Vietnam.

Longtime television newsman Walter Cronkite, who presided over the *CBS Evening News* during the war and was now on the eve of his retirement, interviewed the president in early March 1981. Although not without critics, many Americans thought of Cronkite as an avuncular and trustworthy gentleman who turned against the Vietnam War in 1968 in what seemed to be a considered and thoughtful process. Many viewers, therefore, probably did not perceive his questions to the president as politically motivated or obviously biased.

Cronkite asked Reagan directly, "Do you see any parallel in our committing military advisers and military assistance to El Salvador and the early stages of our involvement in Vietnam?"[26] Reagan responded, just as directly, "No, Walter, I don't."

Instead, Reagan said that the difference between the two situations was "profound." He explained that the American interest was in "offering some help against the import ... into the Western Hemisphere of terrorism, of disruption.... Our problem is this whole hemisphere and keeping this sort of thing out." About the question of sending American military advisers to the region, Reagan added that the purpose of such advisers was in going "down there to train. They do not accompany them into combat."[27]

Reagan's comments in the remainder of this interview made it clear that his view of the situation in El Salvador was, indeed, part of the larger picture he harbored of a tenaciously opportunistic and belligerent Soviet Union. As part of this worldview, he criticized the Soviet role in Afghanistan and explained that his hard-line attitude towards the Soviets was a just response given that "They have told us that their goal is the Marxist philosophy of world revolution and the single one-world Communist state.... Remember their ideology is without God," and that to them, "nothing is immoral if it furthers their cause."[28]

As the news media recognized, Reagan had brought attention to the conflict in El Salvador, but he had done so at a price. Still only weeks in office, the new administration ignited, inadvertently it seemed, a wide-scale and sometimes passionate response that located public fear of "another Vietnam" near the center of debate.[29] Consequently, upon confirmation that 15 Green Berets from the U.S. Marine Corps had been sent to provide training, along with $60 million to assist in the fight against the Salvadoran rebels, members of the Senate were said to be "wary of [a] Vietnam sequel."[30]

These developments were met with strong opposition in the U.S., where there were protests almost immediately in many locales.[31] In the nation's capital, more than 20,000 people, chanting "No draft, no war; U.S. out of El Salvador," participated in what *The Washington Post* called a "demonstration reminiscent of the anti-war protests during the Vietnam era."[32] The reappearance of candlelight vigils and demonstrations, which had not been seen very often since the end of the war, was a pointed reminder of the turbulent war years. In Washington, Senators and members of Congress received a heavy volume of mail against American military involvement in El Salvador, and a poll published in *The New York Times* further confirmed that many Americans were fearful of a "new Vietnam."[33]

By April 1981, the Vietnam War comparison was firmly entwined in perceptions of the administration's El Salvador policies. An NBC News–Associated Press poll found that 53 percent of respondents thought that the prospect for American actions in El Salvador turning into a "Vietnam-type situation" was "very likely" or "somewhat likely."[34] National publications added their thoughts on the subject, as seen, for instance, in an article entitled "No More Vietnams," which appeared in *The National Review.*[35] The El Salvador situation continued to simmer, though attention to it in the media waxed and waned over the remaining months of 1981.

If Reagan had been more successful in changing public perceptions of the war to a view in which it was seen as "a noble cause," the constant raising of Vietnam War comparisons may not have been a problem for the administration. This view, however, was never fully embraced by the public. The war remained a divisive and painful symbol, and its invocation in relation to Reagan's policy agenda in Central America proved to be a significant political obstacle.

Although Reagan's retelling of the Vietnam War story, emphasizing the perceived nobility of its purpose, had some resonance in the American public, it appears that this was primarily as it grappled with questions of the war's many veterans. It was obvious that Reagan had been less successful in moving broader public perceptions of the war in terms of his view about its centrality in global politics and the decades-long struggle between the West and the Soviet spheres of influence. For Americans, the reframing of the war was thus incomplete, and a strong undercurrent of discomfort with the perceptions of the war's legacy — of what the president called the Vietnam Syndrome — proved difficult to dislodge from public understanding.

Public attention to El Salvador lost some intensity in the final months of 1981, but resurfaced in full force when the Reagan administration announced that it would seek $100 million in aid for El Salvador the next year. A series of high-profile articles and commentaries appeared in leading publications, calling specific attention to the question of whether or not the situation in El Salvador would turn into something resembling the American experience in Vietnam. A piece in *Time* stated bluntly" "El Salvador: it is not Vietnam."[36] In another example, Anthony Lewis, who had already written in *The New York Times* his opinion that the Reagan presidency was marred by "blunder, incoherence and policy disaster,"[37] countered Assistant Secretary of State Thomas Enders' statement that El Salvador "is not Vietnam." Lewis asserted that "there are some similarities— and some reasons to worry about the analogy."[38]

When, at a February news conference, Reagan attempted to explain his view that the comparison between the two situations was a mistake, the version of events he gave for what had happened in Vietnam may have made matters worse. The press characterized Regan's knowledge of history about the Vietnam War as "confused" and seeming to "clash with widely accepted accounts of the past."[39]

By March 1982, the administration announced that it did not have plans to send combat troops to El Salvador, but the controversy continued. Haig attempted to justify Reagan policies with reports that the U.S. had evidence that the Salvadoran rebels received direction from outside nations.[40] By then, however, in the view of *New York Times* writer Adam Clymer, "the Reagan administration seems to have lost control of the political agenda it dominated throughout 1981" and public opinion was "running against" Reagan about matters such as El Salvador.[41] The administration subsequently announced that it sought talks with the Soviets and others regarding the issue, but the public's fears were already aroused. Now, fully 60 percent of respondents in a CBS-*New York Times* poll reported fears that the El Salvador situation would evolve into a situation resembling the Vietnam War.[42]

Legislative elections in El Salvador were held in March 1982. This event elicited praise from President Reagan. Events in El Salvador were briefly overshadowed by an attempt (not politically motivated) to assassinate Reagan on March 30, in which the president was shot and hospitalized. As would be expected, this event, and news of his speedy recovery, captured headlines temporarily. When it was clear that this crisis was passed, however, politics continued. The El Salvador matter had not been resolved, and in coming months the issue would again move, quite literally, to the front pages of American newspapers.

The Vietnam Veterans' Memorial

The Vietnam War already had been raised as a cautionary example in discussions about the problems in Central America, and it was clear that the war still held deeply negative associations for much of the American public. Discussions of war as a foreign policy had become largely separated from public discourse about Vietnam veterans, however. That picture continued to change.

Throughout this time, there was a persistent undercurrent of hope that some of the soldiers listed as missing-in-action might yet be returned alive. Popular sentiment on this ran strong, as many Americans continued to think about those who had served in its military during the war. The mass media's new view of Vietnam veterans, as seen in television, was evidence of changing interpretation in the popular culture. The ways in which the veterans were regarded in civic culture was changing, too. Perhaps nowhere was the symbolic sea-change, and the controversy it invoked, more perceptible than in the struggle to build a national memorial for veterans of the war.

The Vietnam War presented a new complexity to the national tradition of formally honoring military veterans after war. In the past, war memorials and monuments commemorated not only those who had served and those who had died, but also were testaments to the American victories that had resulted from the sacrifices of the soldiers. Memorials to veterans of previous wars were usually monuments to the nation itself, proclaiming a story in which the good of the U.S. had triumphed over the evil of aggressors. In the case of the war in Vietnam, of course, there was no victory to valorize, and it was hard to say, with any widespread agreement, exactly how the events fit into a narrative of good and evil. Moreover, there were still conflicted feelings about the men and women who had served. Some civilians, and some of the many veterans, were anxious to forget the war that was so different from the seemingly unambiguous World Wars. (The same could not be said of the so-called "forgotten" war in Korea, public memory of which seemed in many ways eclipsed by the long duration and trauma of the Vietnam War.)

In spring of 1981, it was announced that a Yale University student had won the competition to design the Vietnam Veterans Memorial that would be built in Washington, D.C. The design that 21-year-old Maya Lin submitted envisioned two large, black granite walls, to be arranged in a V-shape and built into the selected location. Inscribed on the walls would be the names of each of the 58,000 American military personnel known to have died in the war. Praising Lin's vision, the judges for the competition cited her proposal as "contemplative and reflective ... [and] superbly harmonious with its site."[43]

The selected design was not greeted with universal enthusiasm, however. In an opinion piece in *The New York Times,* for example, Tom Carhart,

VID L CLIMER · THOMAS G EDGREN · MICHAEL R HALIBURTON
· CALVIN W RAMSEY · CARROLL E RAYMER Jr · ROBERT L RICE Jr
ON · GARY D SENGSTOCK · JOE N SMITH · WILLIAM W WALKER
· PONDEXTUER E WILLIAMS · DON W AVERY · KIRK O BARKLEY
SHAWN G CANNON · ROBERT W ELLIOTT · WILBERT J JONES Jr
· ANTHONY V MARTINEZ · WILLIAM F McNULTY · JOE REYNA Jr
IAEL A CAFFEY · JOHN E CROWLEY · JOSEPH F MARCANTONIO
ANTHONY G KUBELUS Jr · WILLIAM H KUSCH · DANNY L EVANS ·
ARD W McFARLAND · JAMES D BRADLE · KENNETH J SORENSEN
E · GARY J WINTER · DONNIE D ASBURY · ANTHONY L RAMSEY
OS PIZARRO-COLON · THOMAS L PORTER · WALTER L REDDING
IIK · ALAN W ASHENFELTER · JAMES A BROWN · DAN G FEEZELL
CHARLES K PUDERBAUGH · JIMMIE D RYALS · BLAIR H SIMPSON
SSELL L BAHRKE Jr · ALAN B CHEESEMAN · DONALD C COLLINS
IICHAEL A GAGE · NICKALAS PEREZ GURNIAS · JAMES C JUNGE
TON · GEORGE D HENRY Jr · LESTER E OONK · JOHN P POWELL
GORY C STITT · LAWRENCE G SWARBRICK · ROBERT H WESTON
NILLIAM E BARRITT · MICHAEL J BRENTON · DENNIS H HERRICK ·
RANKLIN K NELSON · HECTOR D OYOLA · ALVIN L PEMBERTON
OUGLAS THOMPSON · DUANE E WALDRON · DANIEL C UPTON
· WARREN C ANDERSON · WILSON P BAILEY · JAMES C BECKER
SER · CURTIS COOPER · BEN JACKSON Jr · DONALD R HILLIARD
I · JAMES W MATTHEWS · JOHN E McGUIRE · PETER A SCHMIDT
S Jr · BILLY N JOHNSTON Jr · STEVEN R OTT · ROBERTIS PINKNEY
IFIELD · STEPHEN A SHARP · GARY L WASHENIK · ROBERT A ATER
IE · ROBERT W HART · RICHARD K JOHNSTON · MOSES E JONES
· PATRICK R O'BRIEN · ROGER D PARMENTIER · GUY W PA
OND L STANSBURY II · CHARLIE W TAYLOR · PHILLIP R W
N BOLLMAN · RALPH N DUEMLING · THOMAS L GUN
OMAS H PAPPENHEIM · JOSEPH H SHELTON III · DAV
ON · JOHN E ANTHONY · DENNIS M BAILEY · ROBE
ICO · EVELIO A GOMEZ · TERENCE M KJOS · DAN
NIG · FURMAN D HUGHES · MARSHALL K JONES
HORACE L WARDELL · MICHAEL J DOUGAN
H J KOSOWSKI · ROBERT W LANCASTER RO
AN M WIEGAND Jr · DAVID W YOUNGBLO
IPBELL · GLEN A CHAVEZ · WAYNE R DAV
ILL · GARY L FRAZIER · JOSEPH D GAGNO
N · EDWARD J NOVAK · THOMAS RO
ND S BRAMWELL · CLARENCE BRO
NES · ARTHUR MEDINA · DAVID W
SIMES Jr · SAM E STOUT · EVERE

who had graduated from West Point and was later a civilian lawyer in the Pentagon, wrote of his belief that the Lin design was a "black gash of shame and sorrow, hacked into the national visage that is the Mall" and that it was "pointedly insulting to the sacrifices" of the veterans it claimed to honor.[44] He further stated that "The jurors know nothing of the *real* [sic] war in Vietnam.... It may be that black wall sunk into a trench would be an appropriate statement of the political war in this country. But that is *not* [sic] the war whose veterans the Fund has been authorized to memorialize."[45] The writer was not alone in his views, as the selected design deviated from commonly held public expectations about what a war memorial should be. *The National Review* similarly complained, asserting that the focus on the many names of individuals drew away attention from the deaths being made for "a cause" and that "The invisibility of the monument on ground level symbolizes the 'unmentionability' of the war."[46]

The design was unusual in comparison to traditional war memorials and public monuments. Its stark simplicity was devoid of grandeur. Instead, the design offered huge black slabs, sunk below street level, with funereal overtones. For some people, the shiny black surface — as opposed to the white stone often used in public monuments — seemed to overly accentuate a sense of morbidity that outweighed a feeling of honored remembrance. Some also questioned the numbing effect of the row after row of names that listed each of the soldiers who had died. Interestingly, the Memorial itself thus offered no heroic representation of the fallen soldiers and, in fact, yielded very little information about the war itself.[47] To a great extent, then, the effect that the Memorial had on viewers depended upon the knowledge, opinion and context that visitors brought to it.[48]

This seeming ambiguity of the Memorial led to some speculation that it might be used as a powerful symbol in political efforts to create a revisionist public memory of the war.[49] Alternatively, some observers found the Memorial to be a deeply personal place of silence, reflection or private commemoration[50] or a place where visitors could confront their own emotions in a search for redemption, amid lingering feelings of guilt and sorrow resulting from the war.[51] Indeed, the Memorial was seen as enigmatic in many respects, allowing for — or perhaps reflecting back — the multiple interpretations of the Vietnam War that remained unresolved, not only at the time of its unveiling, but also for decades beyond.[52]

Opposite: Although initially the design for Vietnam Veterans Memorial sparked some controversy, the Wall soon came to be a highly revered monument. It often evokes powerful emotional responses from visitors, who sometimes leave flowers, messages and mementoes in honor of loved ones whose names appear on the huge black slabs. Photograph: National Park Service.

Though responses were generally positive, some of the controversy about the design continued upon the Memorial's unveiling in 1982. The occasion of its appearance prompted magazine articles presenting a wide range of views, with titles such as "Refighting the Vietnam War,"[53] "Honoring Vietnam Veterans—At Last,"[54] (both appearing in *Newsweek)* and "Monumental Folly"[55] (in *The Progressive*). Even general interest magazines took note of the Memorial; the widely read *People Weekly* reported that the new Memorial "raises hope — and anger."[56]

Some aspects of the design remained difficult for critics to accept. An article that was published in *The Nation* three years later captured the essence of the complaints from those who had objected to the memorial's design: "They regarded the walls as a symbol for peaceniks. 'A wailing wall for liberals'; ... a degrading ditch"; "the most insulting and demeaning memorial to our experience that was possible."[57] (Even among more moderate voices, some still wished for a realistic and representational sculpture to honor the American war dead. Two years after the Memorial was opened to the public, a representational sculpture was installed as an accompaniment to Lin's original design.)

Soon after it was opened to the public, however, much of the controversy melted away, and the Memorial came to be widely accepted as a place of reverence. As observed in an article in *U.S. News and World Report* on the first anniversary of the unveiling, the Memorial had become "the most emotional ground in the nation's capital" and "a place where Americans make peace with their past.... People kiss it, caress it, salute it, scream at it, pray before it, tape messages to it. It is only a wall, stark and black, but it imposes a spell over those who go grieving there."[58] Indeed, much of the initial controversy about the Memorial evaporated quickly, and Maya Lin's monument came to be called simply, "The Wall." It did not resolve the ambiguities of the war, but it did help to remove the stigma associated with it for Americans who had served in it. The Vietnam Veterans Memorial has remained one of the most recognizable and honored sites in the United States since that time, even as new generations of visitors have encountered it.

Though for many people it was overshadowed by contemporary events and the unveiling of the Memorial, in 1982 another moment for potential closure on the veterans issue came about, as well.

Television Grapples with History

A high-profile news media organization came under fire for its retrospective coverage of the Vietnam War in 1982, although at first it seemed that it was that organization that was on the offensive. In January of that year, CBS aired a documentary report called "Uncounted Enemy: A Vietnam Deception." The program was deeply critical of American military leadership during the war and cast an especially unflattering light on General William Westmoreland, who had overseen American military operations there at the height of the war. The CBS report charged that leading up to the traumatic 1968 Tet Offensive, high-ranking American military officers deceived government officials about enemy forces. Essentially, the charge was that the military leaders had intentionally withheld intelligence information that indicated a substantially higher number of enemy forces than was communicated to Washington. The report claimed that this was an intentional misuse of the intelligence information and that the actions constituted a "conspiracy."[59]

In making its charges, the report included a video-taped sequence in which famed CBS reporter Mike Wallace interviewed Westmoreland. What viewers of the program saw was a close-up video image of a visibly uncomfortable Westmoreland. The arrangement and editing of the material seemed to suggest that Westmoreland was not being candid, bolstering the program's claim of a conspiracy and cover-up. Angered by this portrayal, Westmoreland called a news conference. He disputed CBS contentions, which he saw as untrue and unfair, and the presentation itself, which he claimed was unduly manipulative. Because of these factors, he asserted, viewers were left with a false impression. When CBS refused to grant him air-time to contradict the claims of the report and what he saw as the mistaken impressions that the report gave, he brought suit against the network.

The situation between Westmoreland and CBS was particularly acrid. The retired general sought $120 million in damages for libel. The network, the program's producer, and reporter Wallace found themselves under siege not only by Westmoreland, but also by others who were critical of the report. In an unusual development, the typically non-controversial magazine *TV Guide* ran a story describing the CBS actions a "smear" and calling into question the methods used in putting the CBS report together. The story judged that the network had failed to maintain appropriate journalistic standards.[60] Even an internal investigation at CBS seemed critical of some aspects of the production.[61] The dampening effect of the libel suit was noticeable, as to some it seemed that the press was once again under attack for a Vietnam War story. (The matter went to trial, but it was settled in 1985. CBS issued a mild apology.)

The Westmoreland lawsuit highlighted an increasing disapproval, particularly apparent among the conservatives energized by the Reagan presidency, with the ways in which the Vietnam War was presented to the public.

In the years immediately following the war, widespread public aversion to the topic led to it being discussed and presented somewhat indirectly. Fair or not, just as Americans had previously become somewhat accustomed to looking the other way at the misfortunes that befell Vietnam veterans, it had also been reluctant to embrace a full blown airing of conflicting interpretations of the war.

CBS may have miscalculated the effect that its report would have in reopening wounds that much of the public had been satisfied in putting aside. Discussions and presentations about the war had become more accepted, but these had continued to deal more with after-the-fact consequences and situations than with a thorough reexamination of past controversy about the war itself. Events of the present intruded into thinking about war and peace, however. With the suggestion that the Soviet Union was still deeply menacing and with events in Central America appearing to have significant consequences for shaping the scope and meaning of American power in the world, the Vietnam War could be regarded either as a hurdle to be overcome or an argument for restraint, depending upon one's ideological perspective. In this context, the time was approaching when the underlying polarization of ideological opinion about the Vietnam War would come more visibly to the surface.

Though a number of new books and articles reexamining the war had been published, television played an important part in returning political controversy about the war to the public arena.[62] The controversy surrounding the CBS documentary film was part of that story. Provoking perhaps even more controversy, scrutiny and opinion, however, was the thirteen-hour television reflection of the war broadcast by the public television network.

There had been advance publicity for a Vietnam War-related television project that was already in development in 1980 under the auspices of Boston's public television station, WGBH. Reports indicated that producers there had been assembling what would later be called a "television history" of America's "living-room war."[63] By the time this project, *Vietnam: A Television History*, was completed and broadcast in the autumn of 1983, the political climate in the country had evolved. The changes in attitude about the war that Ronald Reagan championed were more evident, especially among conservative critics of the media.

In a 1983 newspaper article, Fox Butterfield claimed that since the end of the war "The big questions went unasked and unanswered."[64] With increasing scholarly attention to the subject and with publicity in anticipation of *Vietnam: A Television History*, he reported that this was changing. The emerging view that he saw, however, contrasted sharply with

Reagan's interpretation of the war as "a noble cause." Instead, new scholarship argued that the war was even more complex than it originally seemed. As researchers began sifting through records, memoirs and other documents, the picture emerging in their writing suggested that assumptions of liberals and conservatives were questionable and events were more ambiguous than previously realized.

When *Vietnam: A Television History* was finally broadcast in the fall of 1983, Butterfield was again called upon to offer his assessment. Having been stationed by the *Times* in Vietnam for several years near the end of the war, his vantage point was not that of a media critic or political analyst. To his eyes, the PBS project was "extraordinary" and "meticulously researched and carefully balanced." [65] The series received favorable notice in many other widely circulated publications, as well, including *The Washington Post, Time,* and *Newsweek.* In terms of reaching an audience, the series was the most successful documentary that public television had yet aired, with its first episode reaching at least 9 percent of American households during the initial broadcast.[66] (The series was later repeated.)

Yet, as Butterfield noted, the thirteen hour-long episodes in the program contained "something to offend everyone, both hawks and doves." One aspect of the production that was striking consisted of the many excerpts of interviews with leaders and other participants in the war. In the series American viewers saw and heard first-hand reflections from former North Vietnamese enemies, as well as with the more familiar accounts from Americans and allied personnel. For example, Ho Chi Minh's close associate and the longtime prime minister of North Vietnam, Pham Van Dong, appeared in numerous interview segments, often coming across as an elegant and refined elder statesman. (Photographs promoting the series even featured the prime minister and the series' executive producer, Richard Ellison together, suggesting a closeness of association that was perhaps not reflective of the reality underlying the series' production.) Moreover, the intimacy and directness of the television medium in the arranged interview settings gave an almost disarming appearance to some of those interviewed. It seemed to put a human face on an enemy that was, for all its televised aspects during the war itself, still largely unfamiliar to American audience.

Though many observers agreed with Butterfield's appraisal of *Vietnam: A Television History,* others had a very different view. What some had seen as a balanced attempt at objectivity, other observers interpreted as unabashed liberal propaganda. The series had a largely American focus, and thus the complexities and controversies in American thought and action received substantially more attention than did those of the warring factions of Vietnamese. Some of the presentation portrayed the American leaders or military in an ambivalent or negative light, which to some viewers seemed justified and to others was evidence of bias. The impression given of Presidents Johnson and Nixon was often unflattering. In some scenes, American soldiers seemed confused or misguided.

In many important respects, then, *Vietnam: A Television History* did not fit in with the reassessment of history that was part of the Reagan agenda. The program brought renewed attention to past controversy at a time when the administration was arguing for an American presence abroad. As writer Stanley Karnow (who worked on the series and whose book *Vietnam: A History*[67] was promoted in conjunction with the television series) noted, however, in the wake of the Vietnam War experience "people are asking questions about U.S. troops in Lebanon and Central America."[68] The television series helped to amplify attention to the perceived mistakes, missteps and ill-advised policy-making in the war years. It provided a ready-made picture of past events to which contemporary situations could be compared, perhaps unfavorably. The series did not present a view of the war or the world, then, that was welcomed by many conservative observers.

Among the most vocal detractors of the public television series was Reed Irvine, who had founded the organization Accuracy in Media (AIM) in 1969. AIM was established to bring attention to what its members perceived as the widespread and numerous distortions and inaccuracies in the media, and especially in broadcast media. The group's general position was that the mainstream news media had a liberal bias which was largely unchallenged, and that this bias should be engaged and countered. Thus seeing the public television series as a grossly inaccurate and unfair portrayal of what had happened during the war, it soon sought to have a work produced and broadcast that rebutted the picture that emerged from *Vietnam: A Television History*. Within two years, AIM secured the financial sources to mount this challenge, enlisting filmmakers and historians with more conservative views on the war and the services of the familiar and vocally conservative actor Charlton Heston as narrator. Somewhat surprisingly to many of its supporters, the public television network agreed to air this AIM-produced program, *Television's Vietnam: The Real Story*, two years later.

Continuing Crisis in El Salvador

On the international front, 1983 was a challenging year for the United States, in which a number of crises erupted. A commercial passenger jet, Korean Airlines flight 007, was shot down by the Soviets when it veered into Soviet airspace, causing heightened international tensions. In October,

American military forces invaded the tiny Caribbean island nation of Grenada after its leader was murdered. In Lebanon, where U.S. Marines were stationed in an international peacekeeping operation, a truck bomb killed 300 soldiers. All the while, the situation in Central America remained a major issue in American politics.

The El Salvador issue continued to dwell on the minds of the American public. It was emphasized in substantial news media attention, in which perceptions of the situation continued to be shaped by memories of the Vietnam War. In CBS News broadcasts, for example, viewers heard Dan Rather state that Ronald Reagan's language about El Salvador "recalled Southeast Asia" and Lesley Stahl ask more directly, "Is El Salvador turning into another Vietnam?"[69] The White House lobbied hard for its assertive policy position on the U.S. role in Central America, but in doing so the anxieties of some members of Congress, and many in the public, were aroused. The news media coverage was in many ways relentless, repeatedly voicing this theme. Writing in the *New York Times,* Anthony Lewis stated bluntly "Vietnam is in the air, and everybody knows it."[70] It may not have made much difference, however, whether people accepted this way of framing the El Salvador issue at face value; it was raised so often that even the many denials may have unintentionally reinforced the purported parallels.

Meanwhile, despite American aid, the Salvadoran military encountered much difficulty in its battle against the insurgents. As the situation escalated and the rhetoric in Washington became more heated, many Republicans voiced strong objections to the analogy between current events and the past war. Speaking to members of the press in March, Republican Howard Baker complained "El Salvador is not Vietnam.... But the stability of the [Central American] region is of vital concern to the United States. There's a far more credible argument for the domino effect in El Salvador than there was in Vietnam."[71]

But the analogy was too firmly established to be argued away. An opinion piece in *The Washington Post,* which declared that "the echoes of Vietnam are getting louder," was only one of many voices from across the nation that expressed a similar view. A sampling of the titles given to pieces appearing in *The New York Times* in May and June gives additional insight into the use of Vietnam War rhetoric in the policy debate. Among the pieces published were "Salvador Parallels Vietnam; This Time Let's Win,"[72] "Salvador Isn't Vietnam; Illusions Roll On"[73] and "Shaped by the War in Vietnam."[74] As these titles suggest, the actions of the then-present were being viewed through the lens of various understandings of the Vietnam War and what it meant.

In July, the Pentagon asked for a doubling of U.S. military advisers for

El Salvador in the following year, to a level of 125 advisers.[75] A subsequent Gallup poll revealed, however, that a majority of respondents were wary of a new "Vietnam-like commitment" in El Salvador and that almost half did not agree with Reagan's Central American policies.[76] Although there was widespread questioning of its stance, however, the administration pushed the issue forward on the agenda. The controversy was much noted; a front-page headline on the issue read: "The Boiling Point; White House Puts Central American on a Front Burner."[77]

A major story in the *New York Times Sunday Magazine* focused attention on the El Salvador situation and again reinforced perceived parallels with the prior American experience in Southeast Asia. As correspondent Lydia Chavez wrote, "Once again, for the first time since the 1950's, a small group of American military advisers has been placed on the outer edges of American foreign policy."[78] Though noting differences between the military circumstances in El Salvador and what had been the case in Vietnam, the article, and many others appearing at the time in a variety of publications, gave more indication of the linkage between the two that had been firmly established in public perceptions.

Thus, the Reagan's administration's efforts to thwart what it perceived as Soviet interference in Central America and elsewhere continued to be influenced by the war that had ended in the previous decade. The quick American action in Grenada provided a small respite from concerns about a creeping escalation of military involvement in El Salvador. But the war's memory remained powerful. Even perceptions of the seemingly far-removed bombing in Lebanon, in which hundreds of U.S. Marines were killed, were not free from the lingering influence of the Vietnam War.[79]

As Reagan prepared for his re-election campaign in the following year, then, it was clear that the American people had not escaped from the ever-lengthening shadows of the war. Reagan had entered office calling for a conservative renewal in America, which in many respects seemed well on the way to fulfillment. He also had engaged in a highly public political test of wills with the Soviets; the final results of these efforts would not be clear for several years.

Reagan's quest to reframe public memory of the Vietnam War, however, led to more mixed results. It is true that much of American culture had adopted a new and more multi-dimensional way of thinking about American veterans of that war and that these more-positive perceptions reinforced the renewed emphasis on military strength upon which Reagan's foreign policy was based. More encompassing views of the war, however, continued to be negative. Rather than being seen as a "noble purpose," most of the public continued to perceive it as something that should be avoided in conceiving America's place in international affairs. Those perceptions clearly became enmeshed in public discourse about global events of the 1980s. Yet, almost midway through Reagan's "morning in America," the legacy of the war was poised for continued evolution in public awareness.

In coming months, however, the then-secret aid that was funneled to the *contras* — dubbed "freedom fighters" by Reagan — who were fighting the leftist Nicaraguan government would be the source of a significant crisis for the administration.

4

From *Rambo* to *Platoon*

In a small village on New Year's Eve, 1983, a hillside Buddhist temple was doused with gasoline and set on fire. Prior to this arson attack, officials received an anonymous telephone call warning that a "Vietnamese pagoda" had been targeted. In later calls to a local newspaper, the unidentified voice stated that this act of violence was motivated by "flashbacks and nightmares" and the "hell we are still going through."[1] Three American veterans of the Vietnam War were subsequently arrested for the crime. Unlike fictional films relating stories of Vietnam veterans returning to Southeast Asia with unfinished business, however, this incident took place half a world away from Vietnam, in the quiet of a New England winter in Hawley, Massachusetts.

Assuming that the temple was Vietnamese, the arsonists intended the destruction to be an act of vengeance. Prompted by resentment, their actions were fueled by perceptions that Vietnamese refugees in the United States were treated better than America's own Vietnam War veterans. The targeted site was not Vietnamese as attackers imagined, however. Instead, the Buddhist temple had been established by American students of a refugee Tibetan Buddhist who had no ties to Vietnam.

The defendants appeared in a Massachusetts courtroom a few days after the incident. Their attorney characterized the arson as a "symbolic act [aimed] to bring about immediate treatment." Indeed, it was revealed that the defendants were patients at a nearby Veterans Administration hospital, one of several such facilities specializing in the treatment of post-traumatic stress disorder.[2]

These events revealed the lingering pain and disillusionment that was a reality for some American soldiers who had served in Vietnam and for whom the legacy of the war was no abstraction. In most respects, however, this episode was an aberration. The vast majority of the men and women who served in the American military during the war were not left with such debilitating psychological after-effects. Though it is doubtful that few individuals who had served in combat areas were completely unaffected by those experiences, most Vietnam veterans, like veterans of wars before them, successfully returned to society and went about the business of living their lives.

The story of troubled Vietnam War veterans, as manifested in the temple burning episode, called to mind the Vietnam veterans' syndrome, which had been emphasized on screen and in popular culture in the preceding years. Although most Vietnam veterans had successfully rejoined society, many Americans were haunted by the knowledge that some veterans were less fortunate. Indeed, some veterans continued to be plagued by their wartime experience, and they still suffered mentally and physically from its effects. This image of the suffering veteran was powerful and remained unsettling.

Transforming Image of Vietnam Veterans

Into the mid–1980s, memories and perceptions of the war and its veterans continued to evolve. The psychological and physical legacy of the war for those Americans who actually participated in the war continued to differ from the portrayals of such experiences in fictional accounts. On screen, in addition to the affable image of Vietnam veterans seen in television's *Magnum, P.I.,* new movie conceptions appeared, updating a portrait of Vietnam veterans that was first seen in the 1970s. These new film characterizations emphasized the Vietnam veteran as a brooding loner, quietly suffering because of the U.S. government's failure to provide strength in leadership or in moral virtue. Beneath the misunderstood surface in such portrayals, however, was an innate heroic nature, waiting for the opportunity to be enacted.

Variations on this theme ran through many of the screen productions of the era that had the Vietnam War as a subject. In an underlying formula that is common to many of these productions, a wronged or misunderstood veteran is thrust into some new situation. Then, various aspects of the war are recreated, eventually resulting in a symbolic victory through which the nobility of the veteran and patriotic American purpose are vicariously reaffirmed. Basically conservative in tone, in many respects the thematic outline of these films fit within the reframed vision of the war that Reagan had championed.

Among the highest-profile productions in the filmic evolution of Vietnam veterans and the broader Vietnam War theme were the Rambo films starring Sylvester Stallone, of *Rocky* fame. Spanning the 1980s, the three Rambo films captured the changing moods and tastes of American audiences. The first of these was director Ted Kotcheff's 1982 film *First Blood*, an adaptation of David Morrell's novel that introduced the character John Rambo. It paved the way for the next stage in the evolution of film portrayals of Vietnam veterans and its own sequel, the wildly popular *Rambo: First Blood, Part II*. By the end of the decade, the Rambo story was reset in Afghanistan in *Rambo III* (1988), placing the fictional Vietnam veteran in the midst of contemporary international events. After these three film treatments, the Rambo character would come to be the best-known film version of the 1980s-style Vietnam veteran.

In *First Blood*, viewers encounter the drifter John Rambo, a former Green Beret of European-Native American heritage. The latter characteristic allows the film to combine two strands of outsider narrative traditions in American cinematic mythology — the emerging theme of the Vietnam combat veteran and the more familiar theme of Native Americans as noble warriors. (A precursor to this can be found in the 1971 film *Billy Jack*, which also focused on the story of a misunderstood Vietnam veteran of Native-American and European ancestry.) In the story, Rambo is wronged by local authorities. He subsequently escapes into the mountainous terrain of the Pacific Northwest, where he is pursued by an array of well-armed police and military personnel. Once in the forest, Rambo displays amazing physical skills and intuition. For much of the film, Rambo fends off and eludes his pursuers, despite being greatly outnumbered.

Two important themes become evident as the film unfolds. First, the film seems to imply that superb American soldiers, here exemplified by Rambo, could not be the reason the war was lost. If Rambo is any indication, *First Blood* seems to suggest they were too strong, cunning and noble to be the reason for failure. Second, and perhaps more blatant, is the less-than-subtle indictment of Vietnam-era leaders that is suggested when Rambo is betrayed by his former commander. This betrayal is a second victimization for the Rambo character. (The implication is that the first occurred during the war itself when the nation failed to adequately support the military.) Because of the betrayal, Rambo is captured at the end of the film. In keeping with emerging themes in American political culture of that time, this mirrors the idea that failed leadership contributed to the United States' loss of the war.

This first filmic encounter with Rambo shows the character at a transitional stage in screen portrayals of Vietnam veterans. Saddled with the ill-effects of wartime service, *First Blood*'s image of the veteran recalls the image of the socially maladjusted veteran, which was found in films in the previous decade. Audiences see that Rambo suffers from flashbacks of his ordeal as a prisoner of war, and he often strikes back in anger.[3] Rambo's intensely violent responses, however, are shown to be more those of a wronged victim than of a social misfit. Unlike the character of Travis Bickle in *Taxi Driver,* whose violent impulses were rooted in a psychological state so damaged that it was implied he was unfit for society, the film suggests that Rambo's violence is motivated by righteous anger. In this respect, Rambo followed in the footsteps of action-oriented films with vigilante themes that had been popular with audiences in previous years, including the popular *Dirty Harry* films that starred Clint Eastwood.

The level of violence in *First Blood* appeared excessive to some viewers, and film writers took note of the outlandishness of Rambo's heroics on screen. Although according to *The Washington Post* "the script is riddled with grotesquely laughable situations and lines,"[4] *Newsweek* less caustically judged that the film was potentially "crowd-pleasing," even if it represented "a slick piece of manipulation."[5] Regardless of the film's non-realism and the many filmmaking deficiencies asserted by critics, it was a commercial success."[6] A sequel was soon planned.

It would seriously underestimate audiences to suggest that simplistic screen portrayals of the war or its veterans in films such as *First Blood* led audiences to accept these portrayals as essentially accurate representations. Though cloaked in the exaggerated character of Rambo and fantastic plot elements, however, the underlying messages of *First Blood* struck a chord with the American public. This may not be surprising since, if the surface elements of plot and character are stripped away, a narrative consistent with much of 1980s American ideology is apparent. At an elemental level, one finds in *First Blood* a story of the true American fighting for what is right, and of the implied dangers of a big government without genuinely patriotic leaders.

The success of the film assured that its underlying thematic points were widely disseminated. The implicit messages emphasizing the heroism — in this case super-heroism — of the Vietnam veteran stood in stark contrast to the picture of a military-governmental bureaucracy, which is characterized by failure, ineptness and betrayal. As one analysis has suggested, the film symbolically suggests a major failure of American institutions.[7]

The themes were further developed in populist films in the following two years, particularly in *Uncommon Valor* (1983) and *Missing in Action* (1984). In the narrative of the former film, the wealthy father funds a private commando mission to rescue his missing-in-action son, who he has discovered was being held prisoner in a secret compound in Laos. Similar to *First Blood*'s portrayal of the government and military establishment, government agencies in *Uncommon Valor* are shown to be unpatriotic, actively working against the interests of still-imprisoned soldiers. As if to drive home the point with viewers, officials threaten the father when he refuses their demands to terminate the mission.

The next year's *Missing in Action*, directed by Joseph Zito and a vehicle for actor-martial arts expert Chuck Norris, continued with that theme. Norris plays the hero of the film, Col. James Braddock. According to the story, Braddock had escaped from a POW camp during the war, but he remains haunted by the ordeal and is plagued by violent flashbacks to his prisoner days. He cannot forget these terrible experiences and even while watching television is confronted with news stories of MIAs still in captivity.

The film implicitly suggests that Braddock's subsequent rescue mission would have been unnecessary were it not for the misguided American government's pitiful failures.[8] Instead, it is left to the almost mythic American soldier, Braddock, to save the day. By virtue of his resolve and his individual moral character and physical prowess, Braddock is shown as an antidote to a malaise that resulted in the intense suffering of neglected and forsaken prisoners of war. These themes, which captured the mood of many Americans, would be promoted even more fully in the first sequel to *First Blood*, released the following year.

Changing image of Vietnam veterans in television entertainment. During these middle years of the Reagan era, the Vietnam veteran's image also continued a metamorphosis in television. This theme of Vietnam veterans as heroic renegades, typified by *First Blood,* was toned down and combined with a portrayal of the veteran as a more conventional crime-fighting hero (as seen in *Magnum, P.I.*) in an unlikely action series that was introduced by NBC television in 1983. The running storyline in this series, *The A-Team,* involved a group of eccentric, wise-cracking Vietnam veterans who were fugitives from military authorities. Having been falsely accused of wrongdoing, episodes show their attempts to stay one step ahead of their military pursuers. As they travel around the country, the band of fugitives stumbles onto situations in which they dispense vigilante justice. Their adventures are accompanied by many fist fights, martial arts sequences, car crashes, and other cliché elements from television of this period. The violence, though frequent in the series, is presented in a one-dimensional, mostly cartoon-like way, and much of the time the series aimed for humorous effect.

Although presented ostensibly as a group of non-conformists who were unfairly victimized by the military system, the group ironically continues to replicate standard authority structures. They continue to follow their paternalistic leader, and thus provide the television audience with a way to enjoy the exploits of the band without threatening traditional values.⁹ The experienced actor George Peppard portrayed Col. John "Hannibal" Smith, the male authority-figure for the group, to whom the other members of the band routinely deferred. Harkening back to earlier Vietnam veteran stereotypes, the team also included an eccentric character, "Howling Mad" Murdoch, who had been rescued by the group from a psychiatric hospital. By far the most attention-getting member of *The A-Team*, however, was an actor with the stage name of Mr. T, who portrayed the character called B.A. (Bad Attitude) Baracas. The popular B.A. character provided the series with a potentially dangerous — though here largely neutralized — African-American male with many stereotypical qualities as a complement for the otherwise white cast.

Unexpectedly, *The A-Team* achieved high ratings and was labeled the biggest success of the television season. The Vietnam veteran as fugitive-from-the-law thus became a standard, and in this case blasé, weekly fixture in many American homes. The network had no pretensions that the series was making any important statement about the actual experience of veterans (or anyone else, for that matter). In a candid interview, NBC executive Brandon Tartikoff admitted to a reporter that "I am not going to sit here and say that I am very proud of *The-A Team*. We are not looking for Emmy nominations, but to get blood pumping at the network."¹⁰ In that respect, *The A-Team* fully met the network's goals. It captured a predominantly young, male audience and received much publicity.

With the success of the series, the fugitive aspect of the series eventually was dropped from the storyline. The team was secretly pardoned and then sent on clandestine government missions. The pardon erased the outlaw aspect of the show, and it symbolically restored the fugitives to respectability and acceptance. The characters moved seamlessly from the role as outcasts back to loyal soldiers whose main goal was continued service to their country.

Although the Vietnam War was a necessary, if contrived, element in explaining the team's original motivations, it was nonetheless treated casually. There was no introspection on what the Vietnam War meant to these characters. Instead, the war and the characters' service in it were mostly background elements that provided a convenient excuse for the absurdities of the plots. This may have been an unintended side-effect to the war's pedestrian portrayal, however, especially for the many younger members of the audience. The bland picture of the Vietnam War that the series suggested removed important contextual aspects of the historical war. The divisiveness of the war is essentially absent, and watching episodes of the series, it would be difficult to come away with any sense of what it was about the war that had so troubled younger viewers' parents and grandparents.

In this milieu, one can imagine the feelings of those Vietnam veterans who genuinely were suffering from after-effects of the war as they witnessed often unrealistic, if not outright bizarre, portrayals of Vietnam veterans on movie and television screens. The evolving image of the Vietnam veteran seemed far removed from the actual experience of veterans. A decade after the war, many viewers were too young to have memories of the war era. In that context, the vivid screen portrayals held the potential to influence general feelings and associations about the war, even if these productions were never interpreted as literal history. If few mistook any of these screen presentations as fact, it nonetheless seems reasonable to conclude that the films and television programs reinforced a general mood, or perhaps an orientation, that seems at odds with the historical realities of the war.

The Persistence of the POW-MIA Issue

Films and television shows involving Vietnam War themes may have had unlikely or even preposterous plot elements, but one basic impulse in many of them was already widely evident in American society: the yearning to recover MIA and POW soldiers. Years after the war's end, many Americans never lost hope that at least some of these men would be found alive and returned to their homes and families. Government officials sometimes had less optimism that prisoners remained alive, but they responded to the issue and were increasingly frustrated by their feeling that more information could and should be provided by the communist regime in Hanoi.

Politicians in the mid–1980s often promoted the intertwining Missing-in-Action and Prisoner-of-War (MIA-POW) issue. From the bully pulpit of the presidency, Ronald Reagan's personal interest provided a significant force in keeping public attention focused on this emotional subject. (According to some writers, Reagan's interest in the issue was heightened by the fact that many years earlier, in his days as a Hollywood actor, he had played a Korean War-era POW in the 1954 film, *The Prisoner of War*.[11]) In 1982, for example, military aircraft provided transportation, at public expense, so that more than 450 MIA relatives could attend a convention on the issue.[12] (The practice was repeated in subsequent years.) The next year, the Defense Intelligence Agency began a major new effort to gather and reexamine evidence about the status of MIA and POW soldiers.[13]

By the 1984 election year, the fate of missing servicemen in Vietnam was a prominent national issue. In February of that year, Assistant Secretary of Defense Richard Armitage and National League of Families executive director Ann Mills Griffiths led a high-level delegation to Vietnam for renewed discussions about missing American soldiers.[14] Another delegation, from the Vietnam Veterans of America, was led by its president Robert Muller to Cambodia and Vietnam in search of more information that same year.[15]

For many Americans, however, suspicions were not calmed by these visits. In July, after the Vietnamese government returned the remains of eight more American servicemen, a Pentagon official bluntly stated, "We believe they [the North Vietnamese government] have knowledge of other remains."[16] Speaking about efforts to account for the missing on the occasion of National MIA-POW Recognition Day in 1984, the president promised that "we will not rest" in the efforts to resolve the issue.[17] In that period, the distinctive black MIA-POW flag flying in the wind became an increasingly familiar sight across the U.S., providing a visible reminder of those who had not returned.

The goal of gaining the return of missing-in-action and prisoner-of-war soldiers, or their remains, had become a national quest. By the mid–1980s, the MIA-POW rhetoric was firmly part of the political arena. As time continued to pass, however, the issue became increasingly more difficult to sort out. Though official rhetoric often emphasized the search for information and the return of the deceased, many people retained hope that it would be the living, not the dead, who would be returned to American shores. Few politicians or officials, whether conservative or liberal, wished to be seen as giving up the search, which by this time was discussed in a decidedly patriotic tone. Moreover, for the new Cold Warrior Ronald Reagan and his conservative allies, the prominence of the issue kept the image of untrustworthy and potentially devious communist adversaries highly visible in the public sphere.

Complicating attempts to understand the MIA-POW issue were the confusing and sometimes ambiguous realities of warfare in a faraway place. In fact, it was difficult to assess exactly how many were really missing because the Pentagon had not been consistent over time in the criteria it used for determining missing-in-action status. During the war, for example, a list of missing-in-action personnel was kept separately from a list of those who were designated in another category, KIA/BNR (killed in action, body not recovered).[18] The latter list included the many cases in which known circumstances dictated that it was all but certain that the soldiers had perished. In many such cases, American military personnel had witnessed the deaths, but warfare circumstances made recovery of the remains impossible. (Examples might include cases in which a jet had been shot down or when combat fatalities occurred in hostile areas or rough terrain, making it impossible to retrieve the body of the deceased.)

By the early 1980s, however, the Pentagon decided to revise its practices and combine the names from the KIA/BNR list with those on its missing-in-action list.[19] With this procedural change, the number of persons cited as missing in public discussions increased. The new, higher numbers varied in different sources, but reports usually indicated that it was in excess of 2,000. Importantly, this new total included a large proportion of cases in which the status had previously been categorized as deceased. Public awareness of this change seems to have minimal, however, which may have contributed to ongoing confusion about the magnitude of the issue.

Of course, given the nature of the warfare in Vietnam, there still was room for a small degree of uncertainty, however minute, and so questions remained about whether at least some of those listed as missing might yet be alive. Some families and loved ones of the missing continued to cling to this hope. Unfortunately, as was the case in World War II, the Korean Conflict, and other wars, in which the large numbers of American soldiers were similarly listed as missing in action and whose remains were never recovered, the exact details about the fates of many of the Vietnam MIAs may never be known. Despite widespread attention to the issue, the years of search did not result in the return of any living MIA soldiers, though occasionally new information about the deceased was learned. Overall, however, for the friends and kin of the soldiers, and for the political leaders and officials who took up the MIA-POW cause, the issue was not one for which a fully satisfactory closure was found.

Families and friends had understandably compelling personal reasons to focus on the issue, and support networks with this aim assured that the issue did not fade from view. In the larger arena of national politics, it is no doubt true that many had genuine empathy for the plight of these soldiers and for their relatives' suffering. Yet, there was also a broader symbolic purpose in keeping the issue in the public eye. The search for MIAs, futile or not, presented an opportunity to make things right for a country which, according to some, had "failed" its soldiers in prosecuting the war. It was a way to restore some sense of honor after, what was for Americans, the war's bad ending. In these respects, the continued attention to the surmised plight of MIAs was fully in concert with the impulse to see the war in Reagan's terms, as a "noble cause." In any case, the news media were reluctant to be caught casting a skeptical eye on persistent assertions that American prisoners of war were still being held, even many years after the cessation of hostilities. For Americans, political rhetoric and fictional entertainment came together to perpetuate the image of the MIA-POW, forsaken in the jungle, as one of the most lasting impressions and legacies of the war. It became a powerful part of what has been called American "mythmaking."[20]

A Second Term

Since Reagan's election in 1980, the United States had confronted many domestic problems beyond the foreign policy issues that commanded public interest. In 1981, for example, the Federal Centers for Disease Control and Prevention (CDC) revealed an unusual increase in cases of a rare cancer, and soon the world learned of a frightening new disease that came to be known as Acquired Immune Deficiency Syndrome.[21] As the 1980s rolled on, other domestic problems surfaced. A growing awareness and fear of widespread drug abuse, for example, led to the famous "Just say no" anti-drug campaign, championed by First Lady Nancy Reagan. Responding to these and other developments, many conservatives lamented what they perceived as increasing moral decay in American society.

But it was the national economy that was the administration's central domestic concern. Eager to reverse the economic woes that Reagan had inherited when he assumed office, the administration pushed a recipe for economic renewal with "supply-side economics"— often called "Reaganomics" during Reagan's tenure — at its center. The administration aimed to reduce tax burdens on businesses in the belief that wealth would "trickle down" for the benefit of all. The mammoth size of government — though not of defense — was an impediment to the nation's economic health in the president's view, and so efforts were made to reduce the bureaucracy and its perceived intrusion into daily life. Reagan embarked on his economic policies, which favored massive tax cuts, reductions in many social programs, and significant increases in defense spending, and by the middle of his first term, the economy began moving forward.

It was in these circumstances that 1980 Democratic vice-presidential candidate Walter Mondale pursued a bid for the presidency in 1984, fending off challenges from fellow Democrats Sen. Gary Hart and the Rev. Jesse Jackson for the party's nomination.[22] Although Mondale's historic selection of a woman, Geraldine Ferarro, as the vice-presidential candidate on the ticket garnered significant attention and rallied some support, in the end there was little that Mondale could do to prevail in light of Reagan's popularity with much of the public. On the domestic side of politics, the recovering economy hindered Mondale's efforts to convince the public of deficiencies or perceived unfairness in Reagan's policies. In international

politics, the image of Reagan as the new Cold Warrior was difficult to overcome.

The Central American foreign policy area did remain a concern during the election year, however. Repeatedly, accounts in the news media
linked continuing American policies in that region to the nation's Vietnam
experience. News commentator John Chancellor, for example, had included
a comparison of U.S. policies in Central America to the Vietnam War on
an *NBC Evening News* telecast in January.[23] In another example, an essay
published in *U.S. News and World Report* asked, is "El Salvador Turning
into 'Vietnam West' for U.S.?"[24] In June, Jesse Jackson claimed that a war
in Central American would have an even worse effect on the nation than
had the Vietnam War.[25] Many times, then, the public encountered assertions that there were parallels between the two situations. This connection
was reinforced throughout print and broadcast media that year.

A prominent public opinion survey conducted in July 1984 showed
that more than 60 percent of respondents saw a danger that Reagan's Central American policies could become like the American experience in Vietnam.[26] This did little to dampen enthusiasm for the popular president,
however. Reagan continued to promote his positive, patriotic vision of a
strong America, one that, in his view, was moving away from the perceived
paralysis of just a few years earlier.

The president also continued to fight the perceived Vietnam syndrome.
For example, one way of refuting negative Vietnam connotations and reinforcing his alternate view of the war as "noble" could be seen when he
invited a Vietnamese refugee to the White House. As the news media
reported, young Chi Luu was the valedictorian at the City College of New
York and bound for further studies at the prestigious Massachusetts Institute of Technology.[27] In publicly extolling this success story, Reagan called
attention to a positive example of the Vietnamese people for whom the war
had been fought.

He pressed his interpretation of the war in other situations, as well.
In a solemn remembrance of fallen servicemen in June 1984, the president
presided over the ceremony that was held for the entombment of the
Unknown Soldier of the Vietnam War. In his remarks, Reagan said, "Let
us, if we must, debate the lessons learned some other time; today, we simply say with pride: Thank you, dear son, and may God cradle you in his
loving arms."[28] These somber remarks were surely the heartfelt expression
of the president's genuine feelings. The occasion also highlighted Reagan's
straightforward qualities, which impressed much of the public.

Another symbolic way of reasserting his positive image of the nation,
thus rebutting the Vietnam syndrome, came with Reagan's observance of

the fortieth anniversary of Allied invasion of Normandy, which was a critical moment in World War II. This again was an opportunity to remind Americans of an unambiguous moral and military victory. As the nation's leader, Reagan once more was able to identify himself within a long tradition of freedom-fighting.

Across an array of political topics, then, Reagan had galvanized support by the time of his official nomination for reelection. Much of the country was satisfied with his economic policies, his seeming straightforwardness, and his enthusiastic vision of the U.S. as the world leader in military and diplomatic affairs. Even his comparatively advanced age was neutralized as a campaign issue, as he joked to the audience of a presidential debate that "I am not going to exploit, for political purpose, my opponent's youth and inexperience."

1984 election and results. Perhaps, then, it was only the large margin of his victory that was in any way surprising about Reagan's landslide success at the polls in November. Winning every state except Walter Mondale's home state of Minnesota, it appeared that the voters had given a strong mandate to the sitting president. Among the public, it is true that there were some reservations about the direction in which Central American policies were headed. For the moment, however, it may have seemed as though public scrutiny and apprehensions in Congress would keep American actions there in check. Although news about this issue diminished and received less attention for a time, in the coming months, unexpected developments would thrust it back to the front pages.

In following the Vietnam War's legacy, the elections of 1984 produced several other results that would be important in future years. In a less noticed Senate race, for example, Massachusetts voters sent John Kerry to Washington. An outspoken member of the Vietnam Veterans Against the War in the early 1970s, Kerry had come to public attention years earlier with his high-profile Congressional testimony against further American participation in the war. He was also identified with the famous protest on the steps of the Capitol, in which disenchanted Vietnam veterans had thrown away their medals. As the junior Senator of a state whose image was dominated by its senior senator, Edward Kennedy, however, Kerry remained out of the limelight for the moment.

In January 1985, Reagan was sworn into office for a second term. At the same time, leadership in the Soviet Union passed to Mikhail Gorbachev, marking the beginning of the demise the U.S.S.R. as the world had known it since the days of World War I. A personal rapport between the leaders of the two superpowers developed at a summit held in Geneva later in the year, which helped thaw lingering tensions. The transition in the Soviet

Union was a sea change, and Gorbachev's calls for *glasnost* (openness in government) and *perestroika* (political and economic restructuring) heralded a new era in which the bitter rivalry between the U.S. and its Soviet adversary soon would radically change. The Cold War contexts of the Vietnam War began to fade from view.

As the end of the Cold War drew near, persistent troubles in the Middle East continued to erupt in frightening episodes of violence. In 1984, a wave of terrorist acts gained worldwide attention. In one case, Palestinian Liberation Organization terrorists hijacked the *Achille Lauro,* an Italian cruise ship, murdering an American passenger, Leon Klinghoffer in October. In another incident, an Egyptian airliner was hijacked and forced to land in Malta, where 59 people died during a rescue effort in November 1984.

For Americans, perhaps the most shocking of these terrorist strikes had occurred a few months earlier. In the summer of 1985, two gunmen seized control of a TWA jet that had taken off from Athens en route to Rome, diverting its destination to Beirut. The hijackers, who were affiliated with the group Hezbollah, held the jet's passengers, most of whom were Americans, hostage. The gunmen issued demands that included a call for worldwide denunciation of U.S. and Israeli policies.

The hijacking developed into a complicated, confusing, and terrifying ordeal that commanded international attention. It appeared on television news broadcasts around the world. As events unfolded, some hostages were released, after which the jet was flown to Algiers, where additional hostages were set free. The aircraft then returned to Beirut. Amid the confusion in Lebanon, which was still gripped by civil war, the hijackers singled out an American passenger who was serving in U.S. Navy. They then beat and murdered him, after which they tossed his body onto the runway. The hijackers were then joined by additional armed men, and the jet flew back to Algiers, where another group of passengers was released. Eventually, the jet returned again to Beirut, where the crisis ended with the safe return of the remaining hostages.

As a global audience witnessed the unfolding crisis on television, one of the most enduring images was captured as television cameras recorded a hijacker holding a gun to the head of the jet's pilot as they leaned out of the open cockpit window for the world to see. The hijacking deeply rattled the American public. The blood-red cover of the following week's *Time* magazine carried the simple legend "HOSTAGE TERROR," a headline that clearly reflected the public's horrified reaction.[29]

By coincidence, the sequel to film *First Blood* had been scheduled for release at this time, in order to capitalize on the tenth anniversary of the

Vietnam War's official end. As the world waited for the conclusion of the hostage crisis, the president unexpectedly called attention to the new film when he spoke with reporters just before the release of the final Flight 847 hostages. "I saw Rambo last night," Reagan reported, "and next time I'll know what to do."[30]

Rambo Comes of Age

Although the character of John Rambo in *First Blood* was a caricaturized figure in many respects, he was at least partially recognizable as an exaggerated version of Vietnam War veterans as Americans perceived them, even if the plot in the film defied credulity. By the time of his next film appearance, however, the character of Rambo became significantly less tethered to the historical war and real world than had been the case in the first film. In some ways, the super-human Rambo appearing in the sequel would act as a force of counter-history, rewriting what had gone before and providing an alternate version of reality in response to the national trauma precipitated by the war.

In the weeks leading up to the release of *Rambo: First Blood, Part II* (often simply called *Rambo*), American movie audiences had been prompted to keep in mind the image of the POW seeking justice and vengeance. The Chuck Norris film *Missing in Action 2* had been rushed to theaters. It told the story of the Norris's Braddock character years prior to the events shown in the original *Missing in Action*. The narrative revisits Braddock's POW ordeal, and as audiences would expect, the villainy and sadism of the Vietnamese captors is fully and graphically displayed.

Though hardly regarded by critics as award-winning material, the first *Missing in Action* film had elicited relatively positive reviews. *Missing in Action 2*, however, received less generous notices. A brief review in *People Weekly* dismissively stated that the film looked so cheaply made "that if the only people to pay admission to see the movie are the actors' families, it should still turn a profit."[31] Nonetheless, the action-oriented Norris had developed a strong following, and *Missing in Action 2* helped prime audiences for the upcoming *Rambo* spectacle.

Rambo: First Blood, Part II was a major, if unlikely, cultural event, highlighting significant contradictions in American attitudes about politics and entertainment. With its creators perhaps sensing a nation ready for vicarious filmic revenge on America's former enemy, the movie set a new industry record by opening on more than 2,100 screens nationwide. It prompted strong reaction. On one hand, *Rambo* was a film that literally caused some theater crowds to break into a rousing chant of "Rambo, Rambo, U.S.A.!" as they cheered the single-handed heroics of the main character.[32] On the other hand, film critics seemed mortified and mystified. A review in *Newsweek* noted the film's "extraordinary violence," which was said to make the visceral depiction of violence in Stallone's *Rocky* films, with their explicit boxing scenes, "look like 'Winnie the Pooh.'"[33] A writer for *The Nation* called the film "at once hilarious and disgusting," asserting that it displayed not only Stallone's "apish ambition" and "the blind ego-mania of a gorilla," but that it represented "twisted history" with "racist images."[34] Writing in *The New York Times* Vincent Canby acerbically concluded that the film "turns into something of a camp classic."[35]

In promoting the film, *Rambo*'s producers aimed to connect the production to public awareness of the MIA-POW issue. As mentioned above, the release date of the film was determined so that the opening would coincide with anticipated media attention on the anniversary of the war's end. The film's debut on Memorial Day weekend may have magnified that effect. *Rambo: First Blood, Part II* aroused unresolved feelings about the war and catered to audience empathies for the surmised plight of MIAs and POWs.

To build on pre-existing awareness about the missing-in-action issue, moreover, the producers sent copies of a documentary film about the issue to media outlets across the U.S. as part of a public relations packet. Aiming to connect fiction with fact, this material suggested various ideas about how to generate Rambo-related news stories by interviewing real Vietnam veterans and MIA relatives.[36] Reagan's seemingly positive mention of the film (see above) was a bonus for an already fully developed publicity campaign.

Little emphasis was placed on dialogue in *Rambo: First Blood, Part II*. This gave many film critics the opportunity to assail the script and Stallone's acting abilities. (One review made a special note of that point in the film at which "Stallone finally manages to grunt out a complete prepositional clause."[37]) Audiences did not seem to mind and were instead drawn to the action, which was even more outlandish than in the original film.

Of the relatively few lines uttered by the Rambo character, however, two serve to make the film's politics clear. First is Rambo's question, upon being summoned for his mission, "Do we get to win this time?" As this makes clear, vanquishing the ghosts of defeat was not merely a sub-text to the film, it was its centerpiece. Whether the film was actually cathartic to audiences in that regard seems dubious, but Rambo's question (to which, it was implied, there was only one legitimate, affirmative answer) could clearly be taken in the context of the then-present time.[38] So, it can be seen not only as an attempt to "rewrite history"[39] of the American war in Vietnam, but also a call to prevent a repetition of that perceived error in the present and future. In this respect, *Rambo* was very much a film with an opinion about the political scene of its immediate time.

In a second notable line, the Rambo character makes his widely quoted statement that it was his— and, by implication, all Vietnam veterans'— simple desire "for our country to love us as much as we love it." *Rambo* thus continues with the line of screen treatments that portray Vietnam veterans as victimized by all sides during and after the war itself. On this point, the film's indictment of those officials who opposed the war is especially striking. As with other films of this genre, it is suggested that those who were against the war effort were immoral, stupid, or worse, and they are equated with those who caused harm to American soldiers by failing to support them.

In *Rambo: First Blood, Part II*, the hero is taken from prison (his punishment from actions in the earlier film) in order to embark on a mission to find, and assumedly to rescue, American POWs who are still being held in captivity in Vietnam. As it turns out, however, the supposed mission was a sham. American officials were going through the motions of a search and were actually determined to thwart any positive result. The reasoning for this is that success might rekindle hostilities about a war now long over and expose the authorities' previous improper actions. Betrayed by the authorities before even starting his mission, then, Rambo's exploits upon his return to Vietnam clearly thrust him again into an unfair and disadvantageous position.

Once in Vietnam, Rambo is aided by a sympathetic Vietnamese woman, but she is subsequently killed. (Again, Vietnamese characters are expendable.) At another point, Rambo is captured by Vietnamese forces and then tortured by his captors under the direction of a Russian military adviser. (The presence of a Russian adviser all these years after the war is never adequately explained.) In one particularly sadistic scene, viewers see Rambo as he is subjected to excruciating electric shocks, which are administered while he is helplessly lashed to a makeshift rack. Later striking out in revenge for these indignities— and, by intimation, to avenge the outcome of the war itself — Rambo violently fights back, giving what critic Canby called "his one-man army demonstration."[40] Single-handedly, Rambo spends much of the film killing numerous enemy forces in a wide variety of super-human displays of violence.

There was little subtly in the film, which exhibits a patriotically anti-communist, pro–American stance from beginning to end. One sequence, which was immediately the subject of media comment, occurs when Rambo stumbles on the bearded, skeletal remains of an American soldier who had apparently been tortured to death while tied in a position resembling that of someone who has been crucified. In the film, Rambo cuts the ropes binding the deceased soldier, freeing the fallen American soldier's earthly remains in a symbolic display of final salvation and liberation.

As press accounts noted, the skeletal figure seemed blatantly designed to evoke the image of the crucified Jesus of Nazareth. Film writers speculated about the intended message. Even mass-market magazines, such as *People Weekly,* commented upon this aspect of the film. According to its reviewer Scot Haller, "The point is this: Jesus may save, but Rambo saves Jesus," which "makes *Rambo* ... insidious and dangerous."[41] Indeed, this film, like others of its type, promotes violence as the solution to problems and suggests that violent revenge is a legitimately moral response to injustice.

There is little ambiguity about who is good or evil in the world as constructed in *Rambo: First Blood, Part II.* Rambo's foreign enemies — the Vietnamese communists and Soviet adviser — are presented as being blatantly and one-sidedly evil. They have few other qualities. Rambo's communist enemies seem to take delight in abusing captured American soldiers, even a decade after the war has ended. It is not apparent why they should choose to continue with this persecution so many years after the war, aside from serving the film's need for personifications of evil. In any case, the implied sadism of the enemy soldiers, in particular, struck some viewers as one element of an overtly racist portrayal of the Vietnamese.

With the passage of time, it may be difficult for contemporary observers to fully appreciate the remarkable enthusiasm that the public showed for *Rambo: First Blood Part II* in the mid–1980s. It was a lively topic of discussion in its day, and it launched scores of tie-in products and screen imitators. Since that time, enthusiasm for the film has significantly faded, but the name of the fictional "Rambo" remains widely recognizable. As much or more than most films, it was clearly a product of its time, and its success in that context suggests that it gave the public, if not film critics, some sense of satisfaction. It was not a penetrating analysis of the Vietnam War or its aftermath, but it did capture lingering discomfort with the past, as well as uncertainty about the present. The film provided a wishful-thinking solution to difficult topics, and already viewers began to imagine suitable locales — the Middle East or Central America were mentioned — for the next Rambo film treatment.

Opposite: As portrayed by actor Sylvester Stallone in *Rambo: First Blood Part II,* the character of John Rambo assumes super-heroic characteristics. Although popular enthusiasm for this film has diminished over time, in the mid–1980s Rambo was arguably the most iconic representation of renewed American patriotism. Photograph: Photofest.

To be sure, audiences often have embraced many types of simplistic entertainment at different times, frequently for not much more than escapist purposes. *Rambo,* too, was an escapist film that may not have affected deeply the political consciousness of many in the audience. Still, the "Rambomania" that followed the public embrace of the film may suggest an amplifying effect on an already-existing set of public attitudes. The film captured a pervasive mood in the United States and presented a simple story that was consistent with Ronald Reagan's vision of America. *Rambo* capitalized on widespread public longings for simple (to some, simplistic) responses to complex problems, for actions rather than words, and, perhaps for some, for renewed American military might rather than diplomacy.

By the time of *Rambo*'s success, several more sober films with Vietnam War themes were in the offing. In the coming months, the public would be presented with new filmic perspectives on the war and its meaning, as well as new contexts in which to interpret them. In late 1986, Oliver Stone's deeply personal and graphic film *Platoon* would more directly revisit the experience of American combat troops in the war. New films would eventually challenge enthusiasm for *Rambo* and that film's fantastical version of recent American history.

The Iran-Contra Affair

In 1986, just prior to the release of *Platoon,* the public became aware of what was later called the Iran-Contra affair. It involved a convoluted series of actions rooted in efforts to somehow get American military aid to pro-democracy Central American rebels, despite apparent Congressional prohibitions from doing so. Many of the details were unclear and contested, and the ultimate historical significance of this episode is not yet fully settled. Still, the Iran-Contra affair was a major scandal for the Reagan administration, in which memory of the Vietnam War exerted a decided influence.

Limitations to presidential military action. From early in his presidency, Reagan favored strong American support for anti-communist regimes and forces in Central America. The so-called Vietnam syndrome was one problem that confronted the administration in efforts to secure direct aid to the anti-communist *contras.* In addition, the legacy of divisiveness between the executive and legislative branches of the federal government during the Cold War and Vietnam War years had a very real impact on the Reagan administration in this respect. The situation called attention to Constitutional matters. At issue was the degree to which the president could carry out military aspects of his foreign policy objectives without Congressional approval.

Congress had long aimed to place some restrictions over presidential military actions and over covert operations. The National Security Act of 1947, which established the Central Intelligence Agency, contained provisions that required prior Congressional notification (or, when circumstances made this unfeasible, for "timely" notification of Congress) for covert operations. A later Congressional action, the War Powers Resolution, further asserted that in cases where military activities exceed 60 days, Congressional approval would be required.[42] (Nixon and some later presidents claimed the Resolution was unconstitutional and hence not binding.[43])

Later, in response to controversies of the Vietnam War era, Congress imposed additional constraints. It addressed secret activities in the 1974 Hughes-Ryan Amendment, attached to the Foreign Assistance Act, stating that covert actions were authorized only if there were a presidential finding that the activities were "important to the national security of the United States." It further mandated that the president was to report such actions to Congress, and that the actions must be brought to conclusion in "timely fashion.[44] A few years later in 1980, the Intelligence Oversight Act required the president to give prior notification to Congressional intelligence committees when initiating "significant" activities such as covert actions, and also required "timely" reporting to Congress, explaining the actions taken.

Finally, during Reagan's first term, amid controversies surrounding his Central American policies, more specific restrictions were adopted. In 1984, the Boland Amendment specifically prohibited further U.S. military aid from the Department of Defense, or any U.S. intelligence entity, to support the *contras*.

Despite the persistently strong desire of Reagan and his associates to send military aid to the *contras*— to aid in what Reagan perceived as their fight for freedom — these various restrictions meant that this could not be accomplished without the consent of a Congress. As Democratic leaders in Congress were opposed, at times voicing concerns about Central American becoming "another Vietnam," it appeared very unlikely that such approval would be forthcoming. Since the administration still wished to aid the cause of the *contras*, members of the White House's National Security Council staff searched for creative ways to navigate around the apparent Congressional restrictions.

Origins of the Iran-Contra affair. The beginnings of the Iran-Contra scandal can be found in secret actions that involved several nations. At first, these did not seem to involve Central America at all. In August of 1985, representatives of the Israeli government presented U.S. officials with a proposal that was aimed to obtain the release of Rev. Benjamin Weir, an American who was being held hostage in Lebanon by a pro–Iranian group. The unlikely plan called for Israel to arrange for the delivery of more than 500 TOW anti-tank missiles to Iran, which in return was to use its influence to secure Weir's release. Israel, not the United States, owned the missiles in question, but the plan was for the Americans to replace those that would be shipped to Iran. Inherent in the plan's logic, then, was the argument that the U.S. technically would not be trading arms for hostages since it did not own the missiles that were to be traded, even if the end result were the same. Robert McFarlane of the National Security Council (NSC) brought the proposal to Secretary of Defense Caspar Weinberger, and arrangements were made to carry it out.

In November, a second round of transactions was proposed, in which the Israelis suggested sending 500 HAWK anti-aircraft missiles to Iran in order to secure the release of all remaining U.S. hostages in Lebanon. During the process of working through the details in Washington, the plan came to the attention of Gen. Colin Powell, who noted that the size of the transaction seemed to mandate Congressional notification. The administration subsequently decided to pursue a modified plan, but it was disappointed with the results. The general framework of these transactions, however, provided the template for a much more complicated, and apparently illegal, set of actions in the coming months.

Ronald Reagan later claimed to have little knowledge of the actions that were being taken in these matters, although it eventually was revealed that in January 1986 he had written an entry in his personal journal that read, "I agreed to sell TOWs to Iran."[45] That decision, as with the earlier deals to ship arms to Iran, remained unknown to Congress or the public at the time. Yet, this decision marked the beginning of a new phase in the transactions. Now it was the Americans—rather than Israelis—who were to directly organize the shipments to Iran, although the arms would still be funneled through Israel.

Following the general outline of the previous secret arms deals, the scheme still aimed to secure the release of hostages. In a variation of the previous procedures, however, a significant mark-up was added to the sale price of the arms shipments. (The offer to Iran under this plan included a mark-up of more than 300 percent, a price at which the Iranians balked.) In addition, there was another new twist to the plan, which significantly complicated the proposed dealings. This was the provision that profits from the clandestine arms sales would be diverted to the *contras* in their fight against the leftist Nicaraguan government. This part of the plan, in the eyes of those organizing the deal, provided an indirect way for the U.S. to send aid to a group it saw as freedom fighters in the continuing struggle against communism in the Western Hemisphere.

Public debate about aiding the contras. While these developments were underway, the administration still worked to gain Congressional approval that would authorize official aid for the *contras*. This led to a vigorous national debate about the extent to which the U.S. should commit aid to the *contras* and their cause. High-profile deliberations in Congress pitted the administration and its allies against an opposition, largely Democratic, that was vocally insistent that the U.S. should not fall into what was repeatedly described as a potential Vietnam War-like situation in Central America. As was widely recognized at the time, the oft-stated sentiment that there should be "no more Vietnams" attached the continuing legacy of that war's discontents to the new political realities of the mid–1980s.[46]

Some Congressional opponents believed they saw uncomfortable parallels between the events in Central America and the situation that had produced the Gulf of Tonkin Resolution in 1964.[47] That resolution had given sweeping authorization for Lyndon Johnson to make war in Vietnam without a declaration of war, and it led to the massive escalation of American military participation in Vietnam during the 1960s. The Gulf of Tonkin Resolution resonated in American politics for another reason, as well. Years after the resolution, it became known that the underlying event that precipitated it—involving a reported North Vietnamese attack on U.S. Navy vessels—was much more confusing and ambiguous than Congress had been led to believe. Many people later came to believe that the Johnson administration had not been forthcoming in providing Congress or the nation with all of the facts, leaving some feeling as though they had been misled.

More general invocation of the Vietnam War weighed on the minds of many opposed to aiding the *contras,* which presented a political obstacle for the Reagan administration. Opponents were outspoken in voicing their concerns. Among those against the president's proposals was Thomas ("Tip") O'Neill, Reagan's begrudging, but usually amiable, Congressional nemesis. Like others wary of the Reagan's plans, O'Neill worried that "The shadows of Vietnam haven't left us."[48] Given the opposition, the test for the administration was to find a way to overcome the roadblock that these protests implied.

A vigorous debate appeared in the news media (especially the print news media), in which editorialists and columnists incessantly remarked on the similarities, or non-similarities, between the Central American situation and the Vietnam War. The issue was very complex, involving partisan worldview differences, and for the most part, the debate followed along familiar ideological lines. In some ways, it centered on questions of balance between America's past and future. Those who emphasized the dangers of "another Vietnam" placed emphasis on their perceptions of past mistakes and argued in favor of a foreign policy that would greatly reduce, in their estimation, the possibility of similar errors by avoiding allegedly similar contexts and situations. By contrast, those who favored the aid located their arguments in questions about what the U.S. should be in the future, with much less emphasis on worry about past mistakes.

In the end, five months of heated debate about *contra* aid eventually resulted in a victory for the administration. This seemed to imply that Congress ultimately rejected the "another Vietnam" label that opponents had sought to affix to the issue.

Secret deals become public. Although the administration won a major battle with Congress about providing aid for the *contras*, developments in the autumn provided a major political threat for the administration and its policies. It began when an aircraft was shot down over Nicaraguan territory in early October of 1986. An American co-pilot died in the wreck, but another American, Eugene Hasenfus, survived the crash and was captured by the Nicaraguan military. Nicaraguan authorities then put Hasenfus on display in a briefing for international journalists, charging that Hasenfus was a C.I.A. agent and that the downed plane had been involved in supplying the *contra* rebels. As what *The Washington Post* called the "first American prisoner of war of the leftist Sandinista government,"[49] Hasenfus and his plight immediately became a major news story.

Making matters worse for the administration, in November 1986, a Lebanese newspaper published claims about the arms-for-hostages deals that also had remained secret until that time. A larger picture that compromised the administration emerged, and within the short span of a few weeks, the secret dealings that had been organized to support the *contras* began coming to light. Having few viable options, Attorney General Edwin Meese subsequently admitted to some of the administration's secret dealings. The revelations caused a media uproar.

In the weeks and months that followed, it became known that National Security Council (NSC) aide Oliver North (a U.S. Marine lieutenant colonel and Vietnam veteran) and others had maneuvered around apparent legal prohibitions against funding the *contras*. Beginning in 1983 and for the next two years, the National Security Council had arranged secret military aid for the *contras*, first under the direction of Robert McFarlane and subsequently by John Poindexter. In addition to diverting profits from the secret arms deals with Iran, the scheme involved the solicitation of funds from private individuals and foreign sources to aid the *contra* insurgency in Nicaragua. North thought such actions were admissible. He believed, for example, that the Boland Amendment, which was approved in 1984, did not technically apply to the NSC because, in his interpretation, the NSC was not officially an "agency or entity of the United States involved in intelligence activities."[50] (Not all agreed with this interpretation.)

By late 1986, the scandal had escalated. Some administration officials resigned, and Ronald Reagan attempted to distance himself from the controversy. The president appointed a bi-partisan, blue-ribbon commission, led by former Republican Senator John Tower, to investigate. In addition, a special prosecutor, Lawrence E. Walsh, was appointed. This raised the possibility that criminal charges would be filed. A November 1986 essay by Charles Krauthammer in *The Washington Post* plainly characterized the political situation in Washington: "What started as a mistake and grew into a fiasco has now become a scandal.... We are about to descend into Northgate, months of endless questions."[51]

Iran-Contra hearings. For the media, the Iran-Contra affair reached its apex during nationally broadcast Congressional hearings that were held between May and August of 1987. Unlike the Watergate hearings of the previous decade, when President Nixon found himself with few defenders, the Iran-Contra hearings showed the effects of an amplified partisan divide in Washington. For many of the president's supporters, it was not at all clear that Reagan's insistence that he was unaware of illegalities in the disputed activities should not be taken at face value. Many Republicans believed that the charges were unfounded and that the allegations were unfairly promoted by the media, which they thought possessed an overtly liberal bias.

Rather than focusing on Reagan in the scandal, however, the news media instead became fascinated with the figure of Oliver North. Though clearly cast as a villain by liberal detractors, North gained much public support, especially from conservatives who viewed his motivations as deeply patriotic. A belief among his supporters was that North had been unfairly victimized because of this patriotism and his outspoken dedication to the cause of the United States. With his unwavering Congressional testimony, many admired North's firm, resolute persona.

Now thrust into the national limelight, North symbolized many of the post–Vietnam themes that were swirling around in both the political and cultural atmospheres in American society. The poised and self-confident Marine recognized that service in Vietnam had deeply shaped his worldview.[52] North saw a clear similarity between Vietnam War and American policy in Central America, and he was determined that there would be no repeat of what he saw as the moral mistakes of the earlier conflict. Believing that it had failed to adequately support U.S. troops and their South Vietnamese allies, North concluded that Congress was culpable in the American debacle in Vietnam. In his testimony to Congress, he blatantly charged that

"The Congress of the United Sates left soldiers in the field unsupported and vulnerable to their communist enemies."[53] Further demonstrating how closely he associated events in the Vietnam War with those in Central America, he also stated:

> It is my belief that what I saw in Vietnam, where I saw the Army of South Vietnam and I saw the Vietnamese marines, one of whom was my roommate as I went through basic school [sic] at Quantico, and who gave their lives for their country, the parallel is to see that in the *campesinos* [sic], the young men and women of the Nicaraguan Resistance, is extraordinarily profound.[54]

The cultural success of *Rambo: First Blood Part II* at this time provided an interesting context for the Iran-Contra Congressional hearings and North's riveting testimony. Indeed, in media portrayals, there are odd parallels between Col. Oliver North and the fictional John Rambo. As encountered in the media, both were shown to see themselves as true patriots who had been let down by the bureaucracy of government and by their own superiors. In *Rambo: First Blood Part II*, for example, Rambo's helicopter is ordered to leave without him when it becomes apparent that in addition to finding photographic evidence of still-held prisoners, Rambo also planned to bring a rescued MIA soldier back with him. According to the film's narrative, this would have deeply compromised the interests of the corrupted bureaucracy, which wanted Rambo's mission to end in failure. Therefore, to prevent Rambo from exposing the truth — and righting a wrong in the process— his superiors betray him. In a larger sense, the film implies that they betray the trust of the American people.

In the image of Oliver North that emerged in the news media, a similar underlying theme is apparent. Like Rambo, he is shown to see himself as a dedicated patriot who has been prevented from championing the ideals of the United States. In this case, putatively immoral Congressional prohibitions such as the Boland Amendment have corrupted American ideals by preventing the United States from aiding freedom-loving *contra* rebels. Following this logic, to uphold the true ideals, official rules cannot stand in the way of heroic action. Again like Rambo, however, North was not greeted with official appreciation after taking what some saw as extraordinary steps to further the cause of freedom. Instead he is accused of criminal acts, attacked by liberal members of Congress, and even abandoned by his superiors in the White House. (He persistently claimed that contrary to statements from the president, Reagan was aware of his activities.) In the end, however, just as the movie character John Rambo was cheered by audiences for is brave attempt to bring about justice, North was transformed by the media into an iconic political figure. He was hailed as a hero by his many supporters.

Congressional hearings about the Iran-Contra affair were followed by criminal trials, in which the special prosecutor obtained several high-profile criminal convictions. These included verdicts against North (in 1989) for obstructing Congress, Poindexter (in 1992) for lying to Congress and Weinberger (in 1992), also for lying to Congress. The convictions were mostly short-lived, however. North had been given immunity as a condition to testifying, and his conviction was soon overturned. Similarly, Poindexter's immunity agreement resulted in a reversal of his conviction. A few years later, on Christmas Eve 1992, George Bush extended presidential pardons to many who had been implicated or convicted in the Iran-Contra affair, most notably former Defense Secretary Weinberger.

North and others had asserted that Reagan knew about the illegal dealings, but there was never sufficient evidence to confirm this. Vice President Bush, a former CIA chief, was also implicated in the scandal, but again no charges were ever filed. Walsh believed that they must have had some knowledge before or after the actions, but there was no compelling evidence connecting them to criminal acts. The 1994 final report of the special prosecutor was unable to fully resolve questions about roles of the president and vice-president in the scandal.

The Iran-Contra scandal weighed heavily during Reagan's second term. In this photograph from 1987, Reagan (center) receives the Tower Commission Report with John Tower (left) and Edmund Muskie. Photograph: Ronald Reagan Presidential Library.

During the heyday of the Iran-Contra affair in 1986 and 1987, it was clear that the legacy of the Vietnam War had played a significant role. The polarizing effect of the War's legacy strengthened, again affirming the deep disparity of thinking about what the war meant, both as a historical event and as a signpost for the role that the U.S. would play in the international arena of the present and future.

Alternative Film Portrayals of the War

The convergence of the second *Rambo* film with the revelations of Iran-Contra scandal served to illuminate the cultural desire to overturn the bitter memories of a lost war. Films such as *Rambo* and *Missing in Action* had revisited the Vietnam War theme by way of seemingly invincible superhuman heroes who displayed, in the words of one writer, "cyborgian immortality."[55] Such cultural representations may have attempted to transform nightmarish memories of the war into less anguishing dreams, accomplished through the mechanism of violent revenge. The culminating effects of the films, one surmises, were intended to be satisfaction and peace, past defeat having been vanquished.

During the months that the Iran-Contra scandal was unfolding, several ambitious films about the Vietnam War were released. These included *Platoon* (1986), *Full Metal Jacket* (1987), and *Hamburger Hill* (1987). The new films portrayed the Vietnam War in a markedly different way, recalling much more of the divisiveness about the war than many of the screen productions in the years just prior. Rather than relying on blatantly oversimplified symbolism and cartoon-like action, this group of films aimed for greater realism.[56] In contrast to the larger-than-life heroes of *Rambo*-styled movies, these films presented a more complex portrait of American soldiers, often emphasizing human weakness and fallibility.

Rambo and *M.I.A.* had displayed a caricatured version of the neoconservative view of both the war and of the state of the nation, in which it is implied that liberalism is antithetical to what is truly American. In contrast, the newer films tended to present views that were more questioning and skeptical of the Vietnam War in general, and thus more in line with the views of those who had expressed fears of "another Vietnam" emerging in contemporary world affairs. The new films also went back to the source. They confronted the war directly. Rather than setting their narratives in the mid–1980s present as had *Rambo*, these films were set during the war as it happened.

Writer and director Oliver Stone's *Platoon* was in many ways the most successful of these films. Stone had originally conceived of the film in the 1960s, after his own tour of duty in Vietnam, but after completing an initial script, the project languished. Although it was to earn substantial critical and commercial success, at first film-industry watchers did not realize its potential impact. Arriving first at a limited number of theaters in late 1986, however, the film quickly generated significant public interest.

Released during the frenzy of the Iran-Contra revelations, *Platoon* was powerful and attention-getting. Although Stone apparently saw lessons in the film that could be applied to the contemporary political scene, as a film set in and about the past, it initially did not provoke debate about then-current U.S. foreign policy. Instead, *Platoon* prompted viewers to think back to the Vietnam War years.

Platoon struck many viewers as a deeply personal, truthful account of what it had been like to be a soldier in the war. The film's combat sequences, in particular, were judged to be highly realistic by many viewers, and this element received special praise from some viewers. One writer went so far as to say "Nobody shoots combat better, period."[57] Stone achieved his effect by photographing the battles so that viewers are in the thick of action, with little hint of what will come next. Ground-level views are common, and at times the enemy abruptly steps out from the haze and just as swiftly is gone again. The violence is visceral. It brought back memories for many Vietnam veterans who saw the film.

The narrative of the film, set in 1967, follows a young recruit named Chris, who has just been sent as a replacement soldier for a platoon taking part in combat missions that year. (Interestingly, the part of the young soldier is played by Charlie Sheen, whose father had played the lead role in *Apocalypse Now*.) The missions are dangerous, and Chris learns that that war is cruel and life can be ephemeral.

Chris soon discovers that the two sergeants in the platoon, Barnes (played by Tom Berenger) and Elias (played by Willem Dafoe), have markedly different moral characteristics.

The conflict that surfaces between the two sergeants is a central part of Stone's narrative. Barnes is a cold, ruthless warrior who sees little humanity in his enemies, perceived or real. Elias, in contrast, though an equally skilled and valiant fighter, has a gentler nature. He searches for humane responses to the seeming madness of the war in which he is a participant. Although many commentators found *Platoon* to be very realistic in many respects, this aspect of the film is more overtly artistic, with convenient embodiments of good and evil available so that Chris can wrestle with the tug of war between the dualities in his own nature.

Director and Vietnam veteran Oliver Stone brought a sense of realism to the image of American combat soldiers in his film *Platoon*. A central part of the story revolves around the moral struggle between two sergeants. Shown here is actor Tom Berenger (center) in the role of Sgt. Bob Barnes. Photograph: Photogest.

In the story, the fighting is brutal. Firefights with the enemy often begin and end abruptly. One harrowing sequence evokes the well-known killings at My Lai, which was the most well-known transgression on the part of American soldiers during the war. In this sequence, Stone shows the American soldiers in a Vietnamese village, where they are trying to iden- tify enemy Viet Cong who are presumably hiding among the villagers. The vast character differences between Barnes and Elias become clearer when one of the villagers is shot and killed while being questioned by Barnes. Out- raged at the shooting, Elias fights with Barnes and prevents another killing. Elias then angrily tells Barnes that he will file charges against him for ille- gal killing when their field operations are over. Before Elias can make good on his threat, however, the platoon engages in an intense battle with enemy forces. Finding he was alone with Elias during the battle, and realizing that there would be no witnesses, Barnes shoots Elias and leaves him for dead. Later, the young recruit Chris discovers Barnes' treachery. He avenges Elias's death by surreptitiously killing Barnes, leaving the sergeant's body to be found as an apparent combat death. Throughout these violent scenes, Stone presents a story in which the usual bounds of behavior — and supposedly simple choices between good and evil — are complicated and warped by the savage conditions of war. As many commentators noted, the film is as much about the struggles that soldiers faced from within as it is about combat with the enemy.

Film critics enthusiastically welcomed *Platoon,* finding it to be a welcome departure from *Rambo*-type films, which were immensely popular successes but mostly failed to impress critics or politically liberal viewers. In contrast to what he claimed were the "revisionist comic strips" of *Rambo* or *Missing in Action,* Vincent Canby hailed *Platoon* as "possibly the best work of any kind about the Vietnam War since Michael Herr's [book] ... *Dispatches.*"[58] According to another assessment in *Newsweek,* "Stone has made one of the rare Hollywood movies that matter."[59] An equally favorable cover-story headline in *Time* magazine declared, "*Platoon:* Vietnam As It Really Was."[60]

The film made an especially powerful impact on veterans. Many agreed that the film made a powerful statement and was a relatively accurate depiction of what it had been like. Not all agreed with the portrayal, however. Some thought that the film's portrayal of American "grunts" gave a false impression, reinforcing negative stereotypes of the Vietnam veteran as irrational, criminal, drug abusers.

Soon after the film's opening, a special screening was held in Washington. In the audience were members of Congress who were Vietnam-era veterans and also some members of the Vietnam Veterans of America, a group that Congress had chartered. The film had a strong effect for many in these viewers; the Associated Press reported that some of the men in the audience wept by the film's end.[61] Democratic Sen. Tom Daschle of South Dakota reported that *Platoon* was "as emotionally draining an experience as I've had."[62] Another veteran commented that "I take issue with reviews that say this is the film for people who were there. I think it's the film for people who weren't there. It'd be good for Sylvester Stallone, George Will and Ronald Reagan to see it."[63]

Although the contrast between *Rambo* and *Platoon* is often thought to be so striking as to preclude seeing any similarities, they are not completely different from one another. For example, both share an American centricity, despite different perspectives what that perspective was. As with previous American films about the war, in both films the Vietnamese are minor players. The American soldiers in *Rambo* are one-dimensional heroes; the Vietnamese are unambiguous villains or victims in some way. The American soldiers in *Platoon* are more fully human, but there is too little attention about the Vietnamese in that film to get any sense of them at all.

Vietnamese foes (and potential friends, for that matter) in Stone's film are essentially faceless. In both films, the sense that the conflict's basic nature was an American experience is reinforced.[64]

In the months following the release of *Platoon*, more films with Vietnam War themes were released. Like Stone's film, *Hamburger Hill* and *Full Metal Jacket* approach the war from the perspective of fighting men in the field.[65] The former film, based on actual events from 1967, follows the bleak story of an especially costly ten-day battle to take a hill held by the enemy. The story focuses on the American fighting men fighting in the operation, showing the many casualties that resulted from the battle. *Full Metal Jacket*, from famed director Stanley Kubrick (whose decidedly wide-ranging oeuvre included *Dr. Strangelove, 2001: A Space Odyssey,* and *Clockwork Orange*) similarly focused his story at the level of individual soldiers. The first part of his film presents a portrait of young men during basic training for the Marines, emphasizing the dehumanizing aspects of that ordeal. The film then moves to an account of a well-known battle in the old imperial city of Hue during the 1968 Tet Offensive. Kubrick's idiosyncrasies are evident in the film, and, as film writers have noted, the first part of the film places a considerable emphasis on gender ambiguities and repressed sexuality, including a derogatory use of the name Gomer Pyle, lifted from the comic television series of the 1960s.[66]

Both *Hamburger Hill* and *Full Metal Jacket* extended, with varying degrees of success, the focus on portraying the experience of American soldiers in Vietnam, though neither achieved the level of commercial or critical success of *Platoon*. What these three films did successfully do was bring a new emphasis on telling the story of the everyday American soldiers who fought in the war, bringing the focus to the level of personal experience and away from the broader commentaries on American politics and society that had been found in films as otherwise disparate as *Apocalypse Now* and *Rambo*.

For film enthusiasts of the late 1980s, a film such as *Platoon* may have seemed, as the film critics suggested, a far superior experience (and perhaps an antidote) to the escapist revenge theme and super-heroics of *Rambo* or *M.I.A.* Oliver Stone's film was honored by an award for Best Picture by the Academy of Motion Picture Arts and Sciences, an acknowledgement unimaginable for *Rambo*, even on the part of its most devoted fans. Yet, the more intimate focus of the newer Vietnam War films, and their attempts to portray the actual experience of American soldiers, may have somewhat limited their broader impact. These were moving accounts, but in attempting to faithfully reproduce the real experiences of American combat troops, the films necessarily evoked a complicated and ambiguous picture. In telling the complexities of the Vietnam experience, and by explicitly including negative aspects—including but not limited to wartime atrocities, drug abuse, sexual assault, incompetent decisions, friendly-fire deaths—the themes presented were reminders not only that young Americans had served their country during the war. These films also vividly recalled the agonizing complexities, poor options from which to make choices, and divisive discontents of the war years, even if that was not foremost in the minds of the directors.

End of an Era

As the Reagan years drew to a close, the political world continued to dramatically change. The president was never completely successful in erasing the lasting influence of the Vietnam War in American politics, but the effects of the so-called Vietnam syndrome were surely less pronounced. Over his two terms, Americans had come together in deciding that Vietnam veterans should be honored and respected, a development that was symbolized in the great public acceptance of the Wall in Washington, D.C. The Wall continued to be a place where Americans journeyed to confront and learn about their past. Younger Americans, who knew little of the war firsthand, encountered the topic in everyday life, as it regularly appeared in mainstream news and entertainment media. At the same time many Vietnam veterans welcomed, at last, the appearance of screen portrayals of their wartime experiences that were recognizable to them.

Under Reagan, the American military was reinvigorated, even if there remained disagreements about the circumstances in which to use it. By the end of his tenure, however, the threat posed by the U.S.S.R. seemed reduced. Soon, democratic impulses in the Soviet bloc would lead to dramatic changes on the international political landscape. It remained to be seen if the Vietnam War's lingering influence would continue into a new era.

5

Vietnam Memories in a New World Order

As the Reagan presidency drew to a close, the world of international politics was rapidly changing. Communism was losing its hold on Eastern Europe, and the Soviet Union was beginning to collapse. Its influence on the international stage weakened even as the communist government's power diminished within its own borders.

These changes were underway by the time of the 1988 presidential campaign in the United States. The Iran-Contra controversy would prove insufficient to derail the candidacy of Reagan's vice president, and the democratic challenger in the 1988 election would never fully capture the imagination of the American electorate. Thus, although Reagan playfully remarked that perhaps he, like the fictional Rambo (appearing yet again in 1988's *Rambo III*), might have liked a third installment, the election of George H. W. Bush seemed like the next best thing for Reagan supporters. Indeed, Bush's triumph over Massachusetts Gov. Michael Dukakis seemed, for many, to assure that the Reagan legacy would live on.

For the United States, too, the world in the waning months of Reagan's second term was in many ways vastly different from the one the he inherited in 1981. American politics and culture had changed much since the war in Southeast Asia. The president had worked hard to vanquish the effects of what he called the "Vietnam syndrome," and the administration had successfully rebuilt the power of the American military. There were still a few stubborn remnants of the old order. Cuba was still in the hands of Fidel Castro, and the U.S. still had icy relations with the communist state of Vietnam. But more importantly, the U.S.S.R., which had been the chief financial, ideological and military sponsor of these isolated nations, was in decline. Around the world, the premises and geopolitical realities that had defined the Cold War underwent a radical transformation, and democracy was on the rise. Perhaps memories of the Vietnam War would be rendered relics of a bygone day as Americans looked forward to a bright new future.

War Memories in the 1988 Campaign

By the presidential campaign of 1988, more than a decade had elapsed since the end of the war. Over the years, the nation had traveled a considerable distance on the road to resolving lingering controversies about the war and the once-young men who had served in Vietnam. In the waning months of the Reagan presidency, his vice president and heir apparent, George Herbert Walker Bush, hardly seemed to be a man who would ignite new controversy about the increasingly long-ago conflict in Southeast Asia. Yet, the Vietnam War resurfaced anew in the midst of the 1988 campaign season.

A major surprise in the Republican presidential campaign that year came just prior to the 1988 Convention, when the Bush campaign announced that Dan Quayle, Republican Senator from Indiana, had been named as Bush's running mate. The youthful 41-year-old, Quayle was a relative unknown nationally, but he quietly had been developing a reputation in Congress during the conservative resurgence in the Reagan years. Quayle served two terms in the House and then successfully ran for the Senate. Serving on the powerful Senate Armed Services Committee, he gained notice for his strong anti-communist and pro-military views. Yet, it was not these Senate activities that attracted notoriety in Quayle's vice presidential bid. Rather, his experiences many years earlier during the Vietnam War years created a media frenzy that for a time riveted public attention.

Years earlier, as a college student eligible for the draft in 1969, James Danforth Quayle had enlisted in the Indiana National Guard. As a practice during that period, National Guard units were not deployed to Vietnam, and so this course of action allowed Quayle to serve in the military without much likelihood that he would see combat. Enlisting in the National Guard had been an option that many young men had considered during those turbulent years as a way of minimizing the chances of being sent to Vietnam, while at the same time providing military service. The political fallout from Quayle's decision, and actions related to it, were profoundly felt in the 1988 campaign, however. With the controversy that emerged, it became apparent that the "healing" of the nation from the wounds of the Vietnam War, which had been declared by administrations since Gerald Ford's presidency, was not yet complete.

The Quayle episode had two major facets that rankled with the American public. The first and most obvious aspect of the story involved the general question about how Quayle's National Guard service should be regarded. As a still-young man who now was seeking an office that would bring him to within a heartbeat of the presidency of the United States, was Quayle's National Guard enlistment to be considered truly honorable military service? Or had it simply been a safe way of avoiding combat? Easy answers were not forthcoming.

It was true that National Guard service was a legitimate means by which a young man could fulfill a military obligation. This circumvented the prospect of being drafted into one of the main branches of the U.S. military, where there were higher odds of seeing a tour of duty involving active combat. National Guard enlistment was, in one view, something of a middle-way course of action in which one neither saw combat duty or resisted the draft to avoid it. It met a legal test, even though to some people it did not seem to be equivalent to service in the regular Army, Navy, Air Force or Marines. Kansas Senator and World War II veteran Bob Dole, who earlier had sought the 1988 Republican nomination for himself, was among those who noted this perceived difference. It was Dole's opinion that, "in my generation, it wouldn't have been looked upon with much favor," adding almost sarcastically, "you knew who was in the Guard and who was in uniform fighting for their country."[1]

The Bush campaign was unprepared for the controversy about Quayle's service, but once it materialized, Bush stood steadfastly behind his choice, even amid mounting speculation that Quayle would be dropped as Bush's running mate prior to the convention. Bush, who as a young man was a decorated fighter pilot in the Pacific theater of World War II, made public statements clearly indicating that he regarded the questions about Quayle's service as little more than "a tempest in a teapot."[2] Such declarations, however, did not quell the rampant attention that the matter attracted from the print and broadcast news media. News accounts closely followed the story, and editorial writers and commentators quickly began to turn out pieces that claimed to shed light on the spectacle. (Interestingly, the camp of Democratic presidential candidate Michael S. Dukakis, former governor of Massachusetts, said little about the matter, apparently preferring to see how much damage would be done to the Bush campaign without entering the fray themselves.)

Ambiguous perceptions about Quayle's National Guard service left him open to criticism from both veterans and Vietnam War opponents. Some veterans shared Bob Dole's chilly reaction to Quayle's military service and were at times harsher in their assessment of the vice-presidential candidate. A front-page story in the *Washington Post*, for example, told of an incident at a church service that Quayle was attending in Cleveland, during which "an angry World War II veteran snarled 'You're a draft dodger' in Quayle's face."[3] In other instances, Quayle was the object of other disparagingly labels. One Vietnam veteran remarked, "It's obnoxious to be hawkish and then picking someone who was a chicken hawk to be vice president."[4]

The view expressed by many war resisters and opponents of the war, meanwhile, often emphasized what they saw as an implicit hypocrisy in Quayle's National Guard service. One former U.S. Marine bluntly stated "We respect people who have the courage of their convictions. We don't respect hypocrites."[5] Another veteran voiced a similar theme, saying, "It was draft avoidance. We have no problem with that. A lot of people saved their lives that way.... We do have a problem with hypocrisy."[6]

Bush and his inner circle continued attempts to downplay the matter while voicing support for Quayle's nomination. Through this tribulation, Quayle also had other defenders, although their enthusiasm was sometimes difficult to detect. James Webb, who had served as Reagan's Navy Secretary, concluded that "Quayle performed valid if not heroic service; he certainly did as much in [sic] Vietnam as Ronald Reagan did in World War II."[7]

Among veterans, it is true that views on Quayle's service were mixed, but many saw little that was wrong with a decision to enlist in the National Guard. To Quayle's supporters, there was an enormous difference between his service during the war years and the actions taken by many young men who had avoided service altogether. Speaking to a group of veterans, George Bush voiced the opinion of many when he pointedly remarked that unlike many of Quayle's generation, "He did not go to Canada, he did not burn his draft card, and he damn sure didn't burn the American flag."[8]

The second major facet of the Quayle controversy concerned this matter of privilege, as new questions were asked about the circumstances under which Quayle had enlisted. The course of action chosen by Quayle in seeking the relative security of National Guard duty, thereby avoiding risk of being drafted into a branch of the military that might have sent him to Vietnam, was controversial, but it was not unique. Among young men of draft age during the war, National Guard enlistment was, in fact, a well-known way to avoid the draft. (This is certainly not to say that all enlistees in the National Guard had this motivation.) Widespread awareness of this, however, meant that during the war there were sometimes more young men seeking to enlist in the National Guard than there were spaces available. For some people looking back on it later, the assumed scarcity of open slots raised questions about how Quayle had managed to secure enlistment in the National Guard, despite the intense demand. Specifically, they wanted to know if Quayle had come by his enlistment because of preferential treatment.

In fact, to many people it seemed as though Quayle surely had led a charmed life before and after the Vietnam War years. Born into a prominent family whose wealth was derived from a mid-western publishing concern, in some ways Quayle seemed to be the definition of privilege. In 1969, the same year that he received a bachelor's degree in political science from DePauw University, he secured a spot in the National Guard when it was said demand was high. What is more, during the time of his National Guard service (which ended in 1975), he was accepted to law school, despite apparently low college grades. (This, too, was a matter that attracted the attention of political commentators.) After receiving a law degree from Indiana University School of Law in 1974, he briefly held a management position in the family business, and then turned his attention to politics.

Elected to the United States Congress in 1976 and reelected by a large margin two years later, Quayle next set his eyes on the United States Senate. In 1980, perhaps on the coattails of Ronald Reagan, he unseated Birch Bayh, the Democratic senator who, years earlier, had been well known for his opposition to the Vietnam War. In the U.S. Senate, Quayle secured an appointment on the powerful Armed Services Committee, where the young senator earned a hawkish, pro-military reputation.

It is probably true Quayle's apparent good fortune and success after, as well as before, his enlistment in the National Guard influenced the way in which many people thought of him. To some, he was the epitome of an American success; to others, he was simply one more son of privilege.

Questions of privilege and the military draft had been bitterly contested during the war years, and the Quayle controversy in the 1988 presidential campaign reignited some of that controversy. As mentioned above, in the 1960s, many young men made the same choice to enlist in the National Guard as did Dan Quayle, but clearly it was not simply the matter of National Guard enlistment that had prompted questions about the fairness of military conscription during the Vietnam War era. Before the student exemption to the draft was eliminated, young men could usually avoid being drafted as long as they stayed enrolled in college and continued to maintain an acceptable grade point average. Since the college ranks of that era were skewed towards white, middle- and upper-class students, many critics concluded that these young men had an unfair opportunity to avoid the draft that others did not. With Quayle's nomination and the National Guard issue in the spotlight, these old, uncomfortable questions resurfaced.

Perhaps this was, in part, because Quayle's nomination marked the symbolic beginning of the process in which the so-called Vietnam-generation would take the reigns of government. It was an uncomfortable moment nonetheless.

With controversy swirling, Quayle and the Bush campaign now found themselves responding to numerous questions and assertions. Critics complained that the vice presidential candidate had aimed to avoid the draft and was only able to do so because he was a son of privilege. A commentary in the *St. Petersburg Times* put the matter this way:

> More potentially damaging in the long run than how he won a coveted place in the National Guard at the height of the Vietnam War is the picture that emerges of Quayle as someone for whom privilege repeatedly unlocked doors that otherwise might have been closed to him.[9]

As politically embarrassing allegations about Quayle's enlistment circulated, new reports suggested that Quayle's decision to enlist in the Guard came only after he had already passed a pre-induction physical examination. It was only then, according to these accounts, that he told his parents of his intention to join the National Guard, leading Quayle's grandfather, owner of several newspapers, to become involved. It turned out that a senior editor at one of the family-owned newspapers had not only served in the Indiana National Guard, but was a retired major general. Upon being approached by Quayle's grandfather, according to allegation, the retired major general "highly" recommended Quayle to Guard officials.[10] Though it was not suggested that this was illegal, it nonetheless painted an unflattering picture.

Confusion about the exact circumstances of Quayle's enlistment abounded, and news media accounts disagreed about whether Quayle had received any special treatment. The Quayle camp vigorously challenged suggestions that there were no available openings when Quayle sought to enlist, for example, thus seeking to undermine accusations of special favors. A document to this effect, bearing the signatures of the former Indiana National Guard officers, was produced. It stated there was no waiting list at the time of Quayle's enlistment and that the unit in which Quayle served "had vacancies the month before, the month of, and the month after the Senator's enlistment. This has been verified by the unit's official morning report."[11] The statement concluded, "To the best of our knowledge, no influence was exerted to enlist Senator Quayle."[12]

The episode quickly entered the popular culture. As one news account noted, "Quayle jokes have become a staple of late-night television, radio chat shows and work coffee breaks."[13] (One example that was quoted was: "'Why did the chicken cross the road? To get to the National Guard.'"[14])

The issue of vice-presidential candidate Dan Quayle's (right) Vietnam War–era service in the National Guard was a major controversy in the 1998 presidential campaign.
Presidential candidate George H.W. Bush (left) vigorously supported him throughout the campaign. Photograph: George Bush Presidential Library.

To many of Quayle's supporters, not to mention the numerous other men
who had taken the same course of action, the mocking tone may have
seemed unfair and out of context. Yet, the popular culture's tendency to
revel at the imperfections of perceived aristocracy prevailed in the late summer. It did not help Quayle's case that he had already earned a reputation
for making statements that sometimes seemed confusing and garbled. (This
tendency would resurface a few years later when he criticized the fictional
lead character in the CBS comedy series *Murphy Brown*.)

Although the uncomfortable stories about Quayle's National Guard
service were taken by some as a laughing matter, clearly the episode had
raised troubled memories about the war years. Some commentators noted
that the Quayle National Guard controversy seemed to be a resurfacing of
the idea of "Viet guilt" that had been put forward in a 1983 *Esquire* magazine article by Christopher Buckley, who coincidentally at one time had
written speeches for Bush.[15] According to Buckley, this type of guilt could
be found among the men who had avoided military service in Vietnam,
whether through medical or student deferments, a lucky number in the
Selective Service lottery (used in the later years of the war for determining

who would be called up for service), conscientious objector status, or draft resistance means. Although successfully avoiding military service might have seemed a desirable outcome for some men during the war years, Buckley suggested that in the years after the war a sense of guilt would begin to weigh heavily on the minds of these men. In later years, when military service in Vietnam came to be seen, by some people anyway, as a defining moment for the so-called Vietnam generation, Viet guilt was the sense that somehow those who did not participate had missed their generation's call to history, or at the least had taken the comfortable path while others risked, or lost, their lives. The Quayle episode called attention to these vexing thoughts about what was and what might have been.

The news media and mass media made much of the Quayle National Guard controversy. It may seem odd that relatively little was said by Democratic politicians who, one might suppose, may have had the opportunity to reap political benefit from the negative attention that the Quayle matter brought to the Bush campaign. Many Democrats, however, had an equally compelling reason not to mention the matter at all: They had little more to boast about in terms of their own military service backgrounds.

The Wall Street Journal, for example, told readers that New Jersey Senator Bill Bradley chose not to enter the race for the White House because he thought his own duty in the Air Force Reserve would make a poor impression with the public.[16] Bradley, who had been a professional basketball star, once commanded a record salary with the New York Knickerbockers. As the *Journal* stated, "We can imagine the questions ... How did you feel about soldiers dying in Vietnam while you were being paid a half million [dollars] to play games?"[17] Bradley was hardly alone among members of Congress. A survey of members of the House and Senate conducted for the *Washington Times* (and subsequently cited in *The Christian Science Monitor*) revealed that of 203 senators and representatives who had been of draft age during the Vietnam War, 126 had no military experience at all.[18]

Throughout the controversy, George Bush stood by his choice. In Sacramento, Bush told an audience "I'm not going to let some insidious rumor-mongers drive me to change my mind. I'm standing behind Dan Quayle."[19] There is no reason to question his publicly stated reasoning for this. The fact that Bush's own son had also served stateside in the National Guard during the Vietnam War may have reinforced his positive regard for those who had served in the Guard during the war.[20]

Perhaps the most remembered moment in the vice-presidential campaign occurred during the single televised debate between Quayle and the Democratic vice-presidential nominee. Quayle and Texas Senator Lloyd

Bentsen faced each other in Omaha, Nebraska on October 5, 1988. Still reeling from the accusations about his military service, his apparently spotty academic record, and his relative political inexperience, Quayle took the offensive by raising the memory of the Democratic Party's most famous icon, John F. Kennedy. Quayle defended his qualifications for the vice presidency, stating: "I have as much experience in the Congress as Jack Kennedy did when he sought the presidency."

Bentsen, a quarter-century Quayle's elder and an experienced politician who had once defeated George H.W. Bush in a Texas Senate race, then famously rejoined, "Senator, I served with Jack Kennedy. I knew Jack Kennedy. Jack Kennedy was a friend of mine. Senator, you're no Jack Kennedy."

Indeed, it was probably a risky comparison for Quayle, if for no other reason that the Kennedy legacy was shaped, in part, by the often-repeated reference to his role as a PT boat commander in the Pacific theater of World War II and of the heroism associated with that service. (In addition to written accounts about his World War II military service, the 1963 Hollywood film, *PT 109*, had memorialized Kennedy's naval exploits.) Although Quayle may have had a reasonable case to make in comparing Kennedy's early political career to his own, this other aspect of Kennedy's public image presented a marked contrast to Quayle's National Guard service and added an additional implication to Bentsen's admonishment.

Still, the questions about Quayle's service did not derail the Bush campaign. Democratic presidential nominee Michael S. Dukakis, the governor of Massachusetts, had little more success than Quayle in promoting himself in a military light. (Although Dukakis had served in the army in the mid–1950s, he already had left the service prior to major American military involvement in Vietnam.) The Massachusetts governor tried to make the case that he would be a suitable commander-in-chief, but he was largely unsuccessful. During a campaign visit to a military installation, for example, he was photographed riding in a tank, appearing uncomfortable and wearing what looked in photographs to be an ill-fitting, over-sized helmet. This image seemed almost comical to Dukakis's detractors, and it was subsequently used in efforts to deflate Dukakis' White House aspirations.

Thus, by the time of the election in November 1988, any remaining questions about Dan Quayle's National Guard service were not sufficiently powerful to sway the outcome. George H.W. Bush ran an effective campaign, and Michael Dukakis was unable to escape the negative stereotypes that accompanied his background as the governor of what was regarded as America's most liberal state. Much of the American public preferred Bush, who would preserve the conservatism of the Reagan presidency and who could therefore provide a sense of continuity. When the ballots were counted, the Bush-Quayle ticket emerged with more than 53 percent of the vote. (The electoral vote was an even greater victory for the Republican candidate, with Bush receiving 426 electoral votes to Dukakis' 111.)

As Bush prepared to take the oath of office, Americans, like people around the globe, realized that the world was changing. Reagan's successor in the White House looked out on the sweeping transformation that was underway in the geopolitical landscape. In his inaugural address, George H. W. Bush optimistically spoke of the promise of the future and a vision of a "thousand points of light."

Yet, the 1988 election clearly showed that the memory of the Vietnam War continued to be a potent force in American political culture. The actions of the Vietnam generation would continue to be examined and judged in the political realm in coming years, and some of the themes sounded in the Quayle episode would resurface again in the presidential campaign of 2004.

From *China Beach* to *Born of the Fourth of July*

During the presidential campaign and into the years of the Bush administration, American audiences continued to see incarnations of the Vietnam War in film and televised productions. The success of Oliver Stone's *Platoon*, as well as the earlier success of the *Rambo* films, surely enhanced the interest of the film and television industry in taking another look at the Vietnam War as a potential subject or setting. On broadcast television, the CBS television network's Vietnam War series *Tour of Duty* already had attempted to find an audience with combat-oriented stories, and on cable television, HBO's anthology series *Vietnam War Stories* addressed several aspects of the war and gained the approval of television critics. In 1988, ABC countered with the introduction of *China Beach* to its weekly schedule. Although like *Tour of Duty* and *Vietnam War Stories* this new series was a drama, *China Beach* approached its theme from a markedly different perspective: its central characters were American women working in a military medical-recreation compound in Vietnam.

While the role of women in the Vietnam War had not been completely neglected in previous years, this aspect of the war never gained widespread attention in American consciousness. On the American side of the conflict, many women in military service, typically in medical and support roles, had served in Vietnam, though it was seldom discussed. On the other side, things were more complicated. Women were regularly part of Viet Cong operations, which was a jarring thought for American troops who often had thought of women as bystanders or perhaps victims in war situations. Conceiving of women as combatants was largely alien to Americans soldiers and challenged conventional assumptions about gender roles.[21] Indeed, for most Americans this war, like others before it, was regarded as the province of men. Men formed the core of the combat troops on both sides and were more numerously represented in the conflict itself and in later depictions of it. Focusing on the reality that female American military personnel worked primarily in support and care-giving roles, *China Beach* therefore repeated many of the underlying assumptions about the place of women in war, even as it raised awareness of an aspect of the war that had gone largely unnoticed in the United States.

There was no denying that women played a significant part in the American effort in Vietnam. During the Vietnam era, about 265,000 women volunteered for duty, of whom more than 11,000, mostly nursing personnel, actually served in Vietnam.[22] Since 1984, the Vietnam Women's Memorial Project had advocated for the creation of a monument specifically recognizing the contributions of these female veterans, aiming to have it placed at the site of the Vietnam Memorial along with the representational statue of American male soldiers that had been placed there. The Wall itself specifically was created to recognize the contributions of both sexes, and the names of the eight female military personnel who died in Vietnam are recorded there. The subsequent addition of a statue of three male soldiers, however, had led some women veterans to be concerned that the Vietnam experience of American military women was in danger of being forgotten.[23] With the entry of *China Beach* onto the cultural scene, Americans were visibly reminded that women, too, had served in Vietnam.

Although *China Beach* exhibited many conventions common to television dramas, its female-dominated perspective in a war setting was, indeed, noteworthy. Prior to its appearance, depictions of war in American screen entertainment were almost always focused on the activities of male characters. The sorts of films produced about World War II, for example, often had no leading roles for women. The experience of women in war was seldom addressed in such productions, especially in combat-centered works which look at things from the perspective of all-male military units. Widely known films of varying quality — a few examples of which are such disparate works as *Sands of Iwo Jima* (1949), *Stalag 17* (1953), *The Longest Day* (1962), *The Dirty Dozen* (1967), *Force 10 From Navarone* (1978) — showed women, when at all, in subordinate or relatively insignificant roles. (Some of these films were frequently rerun on broadcast and cable television, often extending their influence well beyond their initial theatrical runs.) Motion pictures with Vietnam War themes seldom challenged these conventions, and such 1980s military-oriented films as *Top Gun*, the 1986 box-office sensation starring Tom Cruise, had continued to stress stereotypical male swaggering.

Television series addressing war were not much different in this respect. The 1960s series *Combat!* focused almost exclusively on the men in the unit whose exploits were the center of the show, and even the television version of *M*A*S*H*, probably regarded by its producers as relatively progressive, was sometimes dismissive in its depiction of women as sex objects. With such screen presentations forming the dominant lens through which war had been presented to entertainment audiences in recent decades, it is not surprising that *China Beach* received much media attention because of its female-orientation as well as its use of the Vietnam War as a setting.

A *New York Times* article stated that *China Beach* was evidence of "a more innovative approach" to depicting the Vietnam War "by presenting the war through the eyes of several attractive [sic] women."[24] (The writer does not explain how "innovative" is related to women who are "attractive.") The particular way that *China Beach* focused on women, however, elicited the allegiance of some viewers, while simultaneously alienating others. Some viewers found the series to be a refreshing consideration of the important role women played in the Vietnam conflict. Many viewers were especially impressed with the lead character of Colleen McMurphy, effectively played by Dana Delany, an actress who became an instant favorite with (most often male) television critics. Yet, in some ways the series reflected the soap-opera predilections of a 1980s television world in which series such as *Dallas*, *Dynasty* and *Knots Landing* treated themes of money, power and sex in a highly melodramatic way that also conformed to prevailing assumptions about gender roles.

In a practice familiar to television series, *China Beach* employed stereotypes for narrative purposes, relying on audience familiarity with these conventions to facilitate the creation of dramatic conflict. A similar device had been used in *Platoon*, which several months earlier had played an important role in shaping the entertainment media's new willingness to consider the Vietnam War as a theme. In *Platoon*, oppositional stereotypes had been employed by Oliver Stone to serve dramatic purposes. The two sergeants in *Platoon* — one a humane, quietly heroic, and reluctant warrior, and the other prone to ends-justifies-the-means outbursts of violence — had shown opposing faces of male bravery in time of war. *China Beach* similarly presented characters who exemplified opposing gender stereotypes in a war situation: the caring, supremely devoted and traditional McMurphy character (played by Delany) and a prostitute called K. C. (played by Marg Helgenberger). The well-received performances of Delany and Helgenberger helped to add depth to their characters, but the choice of a nurse and a prostitute as two of the main characters did little to challenge male-dominated stereotypes about the place of women in war. Still, critics (many of whom were men) often celebrated the series, especially in its second and third years. Writing in *The Washington Post*, Tom Shales wrote glowingly of the series, describing it as a "cherished show" that "upholds its high standards.... Even TV this good is rarely this good."[25]

Others, including women who were Vietnam veterans, were not always as enthusiastic about the *China Beach* portrayal of the situation. In one *New York Times* article, a woman who had served as an army nurse during the war noted the limitations of television portrayals of the Vietnam experience: "Characters end up being either superhuman people or rip-roaring stereotypes."[26] Others complained of what they viewed as an excessive emphasis on partying and romance in the series, which ran counter to their recollected experiences during the war. Another woman who had served in Vietnam thought that a series with this topic should make clear that "the war ... [was] not ... an afterthought to partying;" while another added that "You need to portray the sadness and the loss, because that's what war is."[27]

Regardless of differing opinions about *China Beach*, however, it successfully attracted public attention even amid a crowded entertainment media environment. Thus, the subject of American women in the Vietnam War, previously given little notice, was suddenly squarely in the public eye.

China Beach and the Women's Memorial. It was in this milieu that action on the memorial to women Vietnam veterans began to accelerate. On November 15, 1988, a bill signed by outgoing President Ronald Reagan approved the placement of a statue depicting a woman veteran at the Vietnam Veteran's Memorial in Washington, D.C. With this formal commitment, the task of raising public support was reinvigorated.

In the following year, *China Beach* actress Delany lent her support to the project, enlisting her fame as a fictional Vietnam veteran to the cause of authentic military women. On the occasion of Veterans Day of 1989, Delany wrote in USA *Today* that "America has never thanked ... [the American military women nurses who served in Vietnam] for their selfless contributions," adding that "The Vietnam Veterans Memorial has begun an essential healing process for Vietnam veterans, but little has been done to address the needs of women veterans."[28] Clearly, the project had gained official backing and public notice; it would be several more years, however, before the monument would be unveiled in Washington.

After Platoon. Although *Platoon* had established a changed tone for movies addressing the Vietnam War, less realistic, action-oriented treat-

The television series *China Beach* brought new awareness to the service of American women during the Vietnam War. Shown here are series stars Dana Delany (left), who portrayed Colleen McMurphy and Marg Helgenberger, who played Karen "K.C." Koloski. Photograph: Photofest.

ments of Vietnam veterans were still issued. In 1988, two such films were released, extending the franchises of popular Vietnam veteran characters. Memorial Day weekend of that year brought *Rambo III*, in which the hero is deployed to Afghanistan to aid the rebel forces fighting the Soviet presence there. In the film, John Rambo seemed finally to have come to terms with his past. In the series' previous installment, the Soviets appeared in a somewhat secondary light as the vile backers of the Vietnamese communists. Now, they were the primary villains. (Of course, they, too, were about to be removed as suitable cinematic nemesis, as the Cold War was rapidly coming to an end.) Although *Rambo III* was predictably lambasted by critics, the film was still a financial success, albeit on a much smaller scale than the previous entries in the series.

Also in 1988, the Chuck Norris series of Vietnam films debuted another installment. Unlike the Rambo entry, *Braddock: Missing in Action 3* retained its focus on the lingering effects of Vietnam War. The story-line finds James Braddock again returning to Vietnam in a super-heroic effort to free his wife and son, with the plot giving many opportunities for yet another display of martial arts and action sequences that pit the wronged Braddock against rather one-dimensional communist villains. Although it possessed a few new twists, there was little that was original to this narrative. Moreover, in the wake of *Platoon*'s critical and cultural success, the novelties of the *Rambo* and *Missing in Action* films arguably were wearing off, as audiences found other films to satisfy whatever desires they had for action-oriented cinematic heroics.

Oliver Stone's *Platoon* had broken new ground in gaining widespread audience appreciation of the everyday American soldier's experience in Vietnam, even if the subject matter it covered had been approached in earlier films. On television, *Tour of Duty* was an obvious attempt to bring something of *Platoon*'s appeal to weekly television, and *China Beach* had also brought stories from the Vietnam War zone into homes across the U.S. The motion picture world now also responded to the public's newfound willingness to consider the war as a potential dramatic entertainment.

Several Vietnam War films were released in 1989 that adopted a more overtly serious tone, in the vein of *Platoon*. Public response to these movies was mostly mixed. Some of these films were made with an eye towards evoking combat realism and the personal horror of warfare. One moderately successful film of this type was the mid–1989 release, *Casualties of War*, which featured the young actor Michael J. Fox who was then best known for comedic roles on television and in the immensely popular 1985 film, *Back to the Future*. *Casualties of War*, based on a true account that appeared in a *New Yorker* article two decades earlier, stood in stark contrast to Fox's earlier screen appearance, however. Director Brian De Palma presented a bleak portrayal of human frailty and cruelty in a story-line that centered on a squad of American soldiers in Vietnam.

In *Casualties of War*, Fox plays a young soldier who witnesses—perhaps passively enabling—fellow soldiers who commit violent atrocities against Vietnamese civilians. The focal point of the story involves a young Vietnamese woman who is kidnapped, raped and beaten by the American soldiers. The terrible violence of these actions is graphically depicted by De Palma, who had previously directed such films such as *Carrie* (1976), *Scarface* (1983), *The Untouchables* (1987). The level and depth of sexual violence made the film difficult viewing for general audiences, and it was only a modest success financially.

Although based upon a nonfiction account, some viewers of the film may have questioned the appearance of yet another movie that seemed to focus only on the most egregious and aberrant behavior of some American soldiers in the conflict. The negative portrayal of the American military was not limited to soldiers in the field. Like *Platoon*, the military establishment in *Casualties of War* is portrayed as callous and perhaps misguided.

Overall, Vietnam is shown as a setting in which young American soldiers were often far from a moral liberating force, and instead seemed prone to victimizing the very people they had been sent to save from communism.

Born on the Fourth of July. By the 1980s, the Vietnam War had thus been more broadly reconsidered as a topic for screen media in the United States than perhaps at any time previously. Not content with the success that *Platoon* had achieved in bringing his reconstructed version of the war to film audiences, Stone introduced a new Vietnam War film in December of 1989. Stone's *Born on the Fourth of July*, based on Ron Kovic's 1976 autobiography, brought an unflinching portrait of the war's effect on one young American soldier, who returned from the battlefields of Vietnam a paraplegic, paralyzed below the waist.

Stone had met Kovic years earlier and had expressed interest in someday making a film from Kovic's unvarnished account of his experience. The resulting film focused not only on Kovic's tour of duty in Vietnam but also on the emotionally and physically painful process as he later tried to readjust to everyday life as a quadriplegic. The success of *Platoon* enabled Stone to take up the project, even though its bleak and graphic portrait of the life of a severely disabled veteran may have seemed to be unlikely material for a mainstream motion picture.[29]

Stone had realized the difficult nature of his material. He approached the top Hollywood actor and box-office phenomenon, Tom Cruise, with the idea of casting him in the lead role. Having recently appeared in the highly successful, though substantially less ambitious, film *Top Gun*, the popular young star was already familiar to audiences in a role as a dashing young military hero. With Cruise's subsequent agreement to take the lead role in *Born on the Fourth of July*, Stone insured that the film would attract interest, despite its intense and potentially depressing content.

The film's narrative shows Kovic's life from days as an idealistic young soldier to a vocal opponent of the war (he was active in the Vietnam Veterans Against the War group). A major portion of the film deals with his difficult adjustment to private life after returning to the Long Island of his boyhood.

The basic authenticity of Kovic's experience and the reality that the war had, indeed, rendered Kovic paraplegic could hardly be denied. Yet, Kovic also became, as the film showed, an impassioned anti-war advocate in Vietnam Veterans Against the War, a group that may not have seemed representative to the many Americans who knew (or were) Vietnam veterans, and who may not have looked favorably on that group's anti-war activities while the war was still ongoing.

The subject matter was not new; years earlier, *Coming Home* had shown the story of a disabled veteran, and *The Deer Hunter* had focused on the lingering psychological trauma of the war. *Born on the Fourth of July* was more graphic, however, and the after-effects of war's violence have seldom been as portrayed in such a cold, harsh light. The film made an instant impact among film-goers and was widely discussed in the news media.

With *Born on the Fourth of July*, Stone's apparently liberal political leanings began to become increasingly more apparent in his works. In some respects, the film seemed to suggest an interpretation that was very unflattering toward the political-military establishment that had been rebuilt and reinvigorated during the Reagan years. Stone's impulse was quite evident in comments reported in the media, in which he stated that his Vietnam films were intended as an "antidote" to both *Rambo* and *Top Gun*, the latter of which he called "a fascist movie [that] ... sold the idea that war is clean ... to a lot of people who learned nothing from Vietnam."[30]

New York Times film critic Vincent Canby, who judged the film "stunning" and possessing "enormous visceral power," observed that "No other Vietnam movie has so mercilessly evoked the casual, careless horrors of the paraplegic's therapy...."[31] Indeed, Canby concluded that *Born on the Fourth of July* was "the most ambitious nondocumentary [sic] film yet made about the Vietnam experience." Its non-romanticized gaze at the debilitating effects of the war was light years away from the more caricatured portraits of veterans that had appeared (and reappeared) in the *Rambo* and *Missing in Action* films. According to Canby, unlike motion pictures in that vein, in a movie such as *Born on the Fourth of July*, viewers are prompted to "rediscover the seriousness of war ... [and] the value of human life, the galvanizing strength of idealism and the meaning of sacrifice.... It says something about the nature of our popular entertainment today ... that such humanism appears to be a revolutionary concept."[32]

Vietnam War Memories and Challenges to American Hegemony

To the extent that the Vietnam War was related to a global struggle between the U.S. and its democratic allies on the one hand, and the Soviet Union and communism on the other, it could be said that the apparent loss of the war in Vietnam had not prevented an end result that was favorable to the United States. Although Vietnam itself remained a communist state even after the collapse of its Soviet patron, the Soviet threat that was the most important underlying fear of the U.S. in the 1950s and 1960s no longer existed. It could be argued, then, that the battle of Vietnam was lost, but the Cold War with the Soviets was won nonetheless. In any case, the political world in which the Vietnam War had been fought was fundamentally changed in the transformed geopolitical landscape that George Bush labeled a "New World Order."

In the Pentagon, meanwhile, a generation of leaders influenced by the American debacle in Vietnam had envisioned new ideas about any future military struggles in which the U.S. might become involved. Many of the senior staff in the Pentagon had direct experience in Vietnam. These ranks included General Colin Powell, who was appointed as Reagan's national security assistant and was subsequently elevated to chairman of the Joint Chiefs of Staff in 1989. Responding to the changing world of his tenure in that position, Powell came to have new ideas about how the U.S. military should operate. The Powell doctrine, as it later came to be called, was a direct response to the unsatisfactory results of the Vietnam War. It called for military engagement in which there would be clearly defined aims, an exit plan, and a commitment of sufficient force to win. This meant that American military missions should have the support from the American people before any major commitment was made.

Though these may have been a prudent set of principles in light of America's historical experience, to some people these ideas suggested that he might be reluctant to advocate for the use of military force in some circumstances. A *New York Times* piece concluded that Powell was "another of that generation of officers whose Vietnam experience has made them cautious about using military force" and who "share bitter memories that have influenced their thinking."[33] If this reluctance was, in fact, common among Pentagon leaders, it was not always shared by either George H. W. Bush or members of subsequent administrations, who were less steeped in the military culture that resulted from the Vietnam War.

U.S. military action in Panama. Since the early 1980s, American foreign policy had a special focus on Central America, where the Soviets had supported leftist governments and guerilla operations. A different sort of problem boiled over in the Central American nation of Panama in 1989. Panama's de facto ruler, General Manuel Noriega, had been indicted in the U.S. on drug trafficking, racketeering and money laundering charges. Long an irritant to the American government, these accusations, in which Noriega was accused of aiding the infamous Medellín drug cartel that controlled much of the illegal cocaine traffic into the United States, were only the latest in a long line of actions that incensed American officials. Previous accusations against Noriega stretched back two decades and included charges of brutality and despotism, as well as persistent reports that he was profiteering from drug-running.

Tensions had begun to escalate a year earlier, in 1988, when Panama's President Delvalle unsuccessfully attempted to oust Noriega from his position as the Defense Forces commander. Instead, Noriega influenced the National Assembly to remove Delvalle. The U.S. attempted to nudge Noriega from power through various sanctions, but these were unsuccessful, as Noriega assumed full power. The situation thus became increasingly intolerable for the Bush administration, and news reports of "the killing of a Marine lieutenant and the brutal harassment of a Navy officer and his wife in Panama"[34] were the final straw. Noriega had announced that Panama was at war with the U.S.; consequently the administration decided to intervene militarily.

Given the enormous disparity in size and strength between the U.S. Military (which deployed about 25,000 American troops) and the Panamanian Defense Forces under the control of Noriega, it is not surprising that the "invasion" of Panama, as many news accounts called it, was a short-lived affair. Panama's military was hardly a serious foe for American forces. With little war action to report, American news media attention occasionally focused on aspects of the operation that sometimes appeared almost amusing. For example, reports followed efforts to induce Noriega to leave the Vatican Embassy, to which he had fled. In this operation, American forces subjected Noriega to around-the-clock, high-decibel rock and roll music. Blaring from speakers aimed at the embassy were such songs as "Nowhere to Run" and "Pump Up the Volume,"[35] part of a psychological operation intended to drive Noriega into the arms of U.S. captors. As a *Boston Globe* account reported, "Almost as hot a topic as the presence of Manuel Antonio Noriega inside the Vatican Embassy is the deafening music being played."[36] Shortly thereafter, when Noriega was captured and whisked away to stand trial in the U.S. (where he was subsequently sentenced to a prison term of forty years), much of the American press lauded the action and touted the effectiveness of American power.

The successful use of military force in Panama prompted some public recollection of the Vietnam War, as would have been likely with any military action. The extremely short duration, minimal U.S. casualties, and one-sidedness of that action, however, were too dissimilar to the extended trauma of Vietnam to provoke very much comparison. Nonetheless, with the success of Panama added to the previously successful operation in Grenada just a few years earlier, it seemed that the American government was slowly exorcising the ghosts of the Vietnam War, at least as seen in its willingness to resort to military actions in foreign policy.

Even these small, almost minuscule operations in Grenada and Panama were symbolically significant. By establishing successful operations between the time of Vietnam War and the present day, they provided evidence that the most recent American military efforts were not failures. Added to the demise of communism in the Soviet Union and Eastern Europe, these modest military adventures bolstered the administration's confidence that U.S. military force could successfully be used on the world stage. Although the Vietnam War was an unhappy moment in American history, it could be reasoned, for those wishing to follow this line of thinking, that war could increasingly be seen as an isolated episode of the past.

Crisis in the Persian Gulf

A greater test of how far the U.S. had moved beyond the perceived Vietnam syndrome soon emerged. Strife in the Middle East had been a continuing presence in world politics for decades. In this regard Americans typically thought of anti–Israeli violence or they recalled episodes such as the Iranian hostage crisis, the hijacked Pan-Am jetliner, of the commandeered *Achille Lauro* cruise ship, the latter event including the brutal killing of a disabled American passenger.

Although less contemplated by Americans, perhaps because the American stake was not as obvious, it also was true that tensions within the Middle Eastern Islamic world had been growing for some time. During the 1980s, in fact, there was a brutal war between Iraq and Iran, with the U.S. quietly providing some support to Iraq's strongman leader, Saddam Hussein, in part to keep the warring states' attention focused on each other. Ultimately, the decision to provide even modest support for Iraq had unintended costs, as the United States would later embark on war with Iraq on two separate occasions.

In the summer of 1990, Iraq invaded the tiny nation of Kuwait and Saddam Hussein announced that Kuwait was to be annexed. Both the Arab world and the West reacted with alarm, and the United Nations immediately condemned the invasion. Fearing that this would be the precursor of even more strident aggression, perhaps extending to the vital oil resources of Saudi Arabia, the Bush administration reacted swiftly. The U.S. rapidly deployed American soldiers to Saudi Arabia, forming what Bush called "a line in the sand" between the Iraqi and American troops.

Soon, there was a massive buildup of American military forces in the region. It was headquartered in Saudi Arabia, which had agreed, with some restrictions, to allow the large number of American troops to be stationed there. The first wave of deployment rose to 230,000 American troops; they were soon joined by an additional 200,000 soldiers. In a short time, then, the number of American soldiers in the region rivaled the number of troops that the U.S. had stationed in Vietnam during the height of that earlier conflict.

As a *Washington Post-ABC News* poll indicated, the American public generally approved of the Bush's first actions, but the public had fears about an outright war in the Middle East involving American forces.[37] Political rhetoric in the U.S. was feverish. Secretary of State James Baker, for example, said that a failure to confront Iraq could cause "a new dark age."[38] The crisis atmosphere and increasing U.S. military commitment, moreover, quickly raised comparisons to the Vietnam War in a far more vigorous way than had been seen in the Panamanian context less than a year earlier. In the words of one analysis in the news media, "The confrontation threatens to become a protracted stalemate — potentially the greatest challenge to American will since the Vietnam War."[39]

Both the administration and the Pentagon were keenly concerned about the situation taking on the negative connotations of the Vietnam War. They tried to deflect such comparisons in various ways, as could be seen in the organizing of military operations so that the communications about the crisis were handled by Pentagon and other government sources. The military operation that would emerge in the Persian Gulf in 1991, for example, has been described as "designed, by Colin Powell and others, to be the precise opposite of Vietnam: a clear-cut conflict, with limited aims, defined goals, massive force and broad international support."[40]

Despite efforts to distance the Persian Gulf events from the Vietnam War, the earlier conflict continued to influence not only how officials planned for military action, but also how these actions were interpreted by the American public. In some ways, the Vietnam War remained a lens through which leaders, the media and the general public viewed unfolding events in the Persian Gulf. It is probably true that the news media frequent invocation of Vietnam as a point of comparison magnified public awareness. Still, it is doubtful that the media alone were responsible for reminders of Vietnam, since the war had been a persistent presence in American political and media culture over the fifteen years since its end.

In the beginning of the American operation in the Persian Gulf, before it was clear that the crisis would culminate in an overt war, the decision to make a huge troop commitment was a significant challenge for the Pentagon. Not since the Vietnam War had such a large number of troops been assembled for a specific operation involving potentially imminent combat. In fact, to accomplish "what he called a smooth military buildup in the Persian Gulf,"[41] thousands of armed forces reserves mobilized by order of the president. That this was the first time the reserves had been activated since

1968, the year of the Tet Offensive in Vietnam, was not overlooked by the news media.[42]

Moreover, by the end of August one of the most divisive aspects of the Vietnam War on the American home-front was openly discussed. This was the question of whether there would be re-instatement of the draft to meet the personnel needs of the military during the crisis. Surely recognizing the enormous negative potential for undermining domestic support that this question held, officials quickly responded. A Pentagon spokesman aimed to dispel any rumors about the draft's return, stating, "I've had a million questions on that one, but there is no intention to initiate the draft," a view that was affirmed by other officials, as well.[43]

Despite obvious concern about the mounting military preparations and of the looming potential for war, Americans generally supported Bush's actions and downplayed suggestions that the Persian Gulf crisis might evolve into something resembling the Vietnam War. A poll reported in *Time,* for example, showed that almost three-quarters of respondents believed that the U.S. was right "to have become involved in this conflict" and 57 percent did not believe that American actions in the Gulf regions would "result in a situation like Vietnam."[44] Yet, as this *Time* article correctly observed, "Americans initially greet almost any military mission by rallying around the President and the flag. It is almost an involuntary reflex. That was even true of Vietnam.... The critical question is whether Americans have the resolve to see the conflict through."[45] Moreover, as one writer observed, "The wars that condition today's youth are not World War II or even Vietnam, but Grenada and Panama. Both were short and relatively painless, just like Rambo."[46]

Overall, there were few dissenting voices as the nation seemed to be preparing for war. In general, Americans seemed confident about the president's course of action. A cover story in *Newsweek* captured the national mood, noting that "The Vietnam trauma must have truly faded for the assumption once again is that the United States cannot lose."[47] Of course, the context for military action was significantly removed from past conflicts.

As Americans troops amassed in the Middle East, the administration pursued formal United Nations support for dealing with the Iraqis. With diplomatic efforts continuing, there was ample time in the United States for political leaders and the news media to speculate about the crisis in the Persian Gulf. Although there were still relatively few voices raised against possible military action, a sense of anxiousness and trepidation sometimes was evident as American troops gathered in the region during the last months of 1990. Members of Congress and others speculated about what could and should be done to resolve the crisis. During the wait, comparisons to the Vietnam War became more noticeable.

Yet, even as the Vietnam War was raised in relation to current events, such comments were often more cautionary than outright statements of opposition. A major theme went along the lines that if military action were to be inevitable, then American troops should have full support of Congress and the American people. This thinking reflected perceptions about the lack of support that American soldiers received during the Vietnam years.

"The aura of Vietnam hangs over these kids," said Pennsylvania Democratic Congressman John Murtha, who explained that "Their parents were in it. They've seen all these movies. They worry, they wonder."[48] Caution about the potential for extensive ground combat was a special concern. Republican Senator John McCain, a former Vietnam POW, stated that the U.S. needed to avoid "a land battle in which we trade American bodies for Iraqi bodies.... [and that] I don't believe the American people will support a war of attrition any longer, even if our vital interests are clearly at stake."[49]

In this political milieu it was evident to members of both parties, then, that war, if it were to come, should be swift and the Pentagon should seek to spare American lives to the fullest extent possible. These were parameters for conflict that were consistent with those that Colin Powell and his Pentagon staff had devised in light of their interpretations of what had gone wrong in the Vietnam War. Given these inclinations, it is easy to understand how planners placed great emphasis on long-distance warfare, relying heavily on air and naval power that could inflict military damage on the enemy but that would keep American troops, as much as possible, from combat at close quarters.

Interestingly, it was not only Americans who thought about the potential military conflict in terms of the Vietnam War. Indeed, Saddam Hussein specifically raised the specter of the Vietnam War in televised statements. For example, American news media reported Hussein's ominous prediction, paraphrased in *The Boston Globe*, that the "the United States could suffer Vietnam-like losses in any Persian Gulf conflict."[50] Thus demonstrating knowledge of the anguishing effect that the Vietnam War had on American society, Hussein clearly believed that the thought of significant American casualties would be anathema to the American public. Of course, Hussein's interest in this comparison was specifically calculated to evoke a negative reaction from the American public. Hoping to sway American public opinion, Hussein would continue to link the Persian Gulf situation with Vietnam. Bush and the American leadership, for example, were derisively criticized by Hussein, who claimed that the Americans were too influenced by Rambo films. In a December comment widely quoted in the American press, the Iraqi dictator warned the U.S. that Rambo's victories "will not be played out on the land of Iraq."[51]

Throughout the last months of 1990, the crisis was on the minds of Americans. Surely, after many weeks of preparations some of the national unity on the matter weakened to some extent. As warfare seemed increasingly likely, more voices were raised in opposition to a military solution. There were some large organized protests, such as was seen in Boston on December 1, when 10,000 demonstrators marched against possible war in an event that evoked memories of anti-war protests of the Vietnam era.[52] Other war opponents could be found on national television news programs. *Frontline* (Public Broadcasting System), *Nightline* (ABC), *Face the Nation* (CBS), to cite a few examples, hosted guests who opposed Bush's policies in the Gulf.[53] Yet, although the anti-war advocates were seen in the media and in towns and cities in many parts of the U.S., it would be difficult to conclude that an organized opposition was ever fully established. Such protests of what was impending American military action ultimately did little to change the trajectory of events, and most Americans remained supportive of the administration as international agreement about militarily confronting Iraq continued to grow.

In the news media, Vietnam War veterans were portrayed as having varying views about the situation. On the occasion of Veterans' Day that November, for example, *The Washington Post* interviewed Vietnam veterans at the Vietnam War Memorial and found "mixed views."[54] Clearly uncomfortable with the situation in the Gulf, one veteran commented that "What I think is really sick is that you now have Vietnam vets with kids who are 18 and 19 and 20 who are in Saudi Arabia or on their way over."[55] Voicing a line of thinking that many who opposed war expressed, another veteran was quoted as saying that "we don't have any reason to be there.... The only thing this is doing is making Mr. Bush's Texas friends wealthy."[56] Others disagreed that oil was the main issue. One veteran said flatly "I don't believe it is for oil. I think it is for the world."[57] Another added "I don't like war, but it is something that has to be done."[58]

The president continued preparations while emphasizing his view that the situation was not like Vietnam. Even if war came, he assured Americans that unlike the Vietnam War, in this case "there's not going to be any long, drawn-out agony."[59] He bluntly stated his position often. On the occasion of a December presidential press conference, in fact, Bush declared that the Persian Gulf crisis was not "another Vietnam" three times in a span of only seven sentences.[60]

Although most Americans seem to have remained confident of a positive result in the event that war came, it was widely believed that military conflict in the Middle East likely would not resemble the comparatively easy military actions in Grenada and Panama. Iraq was a significantly larger country with a well developed and battle-tested army. Moreover, as accounts of the vicious war between Iraq and Iran had made clear, Iraq had the potential to use extreme measures should war emerge.

Again, as 1990 drew to a close, the president sought to dispel American anxieties and shore up public support. In addition to the efforts made by Bush and members of the administration to distance the crisis from the memory of Vietnam, top military officials concurred that the supposed similarities were overstated. The field commander of the Gulf operation, Gen. Norman Schwarzkopf, also a veteran of the Vietnam War, noted the superior American military situation in the Gulf. As Schwarzkopf said, "I think we have vastly superior fire power and technology, and I can assure you that if we have to go to war, I am going to use every single thing that is available to me to bring as much destruction to the Iraqi forces as rapidly as I possibly can in the hopes of winning victory as quickly as possible."[61]

As part of the strategy to gain international support for any military action against Iraq, the Bush administration had made some progress working within the framework of the United Nations. The U.N. had already condemned the Iraqi invasion of Kuwait in Resolutions 660 and 661, which were issued immediately after the August incursion. Another resolution was approved by the U.N. Security Council in November, the terms of which required Iraq to relinquish its hold on Kuwait by January 15, 1991.

Meanwhile, the U.S. had successfully brought together a coalition of nations, including the United Kingdom, Canada, and France, which were willing to take part in the ousting of Iraqi forces from Kuwait. Although Hussein made efforts to avert a military response, it was determined that Iraq still did not meet the requirements of the U.N. mandate. In response, the Bush administration went to Congress in January in order to obtain backing for a military response. Congressional approval was promptly secured, and with Iraq continuing to defy the U.N. mandate, a coalition of forces led by the Americans commenced hostilities soon thereafter.

As the three major television networks were broadcasting their evening newscasts on January 16 (in mainland U.S. time zones), massive American air power was unleashed against Iraq. Abrupt flashes in the night sky over Baghdad were reported as viewers watched the beginning of a new breed of televised warfare. By 1991, moreover, the decade-old cable network CNN was a considerable media presence, and the eruption of warfare brought it new prominence. In the U.S. and across the globe, CNN, with its around-the-clock broadcasts and frequent live reports from correspondents in Baghdad, became a source from which viewers sought updates about the war. As discussed below, however, news coverage of this new war would differ markedly from what viewers had witnessed in the Vietnam conflict.

Consistent with the views earlier expressed by both Gen. Powell and Gen. Schwarzkopf, swift, overpowering force was the order of the day. Air power was first directed against the Iraqi air force and air defenses and then to command and control centers. In the years since the last major war in Vietnam, moreover, military technology had been radically transformed. Smart bombs and stealth aircraft delivered lethal initial blows to Iraqi forces. Images from cameras mounted in American missiles as part of targeting systems were released for television consumption, and viewers saw the approach to targets on-screen as if they were watching video games. These images showed very little evidence that humans were involved at all, and surely operated on a different psychological plane from the frequent Vietnam War images, that often focused on human death and suffering.

After crushing Iraqi air defenses and command capabilities, American and coalition ground forces were sent into action beginning April 24. Resistance crumbled quickly, as many Iraqi forces fled the occupied area. Within four days of commencing the ground assault, coalition forces entered Kuwait City. President Bush proclaimed the liberation of Kuwait and announced a cease fire on February 27, effectively ending the war. Having little other choice, Iraq submitted to the demands of the United Nations a few days later, on March 3, 1991. Only a week later, the United States began withdrawing troops from the region.

The United States and its coalition partners had directed massive power and secured the limited aims spelled out in the United Nations resolutions. As a result, Saddam Hussein was temporarily vanquished but not driven from power. In the years to come, this outcome would be seen as a problem. Still, to many American leaders and members of the public, the victory seemed much sweeter than those in Grenada and Panama. The fear and apprehension that emerged during the troop buildup were swept away, and with it, in the eyes of George H.W. Bush, the ghosts of Vietnam seemed to have finally evaporated as well.

Post-Vietnam War effects in news coverage of Persian Gulf War. The Vietnam War's influences on how the Pentagon proceeded were many and extended well beyond battle tactics. As a response to perceptions that the press had played a negative role in the Vietnam War and had helped to undermine public will to fully prosecute that war, by the1990s military officials had policies aimed to prevent a future recurrence of these perceived failings. First, it is important to note that unlike the situation in Vietnam, in which reporters had ready access to field operations without official oversight, in the Persian

Gulf War there were tight restrictions that severely curtailed reporters' access to combat operations. Reporters of coalition military operations had little access to combat situations and were often subject to military escort and oversight. In the post–Rambo patriotic fervor that accompanied the war in the Gulf, much of American society, and perhaps many of the journalists themselves, accepted these limitations. The restrictions caused little stir. In any case, since so many of the coalition's military operations involved long-distance air power, some of the most important military aspects of the war could not be reported in this fashion anyway. The differences in the press access to operations in Vietnam compared to the Gulf War remains striking nonetheless.

The press restrictions meant that in the Persian Gulf situation military press-briefings, which were thought by many journalists during the Vietnam War to have relatively little value, were one of the few ways that reporters could get information about what was happening. Disseminating that information that the leaders of the American-led coalition wished to impart, the briefings were held in official settings at a safe distance from military action. The press-briefing format assured that military officials had a dependable forum in which they exerted significant control about what information was forthcoming and how it would be presented, thereby giving officials the opportunity to help shape interpretations and contextualize the information as it was disseminated. The tighter control on information was a key way in which Pentagon officials aimed to prevent a repeat of Vietnam-era styled reporting from developing in 1991. For their part, the press acquiesced to these circumstances although the very short duration of the Persian Gulf War (especially as compared to the Vietnam War) makes it difficult to know whether a less complacent and more skeptical stance might have emerged on the part of the press if the Gulf situation had stretched over a longer period of time.

The administration's urge to shape public perceptions about the war were also evident in stateside policy. For example, televised images of caskets arriving on U.S. shores had been standard news fare in earlier decades during military operations. Indeed, there are many examples of news images of coffins being respectfully unloaded from military transports at various military bases within the U.S. After the Vietnam War, however, military officials began to think that such imagery could be damaging to morale, and some restrictions on photographing the returning caskets were put into place. With the commencing of hostilities in the Persian Gulf, therefore, the administration issued orders that there were to be no more such photographs. Thus, even if the Persian Gulf War had developed into a conflict that resulted in numerous deaths of American soldiers, a policy was in place to be sure that the sight of multiple caskets being returned for burial would

The triumph of American-led coalition forces in the Persian Gulf War bolstered the popularity of George H.W. Bush and reasserted the might of U.S. armed forces on the world stage. Bush (right) is shown here with Gen. H. Norman Schwarzkopf in Saudi Arabia, November 1990. Photograph: George Bush Presidential Library.

not appear on televised newscasts or in print media. (Indeed, these restrictions were continued into the new war in Iraq in the following decade.)

More generally, however, the swift success of coalition forces in ousting Iraq from Kuwait and forcing Saddam Hussein to accept severe restrictions on Iraqi military action and armament for the future (enforced by "no-fly zones" and persistent weapons inspections in coming years) seemed to validate the Powell doctrine and provide an antidote to the lingering effects of what some called the Vietnam War syndrome. Yet, though Iraq was soundly defeated, Saddam Hussein remained in power. Over time, that result would be seen as an unsatisfying ambiguity by some, potentially casting doubt as to whether the effects of the Vietnam War had, indeed, been fully overcome in the Persian Gulf.

Coming Transitions

In the immediate wake of the Gulf War, it seemed as if George H. W. Bush might be an unstoppable candidate for reelection. Unlike presidential candidates of the Vietnam War era, he had a military victory to his credit. Moreover, a sense of renewed patriotism seemed to have taken hold during the brief conflict in the Persian Gulf. Combined with the knowledge that the Reagan-Bush years had seen the end of the Soviet threat, to most observers it seemed unthinkable that voters would not award Bush with another four years in the White House. The presidential campaign of 1992 would soon make apparent that the American politics were more complex than anticipated, however.

6

Conspiracies and Forgetfulness

In the last weeks of 1991, Oliver Stone's historically based film *JFK* premiered in American movie theaters. The film looked back at the assassination of the president and the alleged role that America's early–1960s Vietnam policies played in that national tragedy. In some ways it was as fitting a herald of times to come as one could expect to find in a Hollywood film. Just as *JFK* was a motion picture that many historians and serious viewers regarded as a distorted account of events and motivations, so, too, were the coming years often marked by increasing public fascination with wide-ranging conspiracy theories, reinvented versions of the past, and suspicions about the motives and actions of American political leaders. In this emerging political climate of the early 1990s, the legacy of the Vietnam War again was ripe for reinterpretation and reuse, even as it continued to be woven into the complicated tapestry of American myth.

At the same time, 1992 saw William Jefferson Clinton step into the national political spotlight. Clinton, the youthful and charismatic governor of Arkansas, would mount an impressive presidential campaign, though one that already would hint at the deeply polarizing and politicized controversies that later would haunt his administration. Vietnam War memories would play a significant role in the 1992 election that was to pit Clinton, a member of the "Vietnam generation" with no military experience whatsoever, against an incumbent who was to be among the last of the World War II veteran presidential candidates. The themes of presidential intrigue and news-media sensationalization were to figure prominently in the coming months and years, as Bill Clinton became a lightning rod for highly contentious partisan politicking as the election year unfolded.

In 1992 the new world order that was proclaimed by George H.W. Bush seemed to be materializing, even if the label was not always applied. The

141

Persian Gulf War had largely swept away the last remnants of the Cold War world, leaving the United States, which viewed itself as the sole remaining superpower, in a position to reassert itself on the world stage. For all the confidence that the nation may have felt after the swift victory in the Persian Gulf, however, international situations would prove to be more complicated and vexing than the many anticipated.

Oliver Stone's *JFK*

The election season was an intriguing context in which Oliver Stone released his next film. Having secured his reputation as a Hollywood box-office winner and *enfant terrible*— in spirit, if not in age — Vietnam veteran Stone continued to be fascinated by the war as subject matter. He had addressed the theme of daily combat in *Platoon* and the plight of disabled Vietnam veterans in *Born on the Fourth of July*. He now turned his attention to the war's origins.

Apparently finding it inconceivable that the United States' descent into the long, costly and bitter war could be attributed to gradually accumulating steps taken by a series of administrations, Stone was drawn to other, more sinister explanations. Encountering hypotheses about the death of John F. Kennedy advanced by authors such as Jim Garrison, a former New Orleans district attorney, Stone discovered a way of thinking about the war's origins that tied together two of the 1960s great traumatic events. Here was a theory that linked Kennedy's assassination to the subsequent eruption of the Vietnam conflict into a full-scale, if undeclared, war.

The basic thesis of *JFK* is that senior American military officials, shadowy men of influence, and government insiders— a group that possibly included the vice president, Lyndon Johnson — had conspired to kill the president in a *coup d'etat*. The narrative suggested that the motivation for the assassination was Kennedy's supposed plan to end the United States military involvement in Vietnam. (It will be recalled that the massive troop build-up occurred after Kennedy's death and was ordered by Lyndon Johnson.) The idea that Kennedy planned a withdrawal, the linchpin to the film's thesis, seems to have been taken by Stone as almost self-evident, though historians noted there was little, if any, credible evidence for it.

For Americans, Kennedy's death had been an almost unparalleled national tragedy, and in retrospect it appeared as a grim precursor of the bitterness that would emerge at the height of American combat in Vietnam. Directly after Kennedy's sudden death, a special bi-partisan investigatory body, the Warren Commission, determined that gunman Lee Harvey Oswald acted alone in the assassination. Almost immediately, however, some people found this conclusion difficult to believe. Beginning in the 1960s, therefore, a long line of conspiracy theories about the Kennedy assassination emerged, ranging from the seemingly credible to the outright fantastic. These theories regularly found an eager audience among the American public, and writing on the subject continued for decades after Kennedy's death. Among these were Garrison's 1988 book *On the Trail of the Assassins*[1] and Jim Marrs's 1990 book *Crossfire: The Plot That Killed Kennedy*[2], both of which were instrumental in providing Stone with a footing for his film.

Garrison was one of the many assassination conspiracy theorists and had already published books on the same topic. His background was unique, however, because he had the distinction of bringing to trial the only criminal prosecution that was based upon an assumed plot to kill the president. In 1967, Garrison prosecuted a New Orleans businessman, claiming in part that this was the man (unnamed in the Warren Report) who tried to arrange legal representation for Lee Harvey Oswald. (Oswald did not live to stand trial; he was murdered by a man named Jack Ruby shortly after being arrested for the Kennedy murder.) Garrison apparently believed that the man had been part of a conspiracy that attempted to cover up compromising details about Kennedy's assassination. At the 1967 trial, however, the man was acquitted of the charges, but Garrison remained convinced that there had been a conspiracy and a cover-up. (It was later confirmed only that the man did have a minor relationship with the C.I.A.) Undeterred in his beliefs, Garrison continued to write about his theories. His later appointment as a circuit court judge lent an air of credibility to his ideas, at least for some readers.

Stone did not create the public's appetite for Kennedy assassination conspiracy theories, but his fame did bring new attention to such conjectures, which many historians thought were clearly misguided. This may not have amounted to much if the film had been a pedestrian production, but it turned out that even Stone's critics were impressed with the film-making prowess in *JFK*. Indeed, the film was among the most visceral treatments of the theme in any medium, and Stone displayed a deft ability combining a number of film-making techniques to vividly bring his version of events to life. The conspiracy theories in *JFK* thus garnered much media attention.

By this time, Oliver Stone's reputation as a Hollywood maverick and apparent government critic were sufficient to make *JFK* news before the film was even released. An early draft of the script had been leaked months before the film's premier. The news media subsequently published stories that reported preliminary reactions to the upcoming film. The negative tone in some of these pieces suggested that the film would find a cool reception among many political commentators. *The National Review,* for example, dismissed Stone as "just another Hollywood liberal infatuated with the Sixties and with Kennedy, and who thinks that national politics are conducted on the same principles as Hollywood studios."[3] Commentators may have had a negative impression of the as-yet-unreleased film, but the advance publicity helped assure that Stone's re-envisioning of Kennedy's role in the Vietnam War's history would receive an ample public airing.

In one respect, Stone's account was similar to many of the other Kennedy conspiracy theories that had been advanced; it lacked very much directly supporting evidence. Indeed, the theory seems largely pieced together from very specific readings of evidence. This evidence appears at most to be suggestive and is surely not indisputable evidence of a conspiracy. The film's assumption that Kennedy intended to withdraw from Vietnam has been especially contested. As *New Republic* writer Ronald Steel noted at the time, the director attached much significance to Kennedy's comment that "in the final analysis, it is they [the South Vietnamese] who have to win or lose this struggle," giving the impression that Kennedy had declared his intent to reverse course in Vietnam.[4] Stone emphasized this point in the film, but he failed to include the entirety of Kennedy's remarks. Indeed, a very different impression is given if one considers the rest of Kennedy's statement, in which the president said, "But I don't agree with those that say we should withdraw. That would be a great mistake."[5]

The underlying motif in the film — that some American leaders whose dedication to American values and ideals was highly corrupted — was not very far from the portrayal that some leaders received in films of the *Rambo* vein. Indeed, the *Rambo* films may have treated both American military and political leaders more gently, since for the most part the worst traits that were intimated were those of cowardice and stupidity. *JFK,* by contrast, implied the much more incendiary — and many historians would say preposterous— theory that the Vietnam War, which erupted after Kennedy's death, was the result of a traitorous and murderous plot to kill the president.

The film generated a quandary for media critics and political writers. As a film, it was a first-rate production, with impressive direction, production values, and acting. (Even critics of the film favorably noted Kevin Costner's acting in the district attorney role.) On one hand, as a director Stone had delivered a bravura performance, in which he took advantage (some would say in more than one sense of the word) of the cinematic medium's potential to a great extent. He combined traditionally staged footage, in which a number of Hollywood stars played parts, with staged reenactments and with documentary material. The result was a powerful cinematic brew.

On the other hand, the effectiveness of Stone's film probably amplified criticisms of its underlying thesis. The inclusion of rarely seen true-life footage, such as the home-movie of the assassination known as the Zapruder film (which had been confiscated from its owner by the Warren Commission) helped give Stone's account of the events the look of authenticity. The skillful and artistic manipulation of such real-life scenes with staged ones— often filmed in a way to simulate the look of documentary material — made for a complicated viewing experience. The audience was confronted with a rush of images that were sometimes historically genuine, sometimes pseudo-documentary, and sometimes obviously staged. Indeed, many of those who were highly critical of the film noted that a major part of their concern was in the masterful and effective way that Stone assembled his film. *JFK* was a powerful and persuasive filmic exercise to the point that some critics worried its vivid though fictionalized portrayal of events would eclipse an understanding of events more rooted in traditional historical analysis.

Many mainstream news publications quickly expressed dismay with *JFK*. The *Washington Post* labeled it a film of "absurdities," and *Newsweek* called it "twisted history."[6] *Rolling Stone* recognized the film's complexity, describing it as "a tangled web" that showed "the best and worst of Stone in one volatile package." In the view of its film critic, Peter Travers, *JFK* was, indeed, "riveting" and "often tremendously exciting," and he described its cinematography and editing as "outstanding, creating a vast cyclorama that sets the mind reeling with possibilities and provocations." Yet, his review concluded that "Stone has turned what he considers to be the crime of the century into a disturbing anomaly — a dishonest search for the truth."[7]

Other publications weighed in with opinions of the film. A discussion of *JFK* also appeared in *National Review* in the spring of 1992, in which writer John Simon grudgingly acknowledged that although the film was variously "long-winded, ponderous, or hard to follow ... it is not to be sloughed off easily."[8] An article in *USA Today Magazine* was blunter in its negative assessment: it asserted that *JFK* was a "big lie" that presented a version of history that was "distorted for the sake of propaganda."[9] The article's author, Bruce Loebs, contended that Stone used the "withdrawal myth" that had been advanced by the "pro–Kennedy" historians such as William Manchester and Arthur Schlesinger, who he thought were trying "To shield ... [Kennedy] from the blame for the Vietnam disaster [sic]."[10] According to another school of thought that was expressed by Loebs, although Kennedy and his advisers may have briefly flirted with the idea of withdrawing American troops at one time, the assassination of South

Vietnamese President Ngo Dinh Diem, only weeks before Kennedy's death, had put an end to that thought. Loeb was alarmed by Stone's influence, describing the director as a "brilliant propagandist." He further warned that "Stone's *JFK* cannot be dismissed as a mere movie.... Stone instead follows Hitler's maxim ... that 'the masses fall victim more easily to a big lie than a small one.'"[11]

In these and many other discussions of the film, Stone often was critiqued as if he were an historian rather than a Hollywood director. As an article in *Time* magazine pointed out to readers, however, taking liberties with the historical record was hardly a new phenomenon in the arts. Even Shakespeare had done much the same in his account of Richard III.[12] As to the fear that Stone's version of events would corrupt the understanding of those too young to remember the era, it was argued that "worse things have happened — including, perhaps, the Warren Commission report.... But why should the American people expect a moviemaker to assume responsibility for producing the last word on the Kennedy assassination ... ?"[13]

In published accounts, Stone seemed unmoved by the criticisms of his film. In his view, "The dirty little secret of American journalism ... is that it's generally wrong. Sometimes a little, sometimes a lot, but wrong."[14] In a later interview, Stone remarked, "My name has become synonymous with lunatic conspiracy buff. However, the world is rooted in conspiracy. Every government in the world is rooted in conspiracy...."[15] Indeed, polls had consistently shown that the public had grown skeptical of the Warren Commission's original conclusion that Oswald had acted alone. And for some members of a new generation, for whom the war in Vietnam was a distant event that ended before they were born, Stone's account did not always seem far-fetched. The broader inclination for conspiracy theorizing in American mass culture at that time may have created an almost ideal climate for the airing of Stone's thesis.

Yet, ultimately one cannot conclude that Stone successfully persuaded the public to accept the notion that American policy in Vietnam had been the cause of Kennedy's assassination. After all, a reluctance to agree with the single-assassin theory advanced by the Warren Commission does not lead inexorably to *JFK*'s argument that the government leaders may have been guilty of plotting the crime. It is surely true, however, that Stone's film did little to quell a sense of cynicism about American politics and media that was growing ever more palpable in the 1990s. It may also have reinforced a tendency to view the war in Vietnam as an anomalous event that defied rational explanation.

Clinton, the Draft, and the 1992 Presidential Campaign

After the rapid success of Desert Storm and the wave of national pride and confidence that followed, it may have seemed unimaginable George H.W. Bush would not find an easy path in his quest for a second term as president. More surprising still, perhaps, was that the Democratic challenger who would emerge victorious in November was to be the upstart figure of Bill Clinton.

In his drive to the presidency in 1988, George H.W. Bush had been a staunch defender of running mate Dan Qualyle's Vietnam War-era stateside service in the National Guard. Although to some, Quayle's military service record was slight, especially compared to Bush's own service in World War II, those looking for a military background in presidential candidates found even less in record of Bill Clinton. The Arkansas governor, who was of draft age during the height of the war, had been a student during the war and had no military experience at all. Not long into the campaign, however, controversy emerged concerning Clinton's account of events related to his draft status in the late 1960s. Over the coming months, the issue would doggedly resurface, and it became apparent that Clinton's story had shifted over time. To some, this would seem to be evidence of deceptiveness or truth-stretching, while to others it would appear simply a function of trying to remember events from a quarter century earlier.

Clinton's draft status surfaced as an issue in the days before the nation's first primary election in New Hampshire. This was just weeks after he already had fended off accusations of an adulterous affair some years earlier, and thus the matter of whether he had been a draft avoider entered the public sphere in the context of larger questions about Clinton's moral character.

At first, when rumors emerged that Clinton had tried to avoid the draft, he said that he had been given a draft deferment in 1969 but then gave it up. In explaining the decision, he said, "I didn't think it was right." In taking this action, Clinton said he made him available for the draft like other young men.

Later, details about the circumstances around his draft status were widely circulated, revealing a more complicated picture than had first appeared. Part of the story seemed straightforward. Clinton had been classified as eligible for the draft upon graduation from Georgetown University. His local draft board looked favorably on his intention to go to Oxford University for further study, and he was not immediately called up. The next summer, when Clinton was still eligible for the draft and could have been called, he decided to sign up for the R.O.T.C. at the University of Arkansas, which removed him from draft eligibility until the following year.

Rather than entering the R.O.T.C. and studying at Arkansas, however, Clinton instead returned for another year at Oxford. (During this time the Nixon administration decided that graduate students could finish out their current academic year of study even if called up, and so as it turned out that Clinton would not have been drafted during that year in any case.) The following year, however, Clinton did give up his deferment, after which he was again classified as eligible for the draft on October 30.

Remarkably, less than month after giving up his deferment, the Selective Service switched the method used to call up draftees. Under the new procedures, the young men who were actually selected for induction were chosen in a lottery; they were only eligible for the draft for one year. The procedure was simple: All possible birth dates for a given year were written on ping pong balls, which were tumbled together in a large rotating drum. To determine the order in which young men would be called, individual ping pong balls were taken one by one from the drum, generating a list of birth dates in rank order. This was the order in which men were drafted. Consequently, those with birth dates appearing at the top of the list were the first to be called up. Since more men were eligible than needed in a given year, however, those men whose birth dates were near the bottom of the list had little chance of being drafted.

Based on his birth date, Clinton's number was 311. This meant there was practically no chance that he would be called up. In the final analysis, according to Clinton's initial version of events, he had done the right thing, and only luck had kept him from being drafted. "The key issue," he said, "is that I made myself available for the draft."

Almost immediately, however, many were skeptical of Clinton's story. The skeptics included not only Republican politicians, as would be expected, but also members of his own party, including Clinton's rivals for the Democratic nomination. Among this latter group was Sen. Tom Harkin from Iowa and Sen. Bob Kerrey from Nebraska, both of whom had served in the military during the Vietnam War. (Harkin was a pilot stationed in Japan, and Kerrey saw combat in Vietnam, where he lost part of a limb and was later awarded the Medial of Honor.)[16] Kerrey commented, "I hope he's telling the truth, but I've got some doubts."[17]

The allegations proved to be a vexing issue for the Clinton campaign, which clearly recognized the potential for it to derail his candidacy. Indeed, as the first primary approached, media reports showed that some New Hampshire voters were "shopping his competition in the wake of reports that Clinton avoided the military draft during the Vietnam War."[18] The reports showed that the reasons for potential wavering support were varied. Some said they would object if it were to be determined that Clinton was a draft avoider. Others seemed to have more pragmatic concerns; they worried that the issue might render Clinton unelectable in the fall. In any case, like Dan Quayle a few years earlier, the issue of Clinton's draft and military status years earlier became a prominent political issue.

Within days, it was widely reported that Clinton's campaign was in trouble. Even a former Democratic official stated, "I think he's in a free fall.... I don't think he can get out of it."[19] Perhaps feeling there was little alternative and that the benefit of making it public would outweigh any damage to the campaign, the Clinton camp then released the text of a letter written long ago to a recruiter in Reserve Officer Training Corps. The text of the letter, which was now reprinted in the news media, did little to clear up the controversy.

The document, dated December 3, 1969, was written while Clinton was studying at Oxford University. Clinton addressed his letter to Col. Eugene Holmes, telling him that it was his "hope that my telling this one story will help you understand more clearly how so many fine people have come to find themselves still loving their country but loathing the military...."[20] Other parts of the letter gave fuel to his critics. For example, he wrote, "First, I want to thank you, not just for saving me from the draft, but for being so kind and decent to me last summer.... In retrospect, it seems that the admiration might not have been mutual if you had known a little more about me."

In the letter, Clinton also explained that the conflict in Vietnam was "a war I opposed and despised with a depth of feeling I had reserved solely for racism in America before Vietnam ..." and that "I have written and spoken and marched against the war." In addition, he noted that he had concluded:

> I came to believe that the draft system itself is illegitimate. No government really rooted in limited, parliamentary democracy should have the power to make its citizens fight and kill and die in a war they may oppose, a war which even possibly may be wrong, a war which, in any case, does not involve immediately the peace and freedom of the nation.

Perhaps the most interesting revelation in the letter, however, was found in these sentences:

> The decision not to be a draft resister and the related subsequent decisions were the most difficult of my life. I decided to accept the draft in spite of my beliefs for one reason: to maintain my political viability within the system. For years I have worked to prepare myself for a political life.... It is a life I still feel compelled to lead.

As Clinton explained, he had signed with the R.O.T.C. with the idea that this "could possibly, but not positively, [help him] avoid both Vietnam

Bill Clinton had been interested in a political career from his earliest days, as became clear during his presidential campaign of 1992. This photograph shows a 1978 meeting between President Jimmy Carter (left) and the young Clinton. Photograph: Jimmy Carter Library.

and [draft] resistance." Yet, he confessed to misgivings for having made this "compromise" with himself "because I had no interest in the R.O.T.C. program itself and all I seemed to have done was to protect myself from physical harm." According to the letter, Clinton then had second thoughts and so he wrote to his local draft board official "stating that I couldn't do the R.O.T.C. after all and would he please draft me as soon as possible." This letter, he said, was "never mailed."

What seemed, for many, to be shocking candor in the letter prompted a fiery reaction from Clinton's political foes. Indeed, the letter had much that arguably could be used as ammunition against him, especially in the wake of the reinvigorated national pride that still seemed evident after the Persian Gulf War. A writer in *The New York Times* pointedly noted that "Bill Clinton's efforts to avoid the draft, epitomized by his agonized letter written that fall from Oxford University,"[21] cast doubt on whether the nation had moved beyond the perceived Vietnam syndrome, after all. Even in 1992, it was said "no national consensus has ever developed as to whether the Vietnam War was just or unjust, whether the draft dodging was justified, or whether the United States could have won with a more determined effort."[22]

The controversy provoked further investigations into the details of Clinton's record. Writing in *The New York Times,* David E. Rosenbaum claimed that from "readily available" sources, Clinton could easily have known he would have had little chance of being drafted when he gave up his deferment.[23] Such reports heightened speculation that Clinton had manipulated the system to his advantage. These accusations fit squarely into the larger picture that Clinton's critics were painting of a man with allegedly deep moral flaws.

At the time when these charges were making political life for Bill Clinton difficult, it can be argued that the lengthening time between the war and the present had been accompanied by a greater reluctance on the part of many to confront the strong divisions that the war had caused on the American home-front. During the twelve years of the Reagan and George H.W. Bush administrations, the military had regained much of its luster, and many Americans dealt with the so-called "lost war" by not dwelling on that aspect of it. Vietnam veterans had earned a much more prominent place of respect in American society than had been the case two decades earlier, while seemingly fewer opponents of that war wished to call attention to their anti-war activities. The American soldier had been invited back into the mainstream of U.S. life; the image of the anti-war protester seemed to be an anachronism. Yet, the private feelings of Americans who had lived through the Vietnam years were often difficult to determine.

Despite the negative potential in Clinton's past draft status, this and other revelations did not end his quest for the White House. Although Paul Tsongas, senator from neighboring Massachusetts and thus viewed by many as a local son, won the New Hampshire Democratic primary with 33 percent of the vote, Clinton posted a respectable second-place finish, attaining almost 25 percent. (Clinton received more votes than Tom Harkin and Bob Kerrey combined.) Thus, he continued to the next phase of the campaign with the knowledge that the allegations about his past behavior might be overcome.

As Clinton emerged as the front-runner in the following weeks, Democrats largely refrained from raising his Vietnam-era record. Still, it was apparent that the issue, linked as it was to larger questions about his character, had the potential to inflict damage.

In late spring, a report surfaced in which it was claimed that Clinton had been sent an induction notice prior to signing up for the R.O.T.C. At first, Clinton denied this account. Later, he said that the notice did not reach him at Oxford University, where he was studying, until after the induction date. In a press release issued by his campaign on April 4, 1992, Clinton explained that he had consulted with his local draft board about the notice, and that the board extended his deferment for an additional semester. This delay had made it possible for him to sign up for the R.O.T.C.[24]

Clinton was a persuasive campaigner, and though questions of this sort continued to trail him, he marched steadily towards the summer Democratic National Convention. In July, he was enthusiastically embraced as the party's choice to challenge George Bush in November. Clinton selected Al Gore, Senator from Tennessee, to be his running mate. Although Gore had not been assigned to a combat unit, he was a Vietnam War veteran, perhaps helping to give the ticket a more balanced look to party faithful.

After the Democratic convention, it became clear that the Republican camp intended to assertively pursue the draft issue. At the Republican convention several weeks later, the Secretary of Labor asserted, "Inside George Bush is the heart of an 18-year-old fighter pilot who risked his life for his country, who did not run from his responsibilities then and does not now. You can't be one kind of man and another kind of president."[25] In a similar vein, Republican Patrick Buchanan said, "When Bill Clinton's turn came in Vietnam, he sat up in a dormitory in Oxford, England, and figured out how to dodge the draft."[26]

In a Chicago convention of American Legion held in late August, Clinton again sought to quiet the issue. He asked those assembled to "judge me fairly, because that's the American way."[27] Adding that he wanted to provide "one final statement to set the record straight," he repeated that "If my number had been called, I would have served, and gone to Vietnam if so ordered, but I won't lie to you, I was relieved when I saw my number was 311, not because I didn't want to serve my country but because I believed so strongly that our policy in Vietnam was wrong.... I know many of you disagree with me. I respect that."[28] The Bush campaign retorted with a statement claiming that Clinton's explanations had been inconsistent.

As September came, the Republicans were determined to push the draft issue further. As one political columnist wrote, "The drumbeat on the draft is clearly escalating.... Almost every day, new press releases come from the Bush-Quayle headquarters, accusing Mr. Clinton of contradicting himself or covering up the truth about why he did not serve in the military in the Vietnam War."[29] Indeed, many Republican politicians repeated the charges that Clinton's draft record made him unfit to hold the position of commander-in-chief of the military and that his apparently shifting explanations were evidence of an underlying untruthfulness.

Democrats tried to defuse the charges. Bob Kerrey said that the president should "call off the dogs" about Clinton's draft record, adding the comment, "God help us, if in 1992, the people who brought us the tragedy of Vietnam use it in a deceptive way to hold on to power."[30] To those who saw Clinton's actions as demonstrations of flawed or insufficient moral character, none of the pleas to drop the draft issue were very convincing. Dan Quayle told a group in Ohio that "Bill Clinton can run, he can dodge, but he can't hide the truth from the American people. Sooner or later, Bill Clinton is going to have to come clean with the American people on how he avoided military service."[31]

For all its controversy, the Republican approach failed to take hold with the public and did not slow Clinton's campaign. By early October, in a three-way contest among Clinton, Bush and the independent candidate, the business mogul H. Ross Perot, Clinton was leading in the polls. Aiming to keep the issue of Clinton's Vietnam War-era activities in the limelight during this time, Bush appeared on the CNN *Larry King Live* program of October 7, saying that Clinton should "level with the American people on the draft, on whether he went to Moscow, how many demonstrations he led against his own country from a foreign soil."[32] (Various reports had surfaced in which it was claimed that Clinton had traveled with a student group to Moscow while he was a student at Oxford.)

A week later, during an NBC *Today Show* interview segment, in which Katie Couric was interviewing First Lady Barbara Bush about the history and décor of the White House, the president unexpectedly walked into the room. Bush then spoke on camera with Couric for the next twenty minutes. The president's criticisms of Clinton's Vietnam-era activities were a central part of this conversation with Couric. Repeating his familiar message, Bush said "I simply do not understand when Americans are in a prison camp in Hanoi and Americans are dying on the battlefield — a lot of kids drafted, didn't have any connections to get out of the draft — I cannot understand an American citizen organizing demonstrations in a foreign land."[33]

That same month, the news media reports indicated that American embassies in London and Norway had been ordered by the State Department to look for any records relating to Clinton's activities during his time at Oxford.[34] Overall, then, the Bush-Quayle campaign continued to hope that Clinton's behavior during the Vietnam War would suggest to voters that the governor from Arkansas would be a poor choice for the presidency.

The Clinton camp, meanwhile, sought to dismiss the barrage of criticism as evidence of a Republican campaign in trouble. They countered that Bush also had questionable past activities for which to account, implying that there was something unexplained regarding his possible involvement in the Iran-Contra scandal a few years earlier. As the campaign neared the end, and finding himself heckled by Clinton supporters at a campaign stop in New Jersey, a frustrated George H.W. Bush declared, "I wish these draft dodgers would shut up so I can finish my speech. Pathetic."[35]

Developments in U.S.–Vietnam Relations

In the weeks prior to the election, George Bush had set in motion a chain of events that would create political difficulties for Clinton in the coming years. These decisions in time would also alter the United States' relationship with its former foe, Vietnam. In a carefully planned ceremony held in the White House's Rose Garden in October, Bush announced that the administration had "achieved a significant, a real breakthrough" with the Vietnamese government in relation to still ongoing efforts to resolve the POW-MIA issue. "It was a bitter conflict," Bush said, "but Hanoi knows today that we seek only answers without the threat of retribution for the past." As a symbolic gesture, the U.S. arranged to send aid for flood relief.

Although attention to it was at some times stronger than others, the plight of the missing POW-MIA American soldiers had never disappeared from the political landscape. In fact, for many months prior to the announcement, a Senate Select Committee on POW-MIA Affairs had been working to gain greater cooperation from the Vietnamese government on this vexing issue, which retained its character as a raw wound for many Americans. (The committee was chaired by Democratic Sen. John Kerry of Massachusetts, the decorated Vietnam veteran who had once been a highly visible opponent of the war, and vice-chaired by Republican Bob Smith of New Hampshire, also a Vietnam veteran. The committee's report judged that there was little basis to think that any American soldiers were still being held.) In the eyes of many who favored improving ties with Vietnam, that nation had recently signaled a greater willingness to cooperate in American efforts to discover the fate of the lost soldiers. Importantly, an indication that previously secret military archives in Hanoi would likely be opened for inspection by American officials was regarded by many, including members of the administration, as important evidence that a change in Vietnam's attitude was at hand.

It may have been that Vietnam's perceived change of heart was pragmatically motivated. The Southeast Asian nation had lost its chief political ally and sponsor with the fall of the Soviet Union, and it was experiencing severe economic problems. Meanwhile, international business executives had begun to eye Vietnam as a potential new economic opportunity. Sensing that other nations were poised to make inroads in Vietnam while they were left behind, some American business had begun to press for the U.S.

to at least lift the decades-old trade embargo with Vietnam, even if full diplomatic relations did not immediately follow.

The Rose Garden announcement returned the issue to a visible place in domestic American politics. In future months and years, the issue would resurrect old controversies.

Clinton prevails. For all the political noise about Clinton's draft record and other alleged shortcomings, he emerged victorious in the November election. In that year's three-way contest for the presidency, Clinton received 43 percent of the vote to George H.W. Bush's 37 percent and independent candidate H. Ross Perot's 19 percent. Still, the draft issue had been an important part in the campaign to discredit him, and it surely helped bolster the attitude of deep skepticism that his detractors would feel about him in the coming years. And the draft issue in the 1992 campaign also was not the last controversy about Vietnam and the legacy of the war in which the president-elect would find himself.

Post-election diplomatic developments. In the weeks following the election, many observers felt that before the end of his term, George Bush would move ahead in normalizing relations with Vietnam. Yet, additional movement on the issue was slow in developing. In mid–December, the Bush administration announced that the embargo was to be softened, though not lifted, and that American businesses would be permitted to enter into contracts with Vietnam that could take effect upon the assumed lifting of the restrictions at a later date. Supporters of opening relations with Vietnam saw this as a positive step, but were anxious to see more. *The New York Times* issued an editorial urging Bush to "finish the last chapter of the Vietnam War," further asserting that "no major P.O.W.-M.I.A. issues remain unresolved.[36]" Indeed, the editorial predicted that delaying further action until Clinton took office would only "invite recriminations from some veterans' groups that resent Mr. Clinton's efforts to avoid the draft."[37]

Predictably, political opponents on the issue were disturbed by any suggestions of easing trade restrictions, but overall, opinion was mixed. Representatives of the Veterans of Foreign Wars favored further loosening of the embargo, while the executive director of the American Legion held exactly the opposite view, stating that his group was "totally disappointed and outraged at the President's announcement."[38] In some respects, it appeared that lingering bitterness from the war would re-emerge in political rhetoric.

The matter still remained unresolved as Bush left office, leaving Clinton with an issue that seemed sure to be contentious for his administration, especially given the controversy about his war-era activities and politics. Anthony Lake, Clinton's National Security Adviser, was assigned to work on the issue. Two months later, the new administration had yet to establish a timetable for further action in U.S.-Vietnam trade or other relations.

Sen. John Kerry kept the issue alive in Washington, saying "Are we not in danger of doing nothing and watching other nations move ahead? Do you perhaps engage the POW-MIA issue by moving ahead more rapidly?"[39] The latter comment reflected a line of thinking that reasoned if more cooperation was needed from the Vietnamese government about resolving questions about POW-MIAs, the best method to obtain that would be to strengthen ties with the old foes.

An opposite view, however, continued to be expressed against any further trade or diplomatic overtures to the Vietnamese. The claim remained that this would constitute rewarding that government for its continuing non-cooperation. By this time, Republican Senator Bob Smith from New Hampshire, also a Vietnam veteran and who was vice chairman of the senate's POW-MIA Committee, had emerged a leading and quite vocal opponent of any further normalization of relations with Vietnam. "Anyone," he said, "who attempts to make the case to the president that Vietnam is being very forthcoming on American POWs and MIAs is simply not being guided by the facts.... Vietnam's cooperation on the clearest cases of last known POWs in their control has been limited at best."[40]

Meanwhile, Clinton had embarked upon changing American military policy with respect to sexual orientation, one of several issues that drew attention away from the matter of U.S.-Vietnam normalization. Although many favored changing policy to allow gays and lesbians to openly serve in the armed forces, others saw this as an extremely negative development and evidence that Clinton was bowing to a special interest. A compromise was eventually struck with the so-called "Don't Ask, Don't Tell" policy, which stated, "Sexual orientation will not be a bar to [military] service unless manifested by homosexual conduct."[41] The policy was a political compromise that removed some of the stigma and legal obstacles for persons with same-sex orientation in military service. It found many critics, nonetheless. The policy did not go far enough for many gay and lesbian advocates, and went entirely too far for many conservatives, especially those with a strong religious orientation. The issue had an effect well beyond its stated topic, however, as observers noted the amount of political capital that Clinton had been forced to use in the process of pushing the issue. As a *New York Times* writer observed that spring, because of the vocal opposition elicited by his prior draft status and the efforts to lift the ban on gays and lesbians serving in the armed forces, he "cannot afford another bruising battle."[42] It seems clear, then, that these other factors also played a part in the slow pace of further normalization of U.S.-Vietnam relations. For the time being, the administration dispatched a retired general to Vietnam to assess the current status of efforts to resolve the POW-MIA issue.

By the summer, the Vietnam issue remained controversial, as exemplified in continued efforts by John Kerry and Bob Smith to promote opposite courses of action. Kerry cited "enormous cooperation" from the Vietnamese and argued for further action on the trade embargo, while Smith said the president should "not be deceived by those who claim enormous progress is now being made."[43] As the disagreement continued, it was largely, though not strictly, along party lines. Indeed, Republican Sen. John McCain of Arizona, Vietnam veteran and former POW, sided with those who sought increased relations with Vietnam. Yet, other Republicans seemed to see things more like Smith. Iowa Republican Charles Grassley asserted that too many concessions had been made and that even with these, Vietnam had responded meagerly.

A milestone in improved relations was passed as the Clinton administration announced a policy change, saying it would not stand in the way of Vietnam's application for international loans. The U.S. trade embargo remained, however, and Warren Christopher, the secretary of state, carefully pointed out that the administration would not move swiftly on complete normalization of relations until unspecified additional measures were taken by the Vietnamese concerning the POW-MIA question.

Into the autumn of 1993, advocates of improved relations continued to press the issue. *The New York Times* said that "sooner or later some American president will find the courage to end Washington's now pointless vendetta against Communist Vietnam. That President might as well be Bill Clinton."[44] The editorial speculated that it was not the POW-MIA issue that was standing in the way, but rather "wounded national pride" and Clinton's "fears of a ferocious backlash." Indeed, it was clear that the skepticism about Clinton on military matters was a factor that continued to impinge upon the administration's actions. It somewhat cast into doubt the younger Bill Clinton's writing about keeping political viability in choosing his personal course of action during the war years.

Other International Crises

As the issue of U.S.-Vietnam relations continued to be a source of controversy, other international situations demanded Washington's attention. Indeed, in the world of global politics, there was no shortage of potential military confrontations during the early years of the Clinton presidency.

Although his lack of military service during the Vietnam years did not keep him from winning the presidency, in some important ways this proved to be a key missing component in Bill Clinton's background in the eyes of critics, who disapproved of the way he handled subsequent matters that were related to America's armed services. Even within the Pentagon, it was widely reported that some senior officers were unsure of Clinton as commander-in-chief because of his lack of service in Vietnam.[45] These doubts became apparent almost immediately.

On the international scene, the Clinton presidency was confronted with several important situations in which the use of American military force was either used or contemplated, and again it is difficult to imagine that questions about Clinton's Vietnam War-era experiences did not color the way in which critics viewed his policies. More generally, in a pattern by now familiar, three overlapping international situations brought comparisons to the Vietnam War back to public attention. These were the crises in Somalia, Haiti, and what was by now the former-Yugoslavia.

Somalia. In the fall of 1993, with the state of relations between the United States and Vietnam continuing to draw attention, the troubles in Somalia were thrust prominently onto the political stage. The situation in the impoverished nation of Somalia had become chaotic. It was the result of a long simmering situation that now threatened to career out of control.

The situation had been developing for a long time. Mohammed Siad Barre, who had come to power in 1969 as the result of a military coup, was ousted from office in early 1991 by a group of opposing factions called the United Somalia Congress. Shortly after removing Siad, however, the coalition broke down, with Mohamed Farrah Aidid and his Somalia National Movement emerging as leading antagonists. In the near-anarchy that followed, a humanitarian crisis became apparent to the outside world. With many Somali citizens facing hunger and deprivation, and with the nation seemingly veering towards complete anarchy, the warring parties agreed to a ceasefire and the presence of United Nations monitors. The immediate results were disappointing, however. As observers noted, food and supplies still were not reaching those in need. Consequently, a month before he left office and in answer to a plea from the United Nations, George Bush had sent 25,000 American troops to Somalia as part of an American-led U.N. security operation, named Operation Restore Hope.

Thus, by the time Bill Clinton took the oath of office, the U.S. military was already on the scene in Somalia. For a time, the operation seemed reasonably successful. An agreement was achieved in March 1993 to end hostilities among the parties, and later the situation seemed sufficiently under control so that the United Nations assumed authority from the U.S. Soon after, American troops in Somalia were reduced to 1200. The violence resumed, however, with several high-profile attacks on peace-keeping troops in the summer months. In August, a contingent of American troops was sent to help with the situation. To at least one editorial writer, these continuing difficulties suggested that "The intervention in Somalia has the appearance of a small-scale Vietnam. The United Nations should avoid the American mistakes of the 1960s and consider extricating itself from the country."[46] Critics in the U.S. Congress echoed the view that Clinton should proceed slowly and obtain Congressional approval for any future military involvement in Somalia.

The situation turned into a horrific public spectacle in October, when American troops searching for Aidid near the Olympic Hotel in Mogadishu encountered hostile gunfire. An ensuing firefight, in which an American Blackhawk helicopter was downed, lasted for 17 hours. By the end, 18 American soldiers were dead and 84 were wounded. The ferocity of the situation, and a deeply troubling reality for the American public, was apparent as television images showed a dead American soldier being dragged through the streets and a wounded American officer from the downed helicopter was shown being taken captive. It was a shocking incident for a nation that, it was said, had overcome the legacy of defeat in Vietnam with the success of Operation Desert Storm.

A chorus of criticism about the American involvement followed. The reports of American troops under attack in Somalia "seemed all too reminiscent of past entanglements abroad — from Vietnam to Beirut,"[47] according to a *Boston Globe* account. Yet, as the chairperson of the National Center for Public Policy Research was quoted saying, "This has become a manhood test of Bill Clinton's foreign policy manhood. He doesn't want to look like a quitter."[48] Though not explicitly stated, it seems safe to assume that perceptions such as this of the situation as a "test" were enhanced, at least on some level, by the earlier attention that had focused on Clinton's strong opposition to American involvement in Vietnam and the alleged lengths to which he had gone to avoid military service in the war.

It may seem somewhat ironic, then, that shortly after the widely perceived humiliation of what came to be known as the Battle of Mogadishu, Bill Clinton is found defending American involvement in a foreign military entanglement. Though it can be argued that Somalia was quite different from the 1960s situation in Vietnam, which was a long-term struggle within the context of a wider Cold War, Clinton's explanation of American participation there seemed like an echo of earlier administration's rationales for participation in war in Southeast Asia. Clinton declared that if the U.S.

withdrew from the Somalia operation "Our own credibility with friends and allies would be severely damaged. Our leadership in world affairs would be undermined.... [and that] We face a choice. Do we leave when the job gets tough or when the job is well done?"[49] To some, it seemed that Clinton, perhaps inadvertently, had "reinforced memories of Vietnam"[50] in his response to the crisis in Somalia.

The immediate effect of Clinton's view of the situation was the dispatching of 5,300 more American troops to Somalia. Yet, it was clear that it was not politically viable to maintain a long-term American military commitment to Somalia. By March 25, though 20,000 U.N. troops continued to patrol the country, American troops were withdrawn.

Haiti. To only a minor extent, an American intervention in Haiti raised some speculation about parallels to the Vietnam War. In 1991, Haitian president Jean-Bertrand Aristide was forced from office in a military revolt, led by three officers who had been trained at the School of the Americas at Fort Benning, Georgia. The Clinton administration watched the situation, while Aristide remained in exile and the circumstances in Haiti grew progressively dimmer. Finally deciding that the time had come to restore Aristide to power, Clinton announced that American troops would invade Haiti unless the military rulers yielded. Through the arrangements brokered by Colin Powell, Jimmy Carter and Sen. Sam Nunn, however, a military assault was avoided. Instead, 20,000 American troops peacefully landed on its shores in Operation Uphold Freedom, and Aristide re-assumed the office. (The security operation was taken over by the U.N. a year later.)

Oliver Stone's *Heaven and Earth*

In late 1993, at the end of Clinton's first year in office, Oliver Stone released yet another film with a Vietnam War theme. *Heaven and Earth* seemed to be a concluding piece to what later became known as his Vietnam War trilogy, perhaps indicating some measure of closure on the subject on the director's part. Rather than returning to the theme as portrayed through the eyes of combatants, however, in the new film Stone focused on the horrific plight of a young Vietnamese woman, who was played by Hiep Thi Le.

Like his earlier Vietnam War films, *Heaven and Earth* was based on true experiences. In this case, the source material had been recorded in two books written by Le Ly Hayslip, on whom the lead character was based. Though clearly aiming to provide an uplifting story of perseverance in the face of terrible circumstances, the narrative of the film is often very bleak

Oliver Stone returned to the Vietnam War theme again in his 1993 film *Heaven and Earth*. Although less popular than his other films about the war, *Heaven and Earth* was noteworthy for showing the war experience through the perspective of a young Vietnamese woman. In this photograph, the film's main character, Le Ly, is portrayed by Hiep Ti Le. Photograph: Photofest

and disturbing. Viewers see the character violently abused by both the South Vietnamese and the Viet Cong. Later, after an impromptu marriage to an American military officer (played by Tommy Lee Jones), she faces a struggle against new setbacks as she seeks to find a better life in the United States.

As with Stone's previous Vietnam War films, the director did not flinch at showing the brutality of war. The film graphically depicts the main character as she is violently victimized, with especially brutal scenes of electric-shock torture and gang rape. In other parts of the film, viewers see a wide array of violence, including scenes of Vietnamese being thrown from a helicopter, gunshots to the head, and suicide. Although Stone may have been attempting to make a larger point, it was unclear whether the public would be receptive to experience that he had created.

In *Heaven and Earth,* Stone suggests that the war was a great catastrophe for all sides. The moral complexity of the conflict is evident throughout the film, and bright spots are hard to find. The darker side of some South Vietnamese and American participants in the war was amply demonstrated, but the Viet Cong were also presented in an equally, if not more negative light. In the view of film critic Roger Ebert, the enemy is portrayed as "brutal, arbitrary, [and] sadistic."[51]

One might argue that Stone's focus of ordinary Vietnamese people during the war should not have been remarkable, but yet this point of view was so seldom portrayed in screen media that it did represent a significant development in the cinema of the Vietnam War. Surely, in the United States, despite significant public attention and memory of the Vietnam conflict over the decades since the end of the war, the Vietnamese people seldom have been recognized publicly as the war's most numerous victims.

Indeed, public reaction to the film was mixed. *Washington Post* writer Desson Howe noted that "For Stone, the latest film is the closing of a circle, the final brushwork on an ambitious canvas," but concluded that the film-maker's "emotional investment reaps little artistic return."[52] Perhaps weary of yet another Oliver Stone foray into this subject matter, film-goers who were seeking serious themes looked to other options. (These notably included Stephen Spielberg's *Schindler's List*, about the Swedish industrialist who saved Jews from the Holocaust, and also *Philadelphia*, director Jonathan Demme's film about an AIDS victim fighting discrimination, which featured the popular actors Tom Hanks and Denzel Washington; both were released during the same time as *Heaven and Earth*.) Stone's reputation assured that *Heaven and Earth* would attract media attention, but it was less successful in attracting audiences. Indeed, the magazine *Entertainment Weekly* dismissively concluded that "Serious subjects make terrible holiday fare. Which is why moviegoers have already rejected Oliver Stone's *Heaven and Earth*."[53]

New Crises

It was a complicated time for the administration, in which the U.S. was called upon to make decisions about whether or not to invoke military means to achieve its objectives. U.S. troops were dispatched to Kuwait, with the aim of preventing any renewed Iraqi invasion of that country. Meanwhile, scarcely gaining notice from the American public, the administration watched as the situation in Rwanda rapidly escalated into what would later be described as genocide. However, the administration was still feeling the sting of events in Somalia, in which American soldiers had perished. Unlike other dire situations, therefore, the administration was anxious to avoid military engagement in Africa.

Bosnia. Throughout this time, a crisis was brewing in the nations that had once formed Yugoslavia. With the end of the Cold War, a largely unforeseen conflict developed as the result of generations-old rivalries and ethnic prejudices among Serbia, Croatia and Bosnia-Herzegovina. When Bosnia-Herzegovina declared its independence from the loose confederation of post-communist Yugoslavian states, these rivalries, which had for decades been suppressed by the defunct communist regime, surfaced in a frenzy of hatred and violence. The region was plunged into bitter and complex hostilities.

As early as 1992, the United Nations had dispatched an international force to maintain the peace in Bosnia. It was clear, however, that the armed forces of Bosnia, Serbia and Croatia, as well as a number of less official paramilitary groups in the region, were intent on exploiting the situation and continuing their military aims. European powers saw this as a primarily a European affair, which was a view that the U.S. initially seemed to endorse. Over the months, however, some leading American politicians and political observers publicly began to ask if this were not a crisis that demanded a U.S. role.

Some political observers clamored for American military intervention. In a parody of the famous slogan "It's the economy, stupid" (from Clinton's presidential campaign), Randolph Ryan wrote "Ground troops, stupid. Now, stupid. Yesterday, stupid! ... U.S. soldiers — roughly 25,000 — assigned to a multilateral peace-keeping force ... is the only way ... to end the paroxysm of ethnic terror by which the Bosnian Serbs are finishing off Muslim culture in Eastern Bosnia."[54] Others found the situation bleak, and possibly "beyond help."[55]

Not surprisingly, the grim situation generated renewed comparison to past crises. Noted *Boston Globe* writer Ellen Goodman asked, "Which is it to be then? Another Vietnam? Another Holocaust?"[56] She continued:

> The lessons of Vietnam are repeated as if we were cramming for an exam. Lessons on the limits of power: Don't get into a war unless you have determined a way out. Don't pretend that you can put your toe into a conflict without putting the body at risk. Don't start without the country's support.[57]

Although Goodman clearly viewed the crisis as having its own unique character, it was again apparent that the Vietnam War cast a long shadow over the American view of these difficult events.

As time passed, and as a parade of disturbing images of civilians under attack in Sarajevo and other cities was broadcast in the evening news, the American public was graphically reminded of the horrors that war inflicts. Accounts of mass killings and organized rapes further raised a sense of urgency about the situation, as reports of "ethnic cleansing" became increasingly familiar. Finally, under the auspices of NATO, the United States joined the multinational peace-keeping effort, providing air power with the aim of keeping the warring parties separated. Although peace was achieved, the episode was a shocking reminder to Europe, as well as the U.S., that demise of the Soviet Union did not mean that the world — or in Europe's case, its backyard — was necessarily safe from the scourge of war.

Looking back at these events it appears that although perhaps less pronounced than in some earlier crises, the lingering influences of the Vietnam

War continue to appear in the shadows as the Clinton administration sought to devise and implement its military policy. That war was still used by advocates of various positions when it served to reinforce their positions, but it can be argued that it also played a less blatant role as one of the factors shaping administration policy. Contradictions abounded. Thus, the same administration asserted both the need to stay the course in Somalia in order to maintain American credibility and to finish a job started — statements in which the distant echoes of Vietnam-era politics were instantly understood — and also seemed reluctant to become militarily involved in the former Yugoslavia, even though the dire humanitarian circumstances were very evident. In perhaps a final irony, news accounts noted the fallout resulting from the administration's apparent non-involvement policy in Bosnia. Internal protests about that policy led to more resignations by Foreign Service officers than any other event except for the Vietnam War.[58]

Trade Embargo with Vietnam Ended

Against the backdrop of these other complex international events, in February of 1994 the administration announced that it would formally end the trade embargo with Vietnam. Seen by most observers as a politically risky move for Clinton — especially given his and the issue's past history — the administration was prompted to make the declaration after a Senate vote that called for the White House to lift the embargo. The Senate declaration, sponsored by John Kerry and others, resulted in 62 favoring and 32 opposing the action, a nearly two-thirds majority that gave Clinton some "political cover,"[59] as Sen. Bob Smith said.

Though a majority in the Senate agreed with the idea, which Kerry said was "to put the war behind us," many of those against the proposal remained vocal in their dissent. Thus, while John McCain concluded that "it's an appropriate time to move forward," opponents such as Bob Smith were sure that such a move was "a mistake."[60] For his part, Clinton insisted that although the embargo would be lifted, that change did "not constitute a normalization of our relationships. Before that happens, we must have more progress, more cooperation, and more answers."[61] After meeting with representatives of veterans groups opposed to the move, the official announcement was made in a White House ceremony.

Half a world away in Vietnam, the lifting of the embargo meant that the trade agreements previously signed by American companies could now be fulfilled. In what seemed to be a widespread sentiment, a Vietnamese high school teacher who was interviewed in Ho Chi Minh City—formerly

Saigon — seemed relieved, saying, "Now at last we are allowed to forget the war."[62] Elsewhere in the city, free samples of Pepsi Cola were distributed,[63] a small symbol of a significant shift in commercial exchange between the two nations. Indeed, American businesses had anxiously waited to re-enter the Vietnamese market, and they immediately seized upon the opportunity that the removal of the embargo provided.

The Vietnamese government, meanwhile, hoped that this would soon signal a willingness by the United States to establish full diplomatic ties. The White House indicated that diplomatic missions would be established in the two capitals to explore further ties. Yet, the matter was to drag on, and it would be some months before this was to be accomplished.

The War in *Forrest Gump* and Other Screen Productions

In the summer of 1994, against the backdrop of a complex and often exasperating political milieu, director Robert Zemeckis's film *Forrest Gump* appeared in theaters throughout the United States. Immediately embraced by audiences, the film featured everyman actor Tom Hanks in the title role. Though the fictional Gump was a hero with very limited intelligence and intellectual capability, he possessed an innate goodness and innocence that served him well. These qualities seemed to enable Gump to wander through history more successfully than most of those who supposedly had more intelligence and stature. Some critics were skeptical of the film's premises; it was, according to one film writer, "literally a tale told by an idiot."[64] Audiences, however, responded enthusiastically to Hanks performance, and it soon emerged as a box-office sensation.

In the film's narrative, Gump is thrust into many important historical situations. Part of the film's appeal was no doubt its special effects, in which Hanks' character appears dropped into actual historical footage, a refinement of an approach used by director Woody Allen in *Zelig* some years earlier in 1983. Gump is shown with American presidents and in important historical events, providing audiences with entertaining examples of cinematic sleight of hand.

Perhaps a bigger part of the film's popularity, however, was its straightforward theme. *Forrest Gump* refuted the cynicism apparent in much of the mass media at the time. In a world where smart people often continued to gets things wrong, *Forrest Gump* showed audiences how simple, trusting innocence could overcome the world's ills.

Writing in *The Christian Science Monitor,* David Sterritt concluded that the film was noteworthy because of its "insistence on raising key issues in recent American history from racial integration to the Vietnam War and the AIDS crisis;" yet these were shown "through a simple-minded hero whose most endearing quality is an ability to miss the point of just about anything."[65] Audiences, he continued, demanded such over-simplifying fare, adding that "in the ongoing struggle between provocative cinema and feel-good entertainment, dumb and dumber still carry the day."[66] Whether or not one agrees with this assessment, it is undeniably true that *Forrest Gump* did greatly simplify major social and political events for the sake of its story-telling.

An important part of the film deals with America during the Vietnam War years. Serving in a combat unit in Vietnam, Gump is shown bravely serving his country and his fellow soldiers. The combat footage was especially notable, applying the latest technological capabilities of film-making to achieve a sense of realism and high drama. Gump's heroics earn him a Medal of Honor; his friend emerges from the war as a disabled veteran.

Anti-war protesters, meanwhile, are shown in a negative light. Spoiled, self-centered and misguided, they appear in unflattering contrast to Gump's innocence, simple patriotism, and devotion to duty. Although conservative writers and pundits seldom have looked to Hollywood films for validation of their views, it was perhaps not surprising that many of them nodded approvingly at what they saw as the underlying patriotic and moral messages of *Forrest Gump*.

Indeed, the political context into which *Forrest Gump* was released played an important part in explaining the film's enormous success. As would be the case throughout his presidency, at this time Bill Clinton continued to be the object of vocal criticism from conservative political opponents. The personal qualities that were often cited in such criticisms were not unlike those that emerged during the 1992 campaign. Critics sometimes conceded that Clinton was, indeed, an intelligent man, but they questioned how he had used this intelligence. To them, he seemed to be an opportunist who lacked moral character and who continued to manipulate the system, just as they concluded he had done in avoiding military service during the Vietnam War. He was, in a word widely used, "slick," and therefore not to be trusted, according to this view. Compared to this deeply negative assessment of the president, then, the fictional Forrest Gump character could seem like a breath of fresh air. The fact that the character was not as smart, not as "slick," as Clinton and other liberal politicians was hardly a handicap, therefore. Instead, in this view Gump showed that intellectual ability was not as important as simple, uncomplicated devotion and traditional moral values.

In any case, *Forrest Gump* was a continuation in the cinematic transformation of the Vietnam War in public memory. Gump the Vietnam veteran, like earlier cinematic Vietnam veterans, was shown as bravely doing a job that others had either refused or avoided. The complexities of the historical circumstances presented in the film (of which the events in Vietnam are only a part) are therefore largely reduced to simpler dichotomies. As a result, in *Forrest Gump,* as in many other screen portrayals of the war, the choices people faced may look clearer than was the case in real history.

Other screen appearance of the war. By the mid–1990s, Hollywood filmmakers began to view the Gulf War as potential subject matter, as was seen in director Robert Zwick's 1996 film *Courage Under Fire,* featuring Denzel Washington and Meg Ryan. Still, the Vietnam War continued to appear in feature films and television in mid-decade, although these productions received far less attention than *Forrest Gump* had attracted.

On television, the 1990s penchant for conspiracy theories was perhaps nowhere more exemplified than in the Fox television network's popular series *The X-Files,* which featured the exploits of two (later four) maverick FBI agents pursuing investigations dealing with government conspiracy, extraterrestrial alien abduction, and supernatural themes. Several episodes in the series drew directly on Vietnam War themes as the basis for their narratives. The episode entitled "Sleepless," first broadcast in 1994, was a frightening rendition of the disturbed Vietnam veteran theme, updated to include a supernatural element. Nonetheless, the episode reproduced, albeit in exaggerated form, some of the stereotypes that previously had been associated with the Vietnam veterans syndrome.

Meanwhile, two films released in 1995 employed a Vietnam War theme that was a somewhat newer interpretation, particularly for mainstream entertainment media productions. *The Walking Dead* and *Dead Presidents* looked at the Vietnam War and its after-effects through the eyes of African-Americans. The narrative of *The Walking Dead,* from writer-director Preston A. Whitmore II, centers on African-American soldiers in an army unit that is ordered to free American soldiers held in a POW camp during the war. The film was only moderately popular with audiences, and critical reception was largely tepid. *People Weekly,* for example, issued a decidedly negative review, pronouncing that "this film, billed as defining the 'black experience in Vietnam,' is so murky and convoluted that it makes the real war seem a model of clarity and common sense by comparison."[67]

Later that year came *Dead Presidents,* a film directed by brothers Albert and Allen Hughes, who had achieved fame upon release of their film *Menace II Society* two years earlier. Their new film was partly based on an account that had appeared in Wallace Terry's well-known book *Bloods: An*

Oral History of the Vietnam War by Black Veterans.[68] *Dead Presidents* premiered at the prestigious New York Film Festival in October, helping assure that it would gain attention from the media.

The story presented in *Dead Presidents* focuses on a character named Anthony Curtis (played by Larenz Tate), who is raised in poverty in the South Bronx. Seeing few viable alternatives, he later enlists in the Marines during the Vietnam War years. Like some other films dealing with the war, the combat sequences in *Dead Presidents* are portrayed intensely and explicitly. In one troubling scene, Anthony encounters a particularly gruesome situation, in which a white soldier who has been sadistically mutilated begs Anthony to kill him in order to end his excruciating pain.[69] Later in the film, the narrative follows Anthony as he returns to life in New York, where he becomes involved in a plot to steal a truckload of money that had been destined to be taken out of circulation by the Treasury Department. The film's exploration of the character's youthful South Bronx and Vietnam experiences and his later fate was intriguing to many film critics. As one writer noted, the film had "unusual interest ... [because of] its probing of the link"[70] between these aspects of Anthony's life.

Taken together, *The Walking Dead* and *Dead Presidents* addressed the element of race among the American military during the war. This important facet of the war seemed only vaguely recalled to the general public, and it was seldom explicitly discussed. Yet, it was certainly an important aspect of the American experience in the war. In the end, however, it is difficult to conclude that these films—or other screen productions dealing with the same topic—deeply penetrated mainstream American perceptions of the war. The war was by then two decades in the past and as a consequence possibly too removed to garner as full a public airing as the subject deserved.

Full Diplomatic Recognition for Vietnam

After months of exploration and preparation, the Clinton administration had yet to agree that it was the time to establish full diplomatic relations with Vietnam. Though there was a broad sentiment that such a decision should be made, some opponents of full recognition remained. Finally, in July of 1995, Clinton seemed ready to move ahead. In Congress, however, it became clear that some opponents would seek to thwart implementation of such a policy if it were announced. No sooner did word of Clinton's apparent decision reach the Congress, in fact, than Republican Sen. Bob Dole of Kansas announced that he would seek to thwart Congressional funding of an Embassy in Vietnam. Because Dole was seen as a prime candidate for the Republican nomination in the following year's presidential contest, his opposition signaled a potential new wave of controversy about the issue.

Yet, Clinton pressed forward with diplomatic recognition, saying it was time to "bind up our own wounds" about the war.[71] He assured the public that the U.S. would continue to insist that the Vietnamese provide a full accounting of missing soldiers, though by this time most authorities long ago had concluded that no missing soldiers remained alive. Critics were not persuaded, however. In condemning the decision, Bob Dole said "all signs point to Vietnam willfully withholding information."[72]

It was not only political opponents of the Clinton White House who objected, of course. Indeed, for some private citizens whose loved ones had been classified as missing in action in Vietnam and who had been dealing with that emotional burden for decades, diplomatic recognition for Vietnam was difficult to accept.

Mid–1990s Politics

In the 1996 presidential campaign that followed, Bill Clinton faced challenger Bob Dole, who resigned his position in order to devote full attention to the campaign. As with the 1992 campaign, the Republican candidate was a World War II veteran. In the 1996 contest, however, Clinton's draft status was much less of an issue. This is not to say that Clinton's politically conservative opponents were more inclined to be satisfied with Clinton's Vietnam-era conduct than four years earlier. The issue remained, though perhaps less visible and specific, in the general questioning and condemning of Clinton's moral character. There was little new to report about it, however, and other issues were more prominent throughout the campaign that culminated with Clinton's victory.

U.S. sends ambassador to Vietnam. In the months that followed, the administration faced a number of domestic and international situations. As a result, final touches remained to be completed in the process of fully implementing the diplomatic relations with Vietnam. Although the two nations had agreed on re-establishment of diplomatic ties in 1995, the U.S. had yet to send an ambassador to Vietnam. On occasions, the fledgling relationship between the two nations remained strained. The administration sometimes chided Vietnam about the Southeast Asian nation's human rights records, and the U.S. continued to look for evidence in still unresolved POW-MIA cases.

In mid–1997, the day to complete a diplomatic relationship finally arrived. On May 9 of that year, some twenty-two years after the last American ambassador had fled the former South Vietnamese capital of Saigon, a new U.S. ambassador arrived in Hanoi. Ambassador Pete Peterson had experience in Vietnam; he had been a prisoner of war in Hanoi for six years during the conflict. The appointment of a man with his background was surely evidence that the Clinton administration was determined to show Americans and the world that the POW-MIA issue remained a concern, even as it embarked on the beginning of a new chapter in American-Vietnamese diplomatic relations. Indeed, the arrival of an American ambassador was, in Peterson words, "a historic event and the beginning of a new era."[73]

A Bright Shining Lie

During Bill Clinton's second term, a firestorm of controversy surrounding Clinton's relationship with a young intern became an enormous media and political spectacle. It was not a milieu in which the Vietnam War seemed to have much relevance.

As national politics focused on events that would lead to the impeachment of the president, the cable network HBO, part of the Time-Warner media conglomerate, released a new production that reconsidered the war. The network's 1998 production of A Bright Shining Lie, based upon Neil Sheehan's well known book of the same name, follows the story of a character named John Paul Vann (played by Bill Paxton), from the early1960s until that character's death in a helicopter crash years later.

Vann is at first portrayed as an enthusiastic participant in the war, acting as an American adviser to South Vietnamese army troops in 1962. His exuberant accounts of apparently successful battles with the enemy are later fed to an eager American reporter. Soon, Vann develops a sweeping confidence that an American-backed victory is achievable so long as the U.S. takes measures to win the hearts and minds of the peasant population. Although Vann briefly returns to the United States, he remains unmoved by growing protests about the war, and even in the Nixon era he remains confident that the U.S. "can win this thing." A journalist working with Vann later sums up both the character's story and that of the nation, saying "Vietnam tore us apart. We went there believing in freedom and democracy, but somehow we lost our moral compass."

Reviews of the production were mixed. One critic wrote that "it travels too lightly to make a firm impression" and that "the passions and convictions that drove the best of the Vietnam War films ... are missing."[74]

Perhaps, however, the political context at the time of the film's release contributed to its relatively modest impact. As the end of the millennium approached, the attention of the American public seemed to be aimed elsewhere.

Developments in U.S.–Vietnam Relations

In 1999, two years after sending an ambassador to Hanoi with the hope of completing a normalized relationship between the two nations, there was some movement in Washington regarding economic policy toward Vietnam, at least on a limited basis. Negotiations between the administration and Vietnamese officials seemed to be progressing, and Clinton determined that American firms doing business with Vietnam should be allowed access to certain government loans and guarantees, which had been disallowed since the 1970s.[75] The administration waived the restrictions, with the House concurring on a more than two-to-one basis. Douglas K. Bereuter, Republican representative from Nebraska, may have summed up the majority view: "Americans must realize that the war with Vietnam is over. Emotional scars remain with many Americans, but it's time to get on with our bilateral relationship."[76]

A year later, after some final stops and starts in negotiations, a comprehensive trade agreement was reached between the two nations. The agreement was formally signed in July of 2000, completing what Bill Clinton called a "historic step in normalization, reconciliation and healing."[77] (It would be another year, only weeks after the dramatic events of September 11, 2001, before the pact was approved by both Houses of Congress and sent to George W. Bush, who signed the agreement into law.)

Clinton visits Vietnam. In the final days of his presidency, even as the final result of the contentious presidential election of 2000 remained in doubt, Bill Clinton embarked on a historic trip to Vietnam. Although for many this may have seemed a fitting final stroke to the steps he had taken in American-Vietnamese policy throughout his two terms in the White House, to others it was a bitter development. According to a representative of the National League of POW-MIA families, Clinton's visit was "32 years too late, and I think he should have gone to his grave without going to Vietnam."[78] To a representative of a Vietnamese-American Women's League, Clinton's trip was "a joke."[79] Noting the widely differing opinions of the president's trip to the former enemy of the U.S., a counselor at the Boston Vet Center commented to a *Boston Globe* reporter, "It's probably a good thing, but it's laced and laden with irony."[80]

Whatever else one might say about his presidency, over Clinton's eight years in office it is difficult to conclude that he fully escaped the 1992 campaign controversies about his preparedness in military matters, which debate about his draft status had helped amplify. To some, he remained a Vietnam-era draft dodger to the end. To others, he may have seemed more a victim of the times, a president confronted by an increasingly complex and unpredictable world.

7

Shadows of Vietnam
in a World Remade

The political divisiveness that escalated throughout much of the Clinton presidency did not abate during the 2000 presidential campaign. Vice President Al Gore claimed the nomination of the Democratic Party faithful. They believed that the Clinton presidency had led to many successes, and they hoped to see that legacy continue with Gore in the Oval Office. Yet, the sitting president remained a lightning-rod figure, capable of eliciting both gushing praise and vehement criticism. Gore undoubtedly saw that too close an association with a president who had been embroiled in bitter impeachment proceedings was a double-edged sword. Like other vice presidents before him, he was eager to step out from the shadow of the current president in his quest for the White House. A main task for his campaign, then, was to capture something of the spirit of the Clinton presidency without coming so close to that flame as to ignite its polarizing effect.

Meanwhile, the Republican Party was eager to end Democratic control of the White House. They engaged in their own struggle to put forward a candidate that had the best chance of bringing this about. The race for the Republican nomination eventually came down to a two-way contest between George W. Bush, the Texas governor who proclaimed the virtues of "compassionate conservatism," and Arizona Sen. (and Vietnam War veteran) John McCain, a candidate who especially appealed to moderate Republicans and who even had a following among some Democrats.

A new millennium was approaching, and as the nation looked forward, many ghosts of the past now received less attention. The issue of Vietnam War-era military service, which had been an issue in Dan Quayle's vice-presidential bid in the 1998 and was again a high-profile part of the first Clinton campaign, was relegated to a minor role. Some supporters of George W. Bush's candidacy did raise questions about McCain's experience as a P.O.W. in Hanoi. In the contest, some Bush supporters attacked McCain. One of those critics had even compared McCain's five-years as a prisoner of war to the experiences of the main character in *The Manchurian Candidate,* director John Oppenheimer's 1962 film set in the aftermath of the Korean Conflict.[1] The comparison seemed aimed to imply that McCain's ordeal, like that of the film's main character, had a profound negative effect on him years after the fact. The accusation thus appeared to imply that his POW experience rendered McCain unfit to become commander-in-chief. The accusation — which seemed mean-spirited to many people, even in presidential politics — did not attract significant attention, however, and it probably had little effect on the party's final selection of George W. Bush as the nominee.

For the first time, the 2000 presidential race featured Republican and Democratic candidates who were both Vietnam-era veterans.[2] This facet of their careers, however, was not a major issue. In popular political culture of the United States, the candidates' military service was part of an era that seemed increasingly remote. The torch of political leadership had passed to the so-called Vietnam generation, which had entered middle age. That generation was not necessarily eager to raise more questions about the contentious war of the long-ago. For younger Americans, meanwhile, there was little reason to focus on experiences from a war that was identified more with their parents' generation more than their own, especially when that war was perplexing and little understood.

War on Film

From the late 1990s into the new millennium, films directly concerning the Vietnam War were infrequent. The Vietnam War had begun fading into memory to some extent, and it remained controversial. It continued to be difficult to tell a film story set in that war without raising other controversies about it in the process.

Although a consensus about the Vietnam War remained elusive, World War II was still the subject of far more agreement. With its far less ambiguous image in public memory, movies with a World War II theme continued to make occasional appearances in American movie theaters. When employing the Second World War as a theme or setting, filmmakers could continue to rely on the public's widespread, if at times impressionistic, shared memory of it as a given background, upon which a new story could be told.

Thus, directors rediscovered World War II as a theme. The narrative of director Steven Spielberg's well-regarded film *Saving Private Ryan* (1998), for example, concerned a rescue mission in World War II. Spielberg captured the intensity of war with explicit scenes of combat violence. With a cast including Tom Hanks and Matt Damon, it was a favorite with movie audiences. Still, setting a big-budget film in World War II was no guarantee of success. The film *Pearl Harbor,* which was released in 2001, received to a decidedly less enthusiastic response. Despite a cast of well-known Hollywood actors — including Ben Affleck, Cuba Gooding, Jr., John Voight, and others — many viewers did not positively respond to director Michael Bay's combination of the story about the attack on Pearl Harbor with a romantic sub-plot. (A critic for *USA Today* wrote that the latter theme was "one of the wimpiest wartime romances ever filmed."[3])

   Tigerland. Along with the World War II films that continued to be produced, new films concerning the Vietnam War occasionally made an appearance. In 2000, the Vietnam War theme appeared once again in movie theaters with the release of director Joel Schumacher's film *Tigerland.* Schumacher had risen to fame as the director of *St. Elmo's Fire* (1985), about a group of self-absorbed college graduates in search of their identities, and had maintained a high profile in Hollywood as the director of big-budget spectacles such as *Batman Forever* (1995) and *Batman & Robin* (1997). For *Tigerland,* however, Schumacher eschewed the approach with which he had earned his fame, and instead embarked on a project that would dispense with Hollywood stars and expensive production values. Shooting his new project in 16mm and relying upon a cast of unknowns, *Tigerland* did have the look and feel of a smaller, more personal production. It evoked a documentary-like appearance on the surface. The combination of this directorial approach and a subject that focused on military training during the Vietnam War was not one eagerly embraced by theater audiences, however.

   Indeed, *Tigerland's* subject was reminiscent of the first segment in Stanley Kubrick's *Full Metal Jacket.* Both showed the darker side of boot camp. Set in 1971, the storyline of *Tigerland* centers on a character named Bozz (played by Colin Farrell, who at that time was a still largely unknown actor to American audiences). Bozz possesses superb capabilities in marksmanship, which brings him certain notice during training, but he opposes the war and frequently clashes with his superiors. Bozz and his fellow soldiers are nearing the end of training and, and as seen in the last section of the film, are scheduled for transfer to a base known as Tigerland, at which they will receive specialized combat training. As they realize, Tigerland is the last stop before combat duty in Vietnam. Finding the system filled with hypocrisy, Bozz sometimes finds creative use of the military's own bureaucratic maze to help comrades avoid that fate.[4]

As one reviewer noted, the film unflinchingly portrays "the discomfort and cruelty of infantry training."[5] The resulting film experience seemed harsh to many viewers. Even film writers found watching the film to be a challenging experience. A *San Francisco Chronicle* critic reported that he "became exhausted from the shouting and abuse."[6] Another critic thought that there were some elements of *Tigerland* that were effective, but largely found the film to "disingenuous" and possessing "the same slick, corny heart" he found in some of Schumacher's other work.[7] Not surprisingly, given such comments, *Tigerland* failed to elicit much enthusiasm from film audiences. Its limited reception in the motion picture marketplace may have suggested that the Vietnam War was beginning to lose, or had already lost, much of its ability to command the attention of American movie audiences.

Troubling Memories

In the relative quiet of the first months of George W. Bush's presidency, a new controversy rooted in the Vietnam War emerged, however. After a high-profile career that included White House aspirations, Vietnam veteran Bob Kerrey left the U.S. Senate in January 2001 to assume the presidency of New York University. For many years, his experiences in the war, during which he was seriously injured, had been a major part of a public persona of the popular Nebraska politician. He seemed to be a man who, like countless others, had served in his nation's military during time of war and had emerged from those experiences with a strong sense of purpose. What the public did not know, however, was that these wartime experiences included at least one incident that had been deeply troubling to the young Kerrey, who had served as an elite Navy Seal.

During the spring of 2001, both the *New York Times* and the CBS News program *60 Minutes II* were in the midst of investigations into this part of Kerrey's service during the Vietnam War. By April, Kerrey realized that these investigations would suggest that a unit under his command had killed a number of civilians, including women and children, during an operation in the village of Thanh Phong in 1969. With a *New York Times* piece slated for publication within days and a CBS broadcast scheduled for soon thereafter, Kerrey hastily arranged to speak about the incident to two other news organizations, *The Wall Street Journal* and the *Omaha World Herald*.[8] Although he may have hoped to pre-empt some of the almost-assured negative reaction by calling attention to the matter himself, the result may not have been much different. Within the matter of a week, the public encountered a blockbuster story, in which the conflicting memories of former comrades-in-arms uncomfortably brought painful remembrances of the war years back into prominence.

The report in *The New York Times* noted that although details about the commando raid were still ambiguous, "one thing is certain: around midnight on Feb. [sic] 25, 1969, Kerrey and his men killed at least 13 unarmed women and children."[9] The incident had a profound effect on Kerrey, who reportedly suffered from nightmares about it for a long time afterwards. Three decades later, he was still troubled, reporting that

> It's far more than guilt. It's the shame. You can never, can never get away from it. It darkens your day. I thought dying for your country was the worst thing that could happen to you, and I don't think it is. I think killing for your country can be a lot worse, because that's the memory that haunts.[10]

As the newspaper story showed, Kerrey recalled the brutal episode, but his memory of it was not complete or clear. This was made obvious in an interview with Kerrey that appeared as part of the *60 Minutes II* story entitled "Memories of a Massacre." It is true that Kerrey never shied away from accepting responsibility for the actions taken in the covert operation that he led. His account, however, suggested other mitigating factors were involved, including darkness that made it difficult to see everything that was happening, as well as the rapidity with which the incident transpired. Kerrey suggested that resulting confusion and unintentional actions had played a major part in the tragic outcome.

According to Kerrey's account of a central part of the incident, he gave the order to fire into a group of huts that he thought was the location of enemy fighters who were shooting at his Seal unit. After the firing ceased, he and his fellow commandos approached the area, "expecting to find Vietcong soldiers with weapons, dead."[11] They did not find enemy fighters, however. Instead, as he recalled, "The thing I will remember to the day I die is walking in and finding, I don't know, 14 or so ... women and children who were dead."[12] Although unable to fully explain the circumstances of the villagers' deaths, Kerrey later hypothesized that perhaps Vietcong foes had used the villagers as human shields before escaping.[13]

Another member of Kerrey's unit that night had very different recollections, which were reported in the *New York Times* and *60 Minutes II* stories. That man was Gerhard Klann, who had also been disturbed about the events in Thanh Phong and who, some years after the event, had once confided his memories of the incident to a navy officer.

In Klann's version, the Seal team realized during their operation that the enemy they were searching for was not in the village, which was in an area under the control of communist forces. But, as Klann recalled, the Seal unit recognized it had another problem: in their search, they had gathered a number of villagers—women and children. As soon as the Seals departed to make their way back to safety, these villagers might very likely report the Americans' whereabouts to Vietcong foes nearby. Reasoning that their "chances would have been slim to none to get out alive," Klann said that the decision was made to "kill them [the villagers] and get out of there." His account also included some disturbing details: "The baby was the last one alive. There were blood and guts spattering everywhere."[14]

Klann's account about how the villagers died differed radically from Kerrey's, but the after-effects on the two men were similar. Just as news reports indicted that Kerrey remained haunted by the incident, Klann could not exorcise the memory of this troubling incident. As Klann told the Times," I can't get it out of my mind. I'd take it back if I could, everybody would."[15]

That war can be cruel is not a new discovery, of course, but revelations surrounding the Thanh Phong incident were unpleasant reminders of war's darker aspects. The fact that the story involved a well-respected political leader, widely admired in his post-war career, added to the story's impact. As a contemporary media event, moreover, the questions raised by the Thanh Phong revelations highlighted changing perceptions about human memory. Indeed, this episode serves as a stark illustration of the fallibility of memory and how little, indeed, memory resembles a photographic snapshot, capturing objective truth. It may never be possible to state with certainty the exact circumstances of events in Thanh Phong that night, but the public airing of the disputed memories revealed how a relatively routine mission ended with the deaths of civilians and a long legacy of guilt and anguish for some of the men who were at the center of action.

September 11 and the War on Terrorism

For Americans, the world changed on September 11, 2001, as terrorist attacks in New York City and Washington, D.C. wrought a horrifying spectacle of death and destruction on the United States. Attacked in its homeland, the deaths of thousands and the dread that further attacks were imminent profoundly altered the American political and cultural landscape, soon causing a series of responses that re-shaped American perceptions of itself and the world. In this frightening new context, the controversies of the Vietnam War may at first have seemed little more than relics from a now-shattered past.

Afghanistan. Having identified the terrorist group Al Qaeda and its leader, Osama bin Laden, as the sinister enemy in a new kind of war, American policy-makers began to plan for a global military response. The U.S. quickly determined the Taliban regime in Afghanistan was harboring bin Laden, and so it became the first target in the new War on Terrorism.[16] In October, the U.S. first began air strikes and then commando raids on Taliban strongholds. A larger number of American troops were deployed near the city of Kandahar a month later, and the city was surrendered not long after in December.

The Taliban government toppled quickly, although it would be some months before the U.S. would deem Afghanistan secure. In the meantime, an interim Afghan government, headed by Hamid Karzai was established in December 2001, and many Al Qaeda and Taliban fighters fled the country. Despite attempts to locate him, Osama bi Laden remained at large. In March 2002, Operation Anaconda, a joint military operation conducted by American armed forces and the new Afghan military, was initiated, further pressuring remaining Taliban and Al Qaeda loyalists. Although sporadic fighting occurred in the following months, by May 2003 the Bush administration declared that Afghanistan had been secured.

War in Iraq

After the demise of the Taliban regime in Afghanistan and with Osama bin Laden still at large, the Bush administration looked to the next possible fronts for its ongoing War on Terrorism. By most accounts, it seems that Iraq had been regarded as a likely new target for some time.

The Bush administration's response to September 11 asserted that nations harboring terrorists would be held by the U.S. to be as guilty as the terrorists. In his State of the Union address of January 29, 2002, Bush had noted that three regimes, which he said constituted an "axis of evil," possessed some of "the world's most destructive weapons." He declared that these regimes presented a clear danger to the U.S. and other world nations. Of the three regimes identified — those of Iran, North Korea and Iraq — it was Iraq that most captured the administration's immediate attention.

The administration was building a case for bringing the War on Terrorism to the regime of Saddam Hussein in Iraq. With Afghanistan toppled, and with Iraq having already been labeled by the president as one of the "axis of evil" regimes, the administration slowly began to make its case public. At the center were concerns, expressed at various times by administration officials, that Iraq was somehow linked to Al Qaeda. It was also said that Hussein's regime was amassing weapons of mass destruction — meaning nuclear, biological and chemical weapons—that it might use or that it might sell or provide to terrorist states or organizations.

In the spring, the administration noted a new direction in military policy that was to have a significant impact on subsequent events. In a major change, the administration announced a revised stance to pre-emptive military strikes. Throughout the Cold War, the defense policy had emphasized containment and carefully balancing power so as not to disrupt peaceful equilibrium. The major enemy in the War on Terrorism, as embodied in the shadowy Al Qaeda organization, was not another nation, however, but rather a confederation of extremists determined to bring violence and bloodshed to American shores. This new kind of enemy would not be restrained by containment policies, according to the administration's reasoning. Therefore, it was determined that American military forces could and should launch pre-emptive military action in order to prevent a recurrence of the nightmare of September 11.

Meanwhile, the administration began lobbying the United Nations to force Iraq into clearer compliance with U.N. mandates, which originally had been imposed a decade earlier and were aimed to assure that Iraq would be unable to pose an international military threat. The Bush administration, had come to believe that Iraq was an international scofflaw and was aggressively seeking to build an arsenal stocked with weapons of mass destruction. The U.S. continued efforts to convince the U.N. to address its concerns about Iraq, and in a September 2002 address to the world body, Bush said that the U.S. would act alone if U.N. backing were not forthcoming. Indeed, the U.S. Congress authorized military action against Iraq a month later, although no military action was immediately taken.

In the following months, the American public and the world waited to see if renewed efforts by the United Nations would secure Iraqi compliance and disarmament, or whether Iraq would instead face the "serious consequences" that had been threatened. At this time, it remained clear that the administration viewed the efforts of U.N. weapons inspectors as ineffective, and continued to believe the regime of Saddam Hussein posed an impending threat to American security. Meanwhile, although the administration assured the public that no decision to go to war had yet been made, a small but vocal opposition to war emerged in both the U.S. and elsewhere.

The war was still several months away, however. In his January 2003 State of the Union address, Bush declared that the U.S. would consider military action against Iraq whether or not the U.N. issued a more explicit authorization of such an action. For some weeks, the administration made further efforts to rally domestic and world support. The Iraqi regime destroyed some missiles in response to the growing crisis, but the U.S.

remained unsatisfied. Finally, on March 19, 2003, Bush decided that the time had come to take military action, and American attack commenced with Operation Iraqi Freedom.

Iraq possessed a stronger and more experienced military than Afghanistan under the Taliban, and a more difficult fight was anticipated, after which American officials said they were confident the U.S. and its allies would be regarded by the Iraqi people as liberators. In fact, the major fighting ended more quickly than many had assumed. Saddam Hussein fled the capital city of Baghdad, which fell less than a month after the fighting began. Indeed, by May 1, 2003, the United States declared victory.

The military actions in Afghanistan and Iraq seemed to bear little resemblance to the Vietnam War. In the post–September 11 world, in fact, many American leaders seemed to suggest that history had passed a watershed moment, apparently believing that the 9/11 trauma rendered much of past history to the status of irrelevant artifacts in a world dominated by an ongoing War on Terrorism.

Yet, the ghosts of the Vietnam War were not so easily dismissed. The long build-up to the war provided many opportunities for reflections on past American wars, in general, and the Vietnam War, in particular. Contrary to many expectations, after initial American military success in Iraq, it soon became clear that victorious American forces would not receive a heroes' welcome like that bestowed on the Allied forces that liberated France in World War II. Instead, new realities of the Iraq war emerged. The news media soon began comparing the situation to the Vietnam War, a trend that would escalate in coming months. An April 2003 article in *Newsweek,* illustrates this point. Written by a supporter of the war, the story reports that "lessons from the Vietnam War are still relevant for the war in Iraq" and that "for a moment last week, it felt like 1967. An overconfident secretary of Defense [sic] with slick-backed hair and a know-it-all style was embarrassed by a ragtag, low-tech army putting up stiffer-than-expected resistance."[17]

The emerging anti–American insurgency became increasingly prominent in the following months. It had become clear that the fall of Baghdad had not translated into a quick end to the violence and American casualties. Comparisons to the Vietnam War continued mounting. Calling the situation "Bush's Vietnam," a *New Statesman* article in June asserted that the apparent military victories in Afghanistan and Iraq were "unraveling."[18] As the writer noted, with increasing frequency, media critics of the war employed the term "quagmire"— a potent and negative word that unmistakably linked the Iraq situation to the Vietnam War.

Of course, supporters of the war and of administration policies regarding the War on Terrorism rejected the association between Vietnam and

Iraq. One writer for the *National Review* concluded that the present war was "No Quagmire" and instead that there were "strong signs of revived public order and economic recovery" in Iraq.[19] Another complained "Vietnam! Vietnam! The mere mention of it sends shudders through Americans," but found that comparisons between the alleged "parallels [between the Vietnam War and the Iraq War] to be mostly superficial."[20] Yet, the earlier war remained a powerful and well-recognized narrative frame, against which the news media and political pundits could compare the situation in Iraq. Moreover, as had also been true in the past, in order to publicly dispute the comparison, administration supporters nonetheless had to refer to it. Thus, even when the comparison was rejected, a link between Iraq and Vietnam was reinforced.

As a quick end to violence in Iraq faded as a possibility, the presidential campaign was beginning. The legacy of the Vietnam War remained in public view. Noting what he saw as "similarities with the Vietnam War," a columnist for the *National Catholic Reporter* asked "Is Iraq Arabic for Vietnam?"[21] In *U.S. News & World Report*, Michael Barone observed, "Over our debates on Iraq and the war on terrorism hangs the specter of Vietnam."[22] The arguments for and against seeing similarities between the two wars raged on as the campaign for the White House approached.

Vietnam War on Film in a New Era

The complexities of the post–9/11 world created a new milieu for the film and television industries. It presented many complexities for film executives who were planning movies with terrorism or war themes, which popular "action films" often included. The social context for film viewers had changed dramatically, and it was unclear how fully audiences would embrace material that focused on such dark themes. The Vietnam War perhaps now more than ever appeared to be a remote tragedy in a vanished world.

Still, even after the trauma of September 11, audiences remained willing to accept war themes in motion pictures. In a film released in late 2001, a particularly troubling incident from the American military participation in Somalia in the early 1990s was brought to the screen. *Black Hawk Down*, from well-known Hollywood director Ridley Scott, featured a cast that included Josh Hartnett, Ewan McGregor, and Sam Shepard. The film captured the chaos and horror of the Mogadishu battle in which American soldiers, vastly outnumbered and trapped in hostile territory, fight their way to safety. *Black Hawk Down* received an enthusiastic response from audiences and many critics. A reviewer for the *Cincinnati Enquire*, applauded

Scott's use of "the tools for making high-end action movies" in telling the story of the Battle of Mogadishu (as it had been called), saying of these elements of movie-making that "for once — they represent the truth."[23]

We Were Soldiers. Only two months later, in February 2002, a new film that centered on the Vietnam War premiered: *We Were Soldiers,* based on a book written by Harold Moore and Joseph Calloway.[24] Unlike the case in *Tigerland* two years earlier, Randall Wallace cast well-known actors in *We Were Soldiers.* Mel Gibson appears in the lead role of Lt. Col. Hal Moore, and the cast also includes Sam Elliott, Greg Kinnear, Madeleine Stowe, and Kerri Russell.

This film focused on a battle that was fought in Ia Drang Valley in 1965, during which American soldiers engaged North Vietnamese troops. It was one of the first major U.S. combat actions of the war. In terms of strategy, the Americans were successful, inflicting heavy losses on their enemy. Yet, although the North Vietnamese dead numbered perhaps two thousand, the Americans suffered heavy causalities, too, with more than 300 killed.[25] If it were a victory, it was one that came with a high cost.

The film has some important differences from many other war films. In addition to telling the story of the battle, *We Were Soldiers* also includes scenes from the soldiers' private lives. This provided a three-dimensional look at characters more than has often been the case in other films with a war theme. In addition, *We Were Soldiers* makes clear that war can be ambiguous and unfair. The high cost of the modest victory is evident throughout the film.

It is not the overarching story of winning or losing the battle or the war, however, that most interests Wallace. Instead, the director focuses on the often unspoken bonds among soldiers and on the pain of surviving when fellow soldiers have been killed. At one point in the film, the Moore character asks, "I wonder what Custer was thinking when he realized he'd moved his men into a slaughter." (Perhaps in more ways than intended, the invocation of Custer's legendary defeat at Little Big Horn pointed not only to a military debacle, but also recalled an episode in which dubious American policy had played a major role.) Overall, *We Were Soldiers* seems to suggest that noble purpose and the honor of those fighting may be more important than specific policies. Indeed, so much does the film valorize these ideas that in addition to dedicating the film to the Americans who died at Ia Drang, it also commemorates "the members of the People's Army of North Vietnam who died in that place."[26]

Surely, in early 2002, after the emotional devastation of the September 11 attacks, prevailing thought in the United States was that a swift and bold military response was both morally justified and necessary. The release of *We Were Soldiers* in this context therefore presents an interesting contrast to contemporary events in a way that *Black Hawk Down* did not. Centering on an American military action gone wrong and the attempt to rectify it, *Black Hawk Down* was at times gripping filmmaking. It did not deal, however, with a situation in which underlying American policies were controversial. In fact, it is questionable whether the American public was ever fully aware of the Clinton administration's foreign policy pertaining to Somalia. In any case, Americans viewed the Somali incident as a mostly isolated event. In contrast, almost all viewers of *We Were Soldiers* knew that although the film focused on a specific battle that had resulted in an American victory, the events in the film are firmly entrenched in the wider phenomenon of the Vietnam War. Few viewers would have been unaware that though the battle at Ia Drang was won, the war would be lost.

Coming near the beginning of military operations in the War on Terrorism, in some ways *We Were Soldiers* stood as a cinematic reminder that decisions about war and peace do not always proceed according to plan. In this respect, it could be seen as a preview of political tensions that would arise in coming months regarding the War in Iraq. Such considerations are perhaps out-balanced, however, by the film squarely traditional and patriotic tone. As several earlier films dealing with the Vietnam War had demonstrated—consider, for example, *The Deer Hunter* and *Platoon*—a motion picture could effectively honor the soldiers who fought in war without engaging in questions about the rightness or wrongness of American war policy. For the most part, *We Were Soldiers* leaves these grander questions unasked, instead examining the characters and what becomes of them. Along these lines, some critics regarded the film skeptically. David Skerritt of the *Christian Science Monitor* saw the film as an example of a trend that minimized the war's larger questions. In his view, *We Were Soldiers* was as a "shameless" example of films that "hack[ed] away all meaningful concern with moral and political questions."[27]

Critical response to *We Were Soldiers* varied, but many reviewers found merit in the film. Writing in the *New York Times*, A. O. Scott judged the film to be an "effective combat epic" that "balances the dreadful, unassuageable cruelty of war and the valor and decency of those who fight."[28] *Rolling Stone* reviewer Peter Travers wrote that this "unabashedly pro-military" treatment of the battle possessed "an impact that transcends politics ... [and] captures the chaos of guerilla warfare."[29] Other writers made glowing assessments. A review in the *San Francisco Chronicle* stated that the film was "one of the best war movies of the past 20 years," especially notable for its "taking in both the battlefield and the home front, the experience of men on the front lines and the women who live in dread of a telegram."[30] Indeed, at the time of its release, *We Were Soldiers* was evidence that the long process, underway since the war's end, of accepting the American soldiers who fought in Vietnam on equal footing with American soldiers in other wars was essentially complete.

The Fog of War. In a very different vein, a documentary film released the following year made the case that the moral footing for the United Sates' participation in the Vietnam War was weak. In *The Fog of War: Eleven Lessons from the Life of Robert S. McNamara* (2003), director Errol Morris explores McNamara's involvement in the war as Secretary of Defense in the Kennedy and Johnson administrations. The film portrays McNamara as having misgivings about the U.S. entering the war, and it suggests that early on he had decided that American participation in it should end. Johnson, it will be recalled, was himself determined not to be the first American president to lose a war, and so McNamara's advice was not heeded. Although this film did not reach a wide, mass-market audience, its release in the context of the Iraq situation made it a work of strong interest to a segment of the public. Some clearly saw the relevance of McNamara's past to other situations. The film shows McNamara's dilemma in the Johnson White House, in which the Secretary felt he had little influence on administration's policy direction in Vietnam. A *San Francisco Chronicle* reviewer sympathized with McNamara's plight, writing, "Anyone who has ever worked for a boss determined to go in the wrong direction knows that feeling — knowing the truth but having no power."[31]

The 2004 Campaign and the Vietnam War

As the 2004 presidential campaign unfolded, it turned out that memories from the Vietnam War had not been rendered insignificant, after all. In the contest that fall, which featured a rivalry in which both leading candidates were Vietnam War-era veterans, major new political controversies erupted about how to judge the candidates' wartime service records. Indeed, whereas the military backgrounds of Al Gore and George W. Bush were hardly an important point of debate in the relative calm of the previous election, in the 2004 election the context of post–September 11 war created a political environment in which the military experience of the candidates seemed to matter much more. Therefore, the actions of the candidates three decades earlier became a major point of contention in 2004 election-year politics.

Thus, in the 2004 presidential campaign, controversies from the Vietnam War rushed back into everyday American politics. As it played out in the news media, the Vietnam War storyline in the 2004 election centered on questions about whether George W. Bush had adequately fulfilled his obligations while serving in the National Guard, as opposed to questions about whether John F. Kerry had deserved the medals he received for combat duty in Vietnam while serving in the Navy.

As with nearly all facets of the 2004 campaign, both of these questions were the subject of heavy politicking by supporters and detractors of the respective candidates. Through the ideological lenses of conservatism and liberalism of the new millennium, then, aspects of the Vietnam War received significant attention, not only in the realm of traditional print and broadcast journalism, but from twenty-four-hour cable television news operations and a new phenomenon, internet-based reports called web logs (more commonly, "blogs"). Many of these reports, focusing on personal and moral characteristics of the candidates, made little effort to place the actions under scrutiny in a broader context, however. Indeed, the Vietnam War itself was often reduced to dichotomous, simplified interpretations that frequently offered little for the uninformed reader or viewer in terms of explaining the historical complexities of the war and the nation's response to it.

George W. Bush and the Texas Air National Guard. After receiving his undergraduate degree from Yale University, George W. Bush enlisted in the National Guard in May 1968. This was the year of the grueling Tet Offensive in Vietnam. Although the American and South Vietnamese armed forces had many successes that year, these were costly victories. From a public relations perspective, the year was a disaster for the Johnson administration. American military casualties ran high, and the American public was growing weary of the war.

George W. Bush entered the Texas Air National Guard in this difficult context. More than 35 years later, his decision became an issue in presidential politics. In ways that were sometimes similar, and sometimes not, to the way Dan Quayle's Vietnam War-era National Guard service was treated in 1988, aspects of George W. Bush's National Guard service became an early source of controversy in the 2004 campaign. As had been the case with Dan Quayle, some critics later questioned whether favoritism had played a part in Bush's ability to obtain placement with the Guard.[32] But unlike Quayle's experience, that was not the aspect of Bush's service that attracted much attention in the 2004 campaign. Instead, the allegations that received the most attention concerned whether Bush had met the terms of his enlistment. Essentially, some questioned whether the president, as a young man, had shirked his duty. For those interested in discrediting Bush, such a revelation would have an obvious use in election-year politics.

As discussed previously, enlistment in the National Guard during the war meant that as a practical matter, there was little likelihood that the recruit would be sent to Vietnam. Still, it was military enlistment and it obligated the recruit to fulfill terms of service. For Bush, service in the Texas Air National Guard led to pilot training. Thus, after joining the National Guard, Bush spent the following year learning to become a fighter pilot, which was perhaps a fitting tribute to his father, who had been a pilot during World War II. After completing this training, and in a manner consistent with standard procedures, Bush was ordered to perform duty one weekend per month at Ellington Air Force Base in Houston.[33]

In 1972, Bush decided to help with the Senate campaign — ultimately unsuccessful — of a family friend in Alabama. Bush was still a member of the National Guard, however, and therefore still had a part-time military obligation to fulfill. Following procedures that commonly were used when a part-time member of the Guard moved from one area of the country to another, Bush filed an application that would allow him to fulfill his part-time military duties at a base in Alabama, rather than in Houston. This was a routine type of request, and unremarkably the application was subsequently approved.

It is in relation to the period, after relocating the venue of this National Guard service to Alabama in 1972, that questions arose in the 2004 campaign.[34] Simply put, opponents of the president claimed that Bush had failed to fulfill the requirements of his enlistment after being transferred to Alabama. Among the first critics of Bush's military record was the controversial film-maker Michael Moore, whose upcoming polemical documentary film *Fahrenheit 9/11*, was expected to be critical of the Bush administration. Moore called Bush a "deserter," a serious allegation that was perhaps too hyperbolic for most Bush critics.[35] Democratic Party chairperson Terry McAuliffe took up the cause, though his toned-down rhetoric characterized Bush as having been "AWOL" (absent without leave), a charge that was still serious, but less heated.[36]

As Democrats began calling for Bush to release more information about his National Guard service, administration officials grew impatient. Scott McClellan, the White House Press Secretary, stated that "This goes to show that some are not interested in the facts on whether or not he served; they're interested in trolling for trash, using this issue for partisan political gain."[37] Some relevant material had been made public earlier (documents were made available in the 2000 campaign but elicited little interest), and in February 2004, Bush ordered additional material relating to his military service to be released. Perhaps unsurprisingly, Democratic critics did not find sufficient answers to all of their questions in this material, and the issue continued to command attention.[38]

A review of the documents led some to conclude that the controversy was much ado about nothing. According to some analyses, when examined as a whole, the record indicated quite clearly that Bush had met the requirements of service. Although it seemed true that the hours of service recorded by Bush during 1972–1973 had dipped from the number in his first years in the Guard, he had still met service requirements. Conservative publications such as *National Review* were keen to point this out.[39]

Mainstream new organizations, however, continued to follow the story as part of the unfolding 2004 presidential campaign. CBS News was among these organizations. In May, it reported that an investigation into the matter showed that although the amount of material was voluminous, Bush's explanations still contained "several holes."[40] In June, the Associated Press went to court, seeking more information from the Air Force. In July, Pentagon officials announced that some relevant information, including part of the payroll records from the disputed timeframe, had accidentally been destroyed in the 1990s. Two weeks later, however, the Pentagon retracted that report and confirmed that the records had been located.

Perhaps the height of the controversy occurred with a CBS News *60 Minutes* broadcast in September that claimed to present documentary evidence which contradicted White House explanations of Bush's service during the disputed period. Lt. Col. Jerry Killian, who had died in 1984, had allegedly written some of the material that was cited. It was this material that attracted the most attention.

Conservatives, who were suspicious that CBS was engaging in unfair attacks on the president, immediately criticized the network's report. Dan Rather, the *CBS Evening News* Anchor who many conservatives thought possessed an overt liberal bias, had narrated the broadcast, but he seemed not to have been deeply involved in the story's production. Yet, after the story was criticized, he vigorously defended it on journalistic grounds. That defense was to be a major issue in the ensuing controversy.

Given the nature of the report, it is not surprising that questions about the authenticity of the source documents were raised immediately.[41] At first, CBS and Rather strongly defended the story, suggesting that allegations about its veracity were unfounded. Within days, however, analyses seemed to indicate that some documents used type fonts that were not created on a typewriter from the Vietnam War era, but instead appeared to have been generated on a computer much later.[42]

A week after the first broadcast, a *60 Minutes* segment addressed the allegations. In one admission, CBS reported that Killian's former secretary believed that the documents in questions were not genuine. However, she told CBS that although she was sure she "didn't type" the documents, she concluded that the "the information in those was correct."[43] The network continued to defend its story. A CBS press release reported, "Mary Mapes, the producer of the report and a well-respected, veteran journalist whose credibility has never been questioned, has a vast and detailed knowledge of the issues surrounding President Bush's service in the Guard."[44] Despite efforts of CBS News to defuse the controversy, however, the barrage of criticism continued.

CBS, it will be remembered, had long been mistrusted by many political conservatives, especially on matters relating to the Vietnam War. From the time when veteran news anchor Walter Cronkite had made editorial comments against the war at its height, to the later lawsuit against network brought by former Gen. William Westmoreland in the 1980s, the network had become a symbol of liberalism and bias for many of the most vocal conservative commentators. Moreover, by 2004 the heyday of three-network (NBC, CBS, and ABC) domination of television news was long over. The cable- and satellite-news networks, such as CNN and FOX, along with newer internet-based news media, had seriously weakened the place of CBS News in the media marketplace. The network had once seemed, perhaps, to be a monolithic and supremely powerful news organization. Now, it was considerably less influential, and it found itself decidedly on the defensive.

The story of Bush's service in the National Guard, therefore, soon became enmeshed in a broader narrative that focused on the credibility of CBS News and, by implication, on the established news media. Fox News, a newer player in the sphere of major television news organizations, and one with a more conservative reputation than its counterparts, closely followed the story and labeled the affair "memogate," a reminder of the Watergate scandal of decades earlier.[45] It reported that "at the suggestion of a CBS News producer," an adviser to John Kerry had spoken to a key figure in the controversy prior to CBS's release of the documents. A spokesperson for Republican Dennis Hastert, the House Speaker, said that CBS should "prove that their sources are telling the truth, especially when they [CBS] have such a bad reputation to begin with."[46]

CBS claimed that despite widespread criticism of its report, "the basic content of [it]—that President Bush received preferential treatment to gain entrance to the Texas Air National Guard and that he may not have fulfilled all of the requirements—has not been substantially challenged."[47]

In the end, however, probably CBS suffered the most damage to its public image in this episode. On September 20, 2004, only days after the report, the network was forced to back down. Dan Rather announced, "After extensive additional interviews, I no longer have the confidence in these documents that would allow us to continue vouching for them journalistically.... We made a mistake in judgment and for that I am sorry."[48] Finding itself immersed in a public controversy and with its reputation tarnished and sagging, CBS launched an independent investigation. As this probe was underway, Dan Rather announced that he would step down from the anchor desk of *CBS Evening News*. Although he did not mention the Bush document controversy in announcing this decision, it was widely thought to have played a large part in his decision.

When the investigation was completed in January 2005, CBS released what another news organization called a "damning" report.[49] The investigation did not conclude that the documents in question were indisputably forgeries, as many critics had alleged, but the report did criticize the network for a number of journalistic lapses.[50] The investigation concluded that the story was aired because of "myopic zeal" and that after criticisms emerged, there had been a "rigid and blind defense" of it that was unfounded. In the wake of the report, Dan Rather was cited by CBS for "errors of credulity and over-enthusiasm." Since he had already stepped down as news anchor and was said to have not been extensively involved in the generation of the story itself, however, his continuing employment relationship with CBS was not severed. The same could not be said for the story's producer, Mary Mapes, who was abruptly fired; three other executives were asked to resign.

John Kerry's swift boat service. During the months that controversy about the president's Texas Air National Guard service was brewing, Democratic candidate John Kerry's Vietnam War-era service also became an issue. This may not seem surprising, given that Kerry's wartime service was already a widely known matter of public record. In fact, his early political career had largely been built upon his high-profile activities as a leading member of the Vietnam Veterans Against the War group. As a member of that organization, his testimony against the war to a Senate committee had been replayed countless times in films and video documentaries about the war.

Undoubtedly, many Kerry supporters had relied upon what they saw as his pristine record. To them, this was armor that would protect the candidate from the kinds of attacks that had been leveled against Bill Clinton, who many people thought had taken extraordinary measures to delay and then avoid military service during the war. Kerry, on the other hand, seemed to be a bona fide war hero, a decorated combat veteran who had been awarded three Purple Hearts, a Silver Star, and a Bronze Star. Indeed, Kerry himself had recorded some of his Vietnam service with a home movie camera — which was itself an unusual thing to do — and in the years since the war, those images had been replayed frequently.

If his supporters thought that Kerry's service in Vietnam would with-stand the scrutiny of his political foes, however, they seriously erred. As members of the Kerry campaign sought to position their candidate as a thoughtful, intelligent, and measured political leader with clearly heroic combat service, a group of Vietnam veterans who opposed Kerry came forward to tell a very different version of Kerry's wartime exploits. The most forceful of the criticisms were mounted by a politically conservative group called the Swift Boat Veterans for Truth. A central claim of Kerry's swift-boat critics was that he had not been forthright in his accounting of actions that had earned him the Silver Star, and they felt Kerry did not deserve that award. A leader of that group, John O'Neill, had already fired salvos at Kerry's account of his Vietnam service in his highly charged book, *Unfit for Command*.[51] The two men previously had encountered each other; more than thirty years earlier they had debated opposing views of the Vietnam War on *The Dick Cavett Show* television talk program.[52]

As is sometimes the case in a combat situation, the incident that led to Kerry's Silver Star occurred quickly, and details about it later emerged differently in the recollections of those who had been involved, or were nearby, when the events occurred. According to most accounts, on February 28, 1969, Kerry led an operation involving three swift boats. When the boats were ambushed, Kerry then put his boat ashore to chase a Viet Cong fighter who, Kerry believed, had fired on the boats. Kerry pursued the ambusher on foot through the brush, and, at some point, shots were fired resulting in the death of the Viet Cong fighter.[53] Several other navy personnel in the area mostly confirmed this basic outline of events. At least one of them concluded that Kerry's actions were, indeed, heroic, and that Kerry had probably saved the lives of American personnel by chasing down one of the ambushers.[54]

But details about the incident were less the subject of agreement. In some other accounts, which appeared in the heat of the 2004 presidential race, the incident was portrayed as far less heroic. It was said that the Viet Cong that Kerry shot was very young, apparently still a boy. It also was alleged that the enemy fighter had been shot in the back as he fled, which differed from Kerry's account. Those siding with Kerry's version of events strongly disagreed.

As the campaign progressed, another incident from the Vietnam War years was raised. Although this incident had largely gone unnoticed until that point, Douglas Brinkley's book *Tour of Duty* had revealed that after leaving the service Kerry met with North Vietnamese representatives in Paris while the war was still ongoing.[55] To some, this appeared to be evidence that Kerry had betrayed the American soldiers who were still fighting in Vietnam, and it added fuel to a political controversy.

Attacks on Kerry's wartime service and subsequent anti-war activities appeared frequently in television advertisements during the 2004 campaign. These ads were financed by so-called "soft money," funds that are intended to focus on issues, rather than promoting specific candidates. Accordingly, the Bush campaign reported that it was not responsible for the ads. A Bush campaign official stated, "President Bush's position could not be clearer. He regards Senator Kerry's service in Vietnam as noble service." Instead, it was claimed, "John Kerry's campaign is the only campaign that has attacked anybody's service in the Vietnam era. Senator Kerry has repeatedly attacked the president's service in the Air National Guard."[56]

Many Democrats were unconvinced that the White House was not involved with the Swift Boat ads. In late August, an attorney working for George Bush resigned after it was revealed he had advised the Swift Boat Veterans for Truth. Kerry's campaign manager subsequently complained, "Now we know why George Bush refuses to specifically condemn these false ads. People deeply involved in his own campaign are behind them...."[57]

In late August, an editor at *The Chicago Tribune* named William Rood wrote about his recollections of Kerry's swift-boat service in the Mekong Delta in 1969.[58] Rood had commanded another swift boat in the operation for which Kerry had been awarded the Silver Star, and in a piece published in the *Tribune* he came to Kerry's defense.[59]

As with the allegations surrounding Bush's National Guard service, the story was frequently highly politicized in media discussions. Media with liberal reputations tended to condemn the accusations against Kerry and the ads from the Swift Boat Veterans for Truth. *The New Republic* asked, "Just how dishonest must a smear campaign be for American journalists to say so plainly — or better yet, ignore altogether?"[60] According to this perspective, the story received significant attention largely because of "television, particularly cable television, with all of its now-familiar pathologies," and that "the effect was to spread lies rather than scrutinize them."[61] On the other hand, media with conservative reputations tended to look at the allegations as evidence of broader questions about Kerry's character and fitness for the presidency.

Rival Documentary Films

Stolen Honor. As the campaign season reached its height, the Sinclair Broadcasting Group directed its 62 television stations to pre-empt regular programming in order to air a documentary film that was critical of John Kerry. The film, *Stolen Honor: Wounds That Never Heal*, took a critical look at Kerry's famous 1971 anti-war testimony before the U.S. Senate. Among the persons appearing in the film was a veteran who had participated in a Swift Boat Veterans for Truth television ad.[62]

The film was directed by Carlton Sherwood, a reporter and Vietnam veteran who later recalled feeling "an inner hurt no surgeon's scalpel could remove"[63] after hearing Kerry's 1971 Senate testimony, during which Kerry suggested that American soldiers had committed war atrocities. Although Kerry was the focus of the film, Sherwood included interviews with other Vietnam veterans, some of whom had been prisoners of war and who had clearly felt betrayed by veterans (such as Kerry) and by celebrities (such as Jane Fonda) who in their view had undermined support for American troops during the war.

The controversy about Sinclair's plan perhaps epitomized the often-vitriolic 2004 campaign. Because the Swift Boat Veterans for Truth ads had already been widely played during the election season, many of these ideas were already known. However, since the planned airing was only a week before the November election, Democratic leaders were outraged. To them and many Kerry supporters, it seemed that Sinclair was unfairly trying to influence the election. Eighteen senators sent a letter of complaint to Michael Powell, son of Gen. Colin Powell and chairperson of the Federal Communications Commission. Sinclair executives found themselves at the center of a bitter debate, and over the following days, the price of Sinclair stock dropped 17 percent.[64] Finally, on October 22, instead of showing all of Sherwood's film, Sinclair aired a special program entitled *A P.O.W. Story: Politics, Pressure and the Media*, in which a portion from *Stolen Honor* was aired. (In later accounts, Sinclair was reported as stating it had never intended to run the film in its entirety.[65])

Fahrenheit 9/11. During the height of the controversy surrounding the Sinclair group's plan to air *Stolen Honor*, Michael Moore suggested that the group broadcast *Fahrenheit 9/11* as an opposing view. The Sinclair group declined Moore's offer.

Moore had come to public notice upon the success of his 1989 film *Roger & Me*, a humorous and openly subjective critique of the General Motors Corporation. More recently, his 2002 film *Bowling for Columbine* had been a controversial but commercially successful look at the issue of guns and gun control in the United States. By that time, Moore was a highly polemic public figure, admired by many liberals for his gadfly films and disdained by many conservatives, who saw him his films as blatant liberal propaganda. It was not surprising, therefore, that his 2004 film *Fahrenheit 9/11*, which probed into the administration's response to September 11, was deeply critical of Bush and his administration.

Released in late June, Moore's notoriety assured that *Fahrenheit 9/11* received substantial attention during the presidential campaign. Predictably, the film was hailed by many liberals and condemned by many conservatives. Film critic Roger Ebert wrote that the film was "compelling" and "persuasive."[66] On the other hand, syndicated columnist Richard Cohen concluded that the film was "utter stupidity" and "so bad it could help Bush."[67]

Moore's focus in *Fahrenheit 9/11* was the response to that event, and especially with the war in Iraq. Yet, in reviewing Bush's record, Moore also raised the matter of Bush's service in Texas Air National Guard. More broadly, by raising questions related to the Vietnam War era in the context of a blistering critique of the Iraq War, Moore gave viewers the opportunity to consider the two events together.

After the 2004 Election

Although it was another close contest, voters returned George W. Bush to the Oval Office. Having secured the second term that had eluded his father, the president was exuberant in victory. Believing that the election had given him substantial "political capital," he set forth an ambitious agenda for the coming months. Yet, the Iraq War stubbornly persisted, and American troop casualties slowly but steadily continued to mount.

As the American public grew increasingly unhappy with the trajectory of events in Iraq, invocations of the Vietnam War were to become more frequent and more pronounced. Public skepticism about the ongoing violence in Iraq grew, and support for the president eroded. In June, almost 60 percent of respondents in a Gallup poll favored withdrawing some or all U.S. troops from Iraq.[68] By the following month, survey results indicated not only that Bush's approval rating had dropped to the lowest point of his presidency, but that the percentage of Americans who disapproved had risen to more than 50 percent.[69] All the while, the rhetorical link between the Iraqi situation and the Vietnam War continued to be made. In August, for example, Chuck Hagel, Republican senator from Nebraska and a Vietnam War veteran, said that the war in Iraq increasingly resembled that prior war and, in language reminiscent of descriptions of the Vietnam War era, raised concerns that the U.S. was "getting more and more bogged down."[70] The administration, of course, resisted the comparison, but even the vice president may have reinforced it when he defended the Iraq War as a "noble cause," invoking the label that Ronald Reagan had fought so hard to attach to the Vietnam War two decades earlier.[71] The controversy continued.

Vietnamese Leader Visits the U.S. In June 2005, as the American public grappled with the ambiguities and difficulties of the war in Iraq, the leader of Vietnam prepared to journey to the United States to meet with the American president, as well as other political and business leaders. Not since the fall of Saigon had such a high-ranking Vietnamese official visited the United States.

On the eve of his departure for America, Prime Minister Phan Van Khai remarked, "During the war, Vietnam and the United States were opponents. Now that thirty years have elapsed since the end of the war, it is our policy to put aside the past and look to the future and a better relationship between the two countries."[72]

In the U.S., some people regarded the visit as a positive sign of progress, while others remained strongly opposed to strengthening ties with Vietnam. Citing human rights allegations, 45 members of Congress wrote to Bush expressing their concerns; one Congressional member described Vietnam's prime minister as a "master of deception."[73]

As the news media dutifully reported, on June 21, 2005, George W. Bush met with Phan Van Khai in the Oval Office. Outside the White House, some demonstrators congregated to protest the historic meeting.[74] The overwhelming majority of Americans, however, seemed not to take much notice. The people of the United States were aware, of course, that Vietnam was a living, breathing nation of the present, but it was the Vietnam War, not the nation of Vietnam, that had become entrenched in American consciousness.[75] Indeed, three decades after the long and painful conflict, America's war in Vietnam endured as a powerful and multi-faceted symbol in American mythology. The country of Vietnam in the present held far less interest.

8

Remembering
and Forgetting

The Vietnam War was America's longest war. Despite the enormous pain that it inflicted on the United States, however, it was not the nation's costliest conflict in terms of lives lost. The number of American soldiers who died in World War II was in excess of 400,000, which was more than six times the number of U.S. military fatalities in the Vietnam War.[1] The death toll for American soldiers in World War I, in which the U.S. was only involved for 18 months, was double that of the war in Southeast Asia. These facts do not minimize the sense of loss, of course. For the families and loved ones of those who have perished in any war, the pain is real and can last a lifetime. Still, the Vietnam War has been represented in American culture as an eminently more painful episode.

On a national scale, after both the First and Second World Wars, the nation quickly moved on. To be sure, it solemnly honored its fallen soldiers and there were residual effects that demanded attention, but the nation accepted the losses and directed its attention towards building the future. After the Vietnam War, however, this was not as easy to accomplish. The war left a legacy of bitterness that proved very difficult to forget or to overcome.

Many Americans, tired of controversies from the 1960s to the Watergate scandal, adopted an inward focus. They were disenchanted with world affairs and with the seeming inability of the government to solve many problems. Looking back at this period, some people conclude that the Vietnam War had been left behind and that the public was anxious to forget about it as much as they were able. To some extent, this appears to be true. But this was never completely possible, partially because of the many visible reminders of the war. Vietnam veterans, in particular, were too numerous to ignore.

The inability to avoid the war's memory was the result of more than these reminders, however. In fact, the end of the war was deeply problematic for the nation. The circumstances of its end, in which the communist North Vietnamese triumphed, were highly dissonant with the picture that American political leaders—and many ordinary American citizens—had of the United States. It was difficult to square the image of a nation that lost in Vietnam with that which had triumphed in the two World Wars. Even the ambiguous Korean Conflict, which essentially had ended in a stalemate, had preserved the pro–Western regime in South Korea, and so while not a total victory, it hardly was equivalent to the seeming complete failure in Vietnam. This knowledge — that America had now "lost" a war — was difficult for Americans to explain to themselves and to square with the picture they had of how things were "supposed" to be. Running counter to the narrative that Americans imagined for the United States, the Vietnam War could not, as an historical artifact, be completely stowed away until some acceptable way of reconciling its inconsistencies with the larger and grander American story could be found.

The perception that the nation had now lost a war was magnified in postwar years because of the high degree of ownership that Americans have assumed for the war. Whereas political figures as different as John F. Kennedy and Richard Nixon both observed at various times that it was ultimately the Vietnamese who would be responsible for winning or losing the war, many Americans— including political elites— seem never to have fully accepted that view. Instead, for the most part, Americans came to believe, and have continued to believe, that the war, though occurring in Vietnam, was about them. The loss, therefore, was theirs.

One source for this way of thinking can be found in the so-called Domino Theory of the 1950s, which provided some of the original justification for American intervention in Vietnam. It was based on the idea that stopping the spread of communism elsewhere was equivalent to protecting the American homeland in the future. According to this way of thinking, American military efforts in Vietnam were part of a grander project about preserving the American way of life. The prominence of this view among Americans certainly was greatly reduced by the time the war ended in the mid–1970s, however. (Later, in the 1980s, even Ronald Reagan's campaign against communist influence did not rekindle widespread fear among Americans that a tidal wave of communism would envelope the world around the United States.) Yet, although the Domino Theory as a way of viewing the world drifted from prominence long before the end of the conflict, the American perception of its ownership of the Vietnam War was unaffected.

There was a complicating factor that added to the ambiguity of the Vietnam War's end and subsequently fueled guilt and recriminations in American politics. This was the fact that the United States had ceased to be a principal party — in any meaningful way — by the time the war finally ended with the fall of Saigon in 1975. This was hardly a more noble or acceptable way to think about the war's end, however. It seemed to suggest that the nation's honor had been compromised.

Thus, it was hard for Americans not to think of the Vietnam War as the lost war. Unaccustomed to losing military conflicts, however, acceptable explanations remained difficult to find. Not long after the war, various re-framings of the war began to appear in American politics and entertainment. In both of these facets of American culture, repeated attempts were made to integrate the historical reality of South Vietnam's demise and America's perceived failure into a bigger American narrative, in which the status and self-image of the United States were not seriously compromised. These efforts frequently looked for a way to find some sort of moral victory in the apparent defeat.

The impulse to confront the Vietnam War in politics and on screen has been an essentially narrative project. The many invocations of the war usually constitute various attempts to tell the story of the war in a way that is consonant with the dominant American themes and values. Realities of the Vietnam War over its long duration were complex and often difficult to fully understand and explain, however. Moreover, as the war transpired, Americans society was highly conflicted about it. To construct an American understanding of it after the fact, then, has often resulted in representations of the war that are highly selective in what they include and that are often radically oversimplified. Popularity in politics, film or television is seldom achieved through elaborate explanation and inconclusive assessments.

Remembered Themes

The Vietnam War has generated an enormous outpouring of published material, films, and political discourse. There is much more information available about it — in both "factual" and interpretive material — than can be consumed as a practical matter. Technically, therefore, there is little, if anything, about any aspect of the war that has been forgotten, at least if the entire record is considered. As mentioned earlier, however, the vast majority of Americans develop their understanding of the war from a much more limited range of sources, of which political news and screen media have been a prominent part. The image of the war that emerges from these influential, populist sources has emphasized a much narrower range of historical information and perspectives than is available. In the process of framing the war for public consumption, certain facets of the war have been emphasized much more than others.

The American soldier. With no victory to celebrate, American political and screen representations of the war have placed their greatest emphasis on the American combat troops who served in Vietnam. War veterans almost always have been held in high esteem in the United States, and they often have been demonstrably rewarded for their service. The G.I. Bill that followed World War II is often cited as an example of the nation's gratitude for the dedicated service of its soldiers during that conflict. A sense that the nation honored its veterans of the Vietnam War was slower in emerging, however. At first, many Vietnam veterans felt they were ignored, and sometimes actively dishonored.

Although it did not come about immediately (and many veterans undoubtedly saw Gerald Ford's amnesty program for draft avoiders and military deserters as an opposite impulse), the Vietnam veteran eventually did emerge as an important political symbol in American politics. The first steps towards post-war recognition of Vietnam veterans in the Ford and Carter administrations were followed by a grand reawakening in the Reagan administration, which extolled Vietnam veterans as it championed a renewal of the armed forces. The unveiling of the Vietnam Veterans' Memorial, and the reverence that it subsequently elicited, was emblematic of the progress that had been made in restoring Vietnam veterans into the mainstream of war veterans and American culture.

Over the years, the image of the Vietnam veteran presented on screen has evolved dramatically. At first, American motion pictures and television usually looked at the war by looking at its veterans after the conflict. (Later, such productions confronted the war experience more directly.) Typically, the storylines of these films emphasized the harrowing experiences of combat and often it was implied that service in Vietnam had rendered them as social misfits, war criminals, drug addicts, or otherwise defective. As in political rhetoric, by the 1980s that picture began to markedly shift. The Vietnam veteran was now not only likely to be portrayed as a heroic figure; he was often seen as a super-hero.[2] The basic nobility of the American soldier in Vietnam was firmly entrenched in screen portrayals, and even in more complex films of the late 1980s and 1990s, this underlying nobility was usually evident in the central characters of films and television shows dealing with the war.

The post-war cultural validation of military service in Vietnam has been so strong that it has prompted many responses. On some occasions, men have apparently found the aura of Vietnam War service to be irresistible. In one celebrated case, for example, a prominent academic historian was publicly exposed for having fabricated a false history of his own life. Joseph Ellis was a highly respected professor at Mount Holyoke College, where he had taught for almost thirty years. Over his successful career, he had won both a Pulitzer Prize and the National Book Award for his historical writing. At Mount Holyoke, one course that he taught was about the Vietnam War. In the late spring of 2001, he stood accused of substantially embellishing his military service record to students in that course, claiming to have served in Vietnam during the war. (Although he had served in the military, this was not accurate.) The *Boston Globe* revealed this false claim, and soon Ellis was the subject of an angry and vocal response in national print and broadcast media, as well as in many internet sources. He subsequently issued an apology and was placed on leave.

At the same time, the image of the war resister continued to be overwhelmingly negative. They have often been presented as somehow misinformed, weak-minded, or un-patriotic. Ironically, this image persists, despite widespread opinion that the war was a mistake, as public opinion polls have shown over a long period.

The responsibilities of government. Another persistent theme, important for creating a Vietnam War narrative that can explain the perceived American failure, can be found in the topic of government responsibilities in supporting the American military. Over and over, in political discourse and in screen productions about the war, one finds a message that stresses that the idea that as the Vietnam War progressed, somehow American leaders had turned away from their responsibilities in prosecuting the war.

Interestingly, it has usually been a responsibility to the American soldiers that has been emphasized, and any perceived responsibility to America's South Vietnamese allies is often, though not always, given far less attention. Although it can be argued that it is implicit that giving full support to the American military would, as a necessary consequence, have resulted in more support for South Vietnam, this potential aspect of the argument is seldom given much attention.

The theme of the U.S. government's responsibility to American troops has played out in many ways over the years. In both the overtly political realm and in Vietnam-themed motion pictures, the enormous attention given to the Missing-in-Action and Prisoner-of-War issue has great symbolic importance in this respect. The overarching narrative of this issue, in both the political and entertainment realms, has emphasized a need for government to more fully discharge its responsibilities to American soldiers.

In politics and on screen, the post-war Vietnam government often has been represented as an untrustworthy and scheming state. In screen fiction and political discourse, it has frequently been portrayed as deliberately withholding information about MIAs and POWs. The perpetual identification of Vietnam as a shifty foe has political usefulness, of course. This allows for many declarations of support for the missing, and for repeated demonstrations of concern for American troops. Some people, though certainly not all, might even regard this as a type of rhetorical atonement. Of course, there are other aspects to the intersecting MIA-POW and diplomatic recognition of Vietnam issue, but the high-profile expression of support for American's missing soldiers is surely a large part of it.

Often, what is implied in the suggestion that the American government and people did not adequately support American troops is the theme that the conflict in Vietnam was a war that could and should have been won. Representations of the war in politics and on screen often suggest that the war was "winnable," and that this would have been the outcome if military support had been greater. Along with this explanation, it is often implied that liberal and other antiwar political interests undermined the American war effort, contributing to the negative outcome.

On screen, audiences have witnessed numerous fictional American soldiers in Vietnam who express—sometimes implicitly, sometimes explicitly—a desire for their nation to show them more love and support. Rambo's famous line, in which he longs for America to "love us as much as we love it", is one of the most obvious examples of this impulse, but it is widely found in Vietnam films and television productions. An implicit message is that Americans should not let this happen again.

Patriotism as the dominant American value. During the Vietnam War years, a popular slogan among war supporters was the phrase, "America: Love it or leave it." The Americans who promoted this slogan were tired of antiwar protesters and those who criticized other aspects of American society, which at the time was undergoing substantial transformation as the result of Civil Rights awareness and other social movements. As this slogan made clear, for many people with this perspective, loving America meant supporting it, almost without question.

This construction of patriotism, in which governmental—especially military—policy, once made, should not be criticized, has persisted in modified form in many quarters of American society. It is an old idea in U.S. political culture that has been reasserted. In political declarations and in screen appearances of Vietnam War-era American soldiers, the correctness of serving the nation without question and hesitation is shown as a strong ideal. (Pacifist impulses, when acknowledged at all, are typically presented as highly unusual or as masks for cowardice.) When, as was the case in the World Wars, there is strong national consensus about the moral rightness and necessity for war, the likelihood that serious reservations will emerge about overall American policy seems slight. The Vietnam War was not a war of that type, however, and within a few years after its beginnings, many questions were raised. The military, needing to bolster its numbers significantly, quickly came to rely upon the draft to meet its needs. Again unlike the World Wars, however, many young men (maybe never a majority) were reluctant to embrace American aims and goals in Vietnam, and they resented be conscripted into service for it. Even though most young men who were called reported for duty, as the proportion of soldiers serving in Vietnam who were draftees increased, increasing opposition to the war could be found, even among the ranks of the American soldiers. Certainly the relatively long duration of the war amplified this effect.

On screen, however, many of the most high-profile characters do not express much interest in thinking about the possible ambiguities of the war, and when, on occasion, some do so, they often conclude that there is little that can be done about it and so it is best just to continue serving without asking a lot of questions. It is, therefore, not a problem when, in many film treatments of the theme, American soldiers seem to have little understanding of what the nation was seeking to accomplish in Vietnam. (It is hard to imagine the popular Rambo or Forrest Gump characters explaining American foreign policy objectives.) Often, however, it is suggested that such matters should not concern them, since their duty was to serve without question. While such obedience is expected in the military, the implication often seems to be that the public also should not ask questions. Of course, some screen portrayals were significantly more nuanced than this, and some even suggest the characters possessed a view of the war as morally ambiguous. This is not the norm in such portrayals, however.

The war as aberration. The war is often presented as a special case, as an aberration in American history. In many instances, the war appears in rhetoric and on screen as an isolated event, usually with important aspects of its historical context missing. Although the Soviets appear — sometimes specifically, and sometimes via surrogates — the Vietnam War is seldom situated in the Cold War realities that actually shaped it. The political reconstruction of the war as a conflict in which the United States could have prevailed, for instance, usually fails to take note of important historical considerations. (As an example, there is usually little mention of Lyndon Johnson's desire to keep the war from expanding into a conflict that would draw in more direct Soviet participation.)

The nobility of American intentions. Ronald Reagan tirelessly championed the idea that although the American war in Vietnam had resulted in a military defeat, the underlying purpose of the war had been a noble one. Indeed, Americans seem to have long approved of spreading democratic ideals in the American mold throughout the world.

Although, as mentioned elsewhere, most Americans have regarded the war as some sort of error, it is not at all clear that this means they have believed that the impulse to stem the tide of communism and preserve what appeared to be a pro–Western, democratic state in a faraway place was not a worthy goal. Indeed, it seems possible, and perhaps likely, that the mistaken aspect of the war that has been cited relates more to the application of this ideal in the context-specific setting of Vietnam than to an overall objection to American goals to achieve such purposes in general. To some people, moreover, the mistaken aspect of the war refers to the judgement that the United States did not go all out to win it.

In any case, despite the prevalence of the view that the war was a mistake, this does not at all logically preclude viewing the intentions of the United States in Vietnam or elsewhere as essentially noble and morally righteous. This, of course, is not the view that was held by many opponents of the war, but it is a view that has resurfaced in other contexts in the years since. Indeed, to some people, the role of the United States on the world stage is interpreted to be one that requires it to intervene in international situations that it finds morally objectionable. In this view, a main problem in the Vietnam War was that American ideals were ineffectively implemented, which is quite different from saying the basic motivation was wrong.

Forgotten Themes

Just as political discourse and screen entertainments dealing with the war have emphasized some themes, other aspects of the war, that were once quite prominent, have received substantially less attention in the years after the war. These themes, a few examples of which are discussed below, do not fit as neatly into a narrative that explains the Vietnam War and its outcome in a way that is consistent with the traditional American story.

Dissent. Although few have forgotten that the Vietnam War provoked an anxious response in the American people that led some to engage in vocal dissent, this aspect of the war's history does not receive substantial attention in many of the recurring representations of the war in mainstream American culture. Those who opposed the war are seen in various ways, but mostly in a negative light. More oddly, perhaps, one finds that there is little representation of any cogent rationale for having opposed the war in the first place, even though public opinion polls have shown that Americans tend to view the war as a mistake.

As time has gone on since the war, it has become very difficult to find political leaders who proudly proclaim that they were among the war protesters during the war. In fact, as the recurrence of the Vietnam War as a theme in presidential politics makes clear, identification with active opposition to the Vietnam is often presented as a decided political liability. In the complicated case of Bill Clinton, for example, although he acknowledged being opposed to the war, he nonetheless made great efforts to avoid being identified as an opponent of the military draft. Even as a young man he recognized this as a potential political liability. His assertion, which not everyone believed, was that was that he was opposed, but would have served then if called to do so. More recently, opponents of John Kerry in the 2004 presidential campaign often pointed to his antiwar activities as a sign of betrayal. The strong efforts that were made to discredit his combat service were likely influenced by perceptions that he had not stood fully behind his nation when it was at war.

In politics, the implication is often taken to be that an antiwar perspective was equivalent to an un–American, anti-patriotic position. Antiwar advocates have often been identified as something resembling a lunatic fringe. The stereotypical image of the antiwar activist as a long-haired, drug-abusing, communist sympathizer continues to lurk in the background in many representations. When stereotyped in such a way, opposition to the war is easy to dismiss. A view in which opponents of the war may have articulate reasons, consonant with American ideals is seldom considered. Frequently, all opposition to the war is construed as a dangerous undermining of support for American soldiers. This leaves few channels open for suggesting significant policy changes in the midst of military actions.

Active political debate about the war, and possible reasons to have supported it or to have opposed it, are seldom seen. The debate is almost never given a very complete airing. Instead, the complexities of the historical war are reduced to the level of slogans. Supporters appear patriotic. Opponents, whether Jane Fonda or John Kerry, are seldom shown to have any reason for their opposition. This simplified, dichotomous portrayal radically misrepresents the arguments that were advanced for and against the war during the war years.

Race. It is widely known that young soldiers from across the spectrum of American racial and ethnic backgrounds served in combat during the Vietnam War. In American politics and screen portrayals, however, this aspect of the war is not examined very deeply. Often, combat duty is shown as a common bonding experience that brings young men from different backgrounds together.

Yet, during much of the time that it was engaged in the Vietnam War, the United States was experiencing upheaval as the Civil Rights movement thrust numerous changes on the social order. Racial tension at times led to rioting in American cities. The American soldiers in Vietnam were hardly isolated from, or immune to, the tumult. The influx of young men into the military unavoidably brought some of the discords of the outside world within the armed forces. Consequently, an examination of the actual experience of American combat troops in Vietnam reveals that racial tensions were widespread. Although this should not be overstated, the issue often has received no attention at all.

The race issue also is apparent in relation to the portrayal of the Vietnamese people themselves. The cultural divide between the American soldiers and the Vietnamese was quite evident throughout the war. For Americans, generally, the culture of Vietnam was understood after the war little better than before it. For this—as well as other reasons relating to the strong American sense of ownership of the war, mentioned above—the Vietnamese are often minor players in representations of the war, whether on screen or in American politics.

When, after the war, the communists led a reunified Vietnam, it is difficult to imagine that the vague and often stereotypical portrayal of Vietnamese persons on film and in public pronouncements did not play some part in the slow pace of progress toward diplomatic relations between the two former adversaries. Of course, other reasons, including ideology, clearly contributed to that situation.

Gender. Although the role of American and Vietnamese women in the war has occasionally surfaced as a theme, attention to this aspect of the war has seldom been pronounced. In emphasizing the role of combat duty and heroism, which remained outside the traditional province of women in American thinking, there has been little opportunity to explore this theme in the many public airings of the war in politics and media.

American military women were formally honored at the site of the Vietnam Veterans Memorial in Washington. The television series *China Beach*, which premiered in the late 1980s, helped to reestablish awareness that American women had served in the war zone. Yet, it is hard to escape the impression that although Americans appreciated such service, it somehow seemed to be viewed as a peripheral activity.

As for Vietnamese women, who were numerous among the war's victims and also were among its combatants, the record of attention is even less substantial. Oliver Stone's *Heaven and Earth* notwithstanding, Vietnamese women have almost never appeared in discourse or screen appearances as three-dimensional people. One seldom encounters representations of these women in which they possess their own ideals, motivations, joys and sorrows. More often, they appear as stereotypes in supporting roles.

Conclusions

It is often supposed that history teaches lessons to those who are willing to learn them. In the case of the Vietnam War, lessons are sometimes hard to find. Among American military and political leaders, the lessons taken from the war were initially pragmatic: that the United States should not engage in military operations without the support of the American people, without clearly obtainable objective, and without a way to determine when to make an exit. In events after the war, these lessons can be seen in the planning and execution of such operations as the Gulf War. To an extent, some have taken these lessons as more relevant to the Cold War world that ended in the early 1990s than to the complicated world that emerged after that time. As time has passed, and especially after the trauma of September 11, 2001, even these apparent lessons do not seem to hold as much weight as was formerly supposed.

American political leaders, meanwhile, also have learned something from the war: to avoid anything that can be labeled as a "quagmire" or as "another Vietnam." The word quagmire, originally a label employed by war opponents as part of their argument that the war was essentially hopeless for the United States, has emerged as one of the most recognizable and powerful political labels in American politics. Instantly calling to mind the war that cost many American lives and was still not won, its application to a situation sends a powerful message.

There are many other lessons that might be taken from the war, of course, but since consensus about it remains elusive, these have been slow to emerge. Although some of the themes mentioned above reflect ideas about the war that do seem widely shared, these and others that could be identified are relatively few and are dependent upon quite specific readings of history. Indeed, the extremely collapsed view of the war that appears in political discourse and the media does not convey enough of a sense of the complexities of the war in Vietnam, or the controversies that it generated in America at that time, to make such conclusions easy to see.

In the many reincarnations of the Vietnam War that have made appearances in politics and screen media since the mid–1970s, it is clear that the war continued to be an important part of how American conceived of their nation and its place in the world over that period. Although the war has surfaced at many times and in many contexts, however, the cumulative picture that emerges from the most disseminated and widespread of these invocations is far from complete and it is far from a rounded view. Instead, the more the war has surface, the more that the overall picture of it has succumbed to an increasingly simplified, dichotomous view.

The war that is so often evoked is not, in a sense, the actual war that ended in 1975. Instead, the Vietnam War of politics, film and television has increasingly been a powerful, though still ambiguous symbol. Even as the generation that fought the war recedes into their golden years, the war remains an emotionally charged topic. Eventually, of course, new large-scale events are likely to push the Vietnam War into a less visible place in the national consciousness. By the time that may happen, however, the Vietnam War will have helped shape events that extended far beyond its time.

Chapter Notes

Chapter 1

1. See Murray Edelman, *The Symbolic Uses of Politics* (Urbana: University of Illinois Press, 1964).

2. See, for example, Maxwell McCombs, Donald L. Shaw, and David Weaver, eds. *Communication and Democracy: Exploring the Intellectual Frontiers in Agenda-Setting Theory* (Mahwah, NJ: Lawrence Erlbaum Associates, 1997) and S. Iyengar, *Is Anyone Responsible? How Television Frames Political News* (Chicago: University of Chicago Press, 1991).

3. Edelman, *The Symbolic Uses of Politics.*

4. Murray Edelman, *Constructing the Political Spectacle* (Chicago: University of Chicago Press, 1988).

5. Robert M. Entman, *Projections of Power* (Chicago: University of Chicago Press, 2003).

6. Erving Goffman, *Frame Analysis: An Essay on the Organization of Experience* (Boston: Northeastern University Press, 1974), 21.

7. William A. Gamson and Andre Modigliani, "The Changing Culture of Affirmative Action," in *Research in Political Sociology*, vol. 3, ed. Richard G. Braungart, (Greenwich, CT: JAI Press, 1987) , 143.

8. See Donald A. Schon and Martin Rein, *Frame Reflection: Toward the Resolution of Intractable Policy Controversies* (New York: Basic Books, 1994) and Donald R. Kinder and Lynn M. Sanders, *Divided by Color: Racial Politics and Democratic Ideals* (Chicago: University of Chicago Press, 1996).

9. J. R. Zeller, *The Nature and Origins of Mass Opinion* (New York: Cambridge University Press, 1992), 13.

10. W. R. Neuman, M. R. Just, and A. N. Crigler, *Common Knowledge: News and the Construction of Political Meaning* (Chicago: University of Chicago Press, 1992), 62.

11. See, for example, G. Gerbner, L. Gross, M. Morgan, and N. Signorielli, "Growing Up with Television: The Cultivation Perspective", in *Media Effects: Advances in Theory and Research*, ed. J. Bryant and D. Zillman (Hillsdale, New Jersey: Lawrence Erlbaum Associates, 1994), 17–41.

12. Such productions have undeniable influence and long tradition in American filmmaking. For example, D. W. Griffith's highly controversial 1915 film *Birth of a Nation* presented audiences with an inflammatory depiction of race relations in the pre- and post-Civil War South. Its racist message was thought to be so effective that it was used as a recruiting tool by the Ku Klux Klan for decades.

13. These, and other aspects of the Vietnam War and American policy, were topics in the 1975 documentary film *Hearts and Minds,* from director Peter Davis.

14. Quoted in "Vietnam Veterans Memorial: America Remembers" *National Geographic,* May 1985, 552–53.

15. See, for example, W. Broyles, W. "Vietnam: A Television History," *Newsweek,* October 10, 1983, 92–93.

16. For a contemporary press account of this phenomenon, see, for example, Vincent Canby, "Revenge Fuels Cold War Movies of the 80's," *The New York Times,* December 8, 1985. For a scholarly reaction to the films, see Gaylyn Studlar and David Desser, "Never Having to Say You're Sorry: *Rambo*'s Rewriting of the Vietnam War" in *From Hanoi to Hollywood: The Vietnam War in American Film*, eds. Linda Dittmar and Gene Michaud (New Brunswick: Rutgers University Press, 1990), 101–112.

17. David A. Cook, *A History of Narrative Film*. 3rd cd. (New York: W. W. Norton, 1996), 950.

18. Richard M. Nixon, *No More Vietnams,* (New York: Arbor House, 1985).

19. George H. W. Bush, "State of the Union Address," as transcribed in *The New York Times,* January 27, 1992.

20. See H. Johnson., *Divided We Fall: Gambling with History in the Nineties.* (New York: Norton, 1994), 48.

21. Hillary Rodham Clinton, *Living History,* (New York: Simon & Schuster, 2003), 140.

22. See Johanna McGeary, Karen Tumulty, and Viveca Novak, "The Fog of War," *Time,* April 7, 2001, 24–32.

Chapter 2

1. These are cited in Rick Berg, "Losing Vietnam: Covering the War in an Age of Technology," in *From Hanoi to Hollywood: The Vietnam War in American Film,* ed. Linda Dittmar and Gene Michaud (New Brunswick: Rutgers University Press, 1990), 44.

2. For example, earlier governmental efforts to suppress the so-called Pentagon Papers, which called into question government explanations, had primed many members of the media and the public to be leery of government pronouncements. The Pentagon Papers episode may have been much more damaging for symbolic reasons than for any of the concrete items it contained.

3. Fred Emery, *Watergate: the Corruption of American Politics and the Fall of Richard Nixon* (New York: Times Books, 1994), 359.

4. Even *Time* magazine, which had no prior history of publishing editorials over the course of its half-century of publication, joined in this chorus of those offering opinion on this matter.See Peter N. Carroll, *It Seemed Like Nothing Happened: America in the 1970s* (New Brunswick: Rutgers University Press, 2000), 152.

5. Ibid., 155.

6. See, for example, his accounts of the rationales for the Nixon pardon and for the draft resisters and deserters conditional amnesty programs in Gerald R. Ford, *A Time to Heal,* (New York: Harper and Row, 1979).

7. This statement is attributed to Major Bob Barrett in Gerald R. Ford. *A Time to Heal.* New York: Harper and Row, 1979.

8. Larry H. Addington, *America's War in Vietnam: A Short Narrative History* (Bloomington: Indiana University Press, 2000), 154.

9. Other international developments also worked to call attention away from Vietnam at this time. The Yom Kippur war in the Middle East had created a crisis in 1973. Also, the complex relationship between the U.S. and the U.S.S.R. continued to flair up in various parts of the world. In 1975, a civil war erupted in Angola, in which a revolutionary faction was supplied money by the Soviets and troops by Cuba. The Ford administration considered aiding the opposition until it was forbidden to do so by a Congress that clearly was fearful of any American involvement with foreign civil wars.

10. This statement is quoted in James Cannon, *Time and Chance: Gerald R. Ford's Appointment with History* (New York: HarperCollins, 1994), 396.

11. See, for example, Andrew Hunt, *The Turning: A History of Vietnam Veterans Against the War,* (New York: New York University Press, 1999), 171–172.

12. This question was part of the Harris Survey conducted between March 15 and March 23, 1973.

13. See Ford's comments on the development and rationale for this policy in Ford, *A Time to Heal,.* 141–42; 181–83.

14. Ford describes his thinking about the decision for the conditional amnesty in Ford, *A Time to Heal,* 181–183.

15. R. J. McMahon. Rationalizing Defeat: The Vietnam War in American Presidential Discourse." *Rhetoric and Public Affairs* 2, no. 4 (Winter 1999): 529–49.

16. This discussion is based on the ratings surveys conducted by the A. C. Nielsen company.

17. *M*A*S*H* was a long-running series and a great success for the network. The series' final episode, which was broadcast February 28, 1983, attracted a Nielsen rating of over 60%, or over 50 million American households, by far the highest-rated television program of its time and still unsurpassed in ratings for sponsored television programs 20 years later.

18. See Berg, "Losing Vietnam: Covering the War in an Age of Technology," 45.

19. Gerald R. Ford, as quoted in James Cannon, *Time and Chance: Gerald R. Ford's Appointment with History* (New York: HarperCollins, 1994), 397.

20. American Institute for Economic Research. "More Inflation in Our Future, Mr. Greenspan?" *Research Reports* 68, no. 14 (23 July 2001), 78.

21. Severeid spoke of this in his commentary that aired as part of the *CBS Evening News* broadcast of May 13, 1975.

22. See Cynthia J. Fuchs, "'All the Animals Come Out at Night': Vietnam Meets *Noir* in *Taxi Driver,*" in *Inventing Vietnam: The War in Film and Television,* ed. Michael Anderegg (Philadelphia: Temple University Press, 1991), 33–55.

23. A Harris Survey of the national population conducted April 16–18, 1975, showed more than 70 percent held a negative view of Ford's performance in this area.

24. The survey was conducted for *Time* by Yankelovich, Skelly and White, May 14–22, 1975.

25. The Federal Election Commission records that voter turnout dropped in every presidential contest from 1960, (when it was 63%) to 1980 (when it was 52.5%).

26. Jimmy Carter, *Keeping Faith: Memoirs of a President* (New York: Bantam, 1982), 125.

27. "Vietnam is Admitted to the U.N. as 32d General Assembly Opens," *New York Times*, 21 September 1977.

28. Steven V. Roberts, "Boat People Brave Adversity to Seek New Lives in U.S.," *New York Times*, January 2, 1978.

29. "America's Duty to the Boat People," *New York Times*, 16 December 16, 1978.

30. "Malaysia to Put 70,000 Refugees Back Out to Sea," *New York Time*, June 16, 1979, 1.

31. See, for example, Henry Kamm, "Cambodian Enigma: Silence and a Scarcity of Refugees," *New York Times*, February 3, 1979.

32. Bernard Weintraub, "Pentagon Is Disputed on Exposure of Troops to Herbicide in Vietnam," *New York Times*, November 25, 1979.

33. This claim, attributed to Dr. Gilbert Bogen, appeared in Richard Severo, "U.S., Despite Claims of Veterans, Says None are Herbicide Victims," *New York Times*, May 28, 1979.

34. This poll was part of the document conducted for the Chicago Council on Foreign relations by the Gallup Organization, November 17–26, 1978

35. Michael Cimino, quoted in Leticia Kent, "Ready for Vietnam? A Talk with Michael Cimino." *The New York Times*, December 10, 1978.

36. Cimino, quoted in Ibid.

37. Vincent Canby, "Screen: 'The Deer Hunter'" *New York Times, December* 15, 1978.

38. Cimino, quoted in Kent, "Ready for Vietnam? A Talk with Michael Cimino."

39. Leonard Quart, "*The Deer Hunter:* The Superman in Vietnam," in *From Hanoi to Hollywood: The Vietnam War in American Film*, ed. Linda Dittmar and Gene Michaud (New Brunswick: Rutgers University Press, 1990), 167.

40. Canby, "Screen: 'The Deer Hunter.'"

41. Karen Rasmussen and Sharon D. Downey, "Dialectical Disorientation in Vietnam War Films: Subversion of the Mythology of War," *Quarterly Journal of Speech*, 77, no. 2 (May 1991): 176–95.

42. Vincent Canby, "The Screen: 'Apocalypse Now,'" *New York Times*, 15 August 15, 1979.

43. The poll of a national sample of the adult population was conducted by Louis Harris and Associates for the Veterans Administration, November 17, 1979 to December 19, 1979 and reported in the Veterans Administration document, "Attitudes Toward Vietnam Era Veterans Survey," (Washington, D.C.: Veterans Administration, July 1980).

44. John Hellman, "Vietnam and the Hollywood Genre Film: Inversions of American Mythology in *The Deer Hunter* and *Apocalypse Now*," *American Quarterly*, 34 (1982): 418–39.

45. The tendency by Americans to place the U.S. at the center of the Vietnam War story is usefully discussed in Arnold R. Isaacs, *Vietnam Shadows: The War, Its Ghosts, and Its Legacy*, (Baltimore: Johns Hopkins University Press, 1997), 145–148.

Chapter 3

1. Hedrick Smith, "Excluded From G.O.P Debate, Four Attack Bush," *New York Times*, February 24, 1980.

2. Ibid.

3. Ibid.

4. Bernard D. Nossiter, "U.N. Assembly, Rebuffing Soviet [sic], Seats Cambodia Regime of Pol Pot," *New York Times*, September 22, 1979.

5. Ibid.

6. See Edward Schumacher, "U.N. Assembly Bids Vietnamese Forces Evacuate Cambodia," *New York Times*, November 15, 1979.

7. Nossiter, "U.N. Assembly, Rebuffing Soviet [sic], Seats Cambodia Regime of Pol Pot."

8. Richard Burt, "Report Charges 'Major Mistakes on Iran Mission," *New York Times*, June 6, 1980.

9. Ronald Reagan, quoted in Howell Raines, "Reagan Calls Arms Race Essential to Avoid a 'Surrender' or a "Defeat,'" *New York Times*, August 19, 1980.

10. Ibid.

11. See Larry Kaagan, "Assertive America," *Foreign Affairs*, 59, no. 3 (1980).

12. See A. Yoder, "The News Media and One World," *Political Communication and Persuasion*, 1, no. 3 (1981): 217–230.

13. Data from a survey conducted by the Gallup Organization, January 25–28, 1980.

14. D.D. Moyer, "Editorials and Foreign Affairs in Recent Presidential Campaigns," *Journalism Quarterly*, 59, no. 4 (Winter 1982): 541–547.

15. Figures from the Federal Election Commission's "National Voter Turnout in Federal Elections, 1960–1996."

16. Peter C. Rollins, "The Vietnam War: Perceptions Through Literature, Film, And Television," *American Quarterly*, 36 (1984): 419–432.

17. See L.C. Spangler, "Buddies and pals: A History of Male Friendships on Primetime Television," in *Men, Masculinity, and the Media*, ed. S. Craig (Newbury Park, CA: Sage Publications, 1992), 93–100.

18. See, for example, Mi Yung Yoon, "Explaining U.S. Intervention in Third World Internal Wars, 1945–1989," *Journal of Conflict Resolution*, 41, no. 4 (August 1997): 580–603.

19. John M. Goshko, "Drawing a Hard Line Against Communism," *Washington Post*, February 22, 1981.

20. See Michael Schaller, *Reckoning with Reagan: America and Its President in the 1980s*, (New York: Oxford University Press, 1992), 143–44.

21. Michael Getler, "U.S. Weighs Arms, Advisers to Bolster Salvador Regime," *Washington Post*, February 25, 1981.

22. A brief story on this appears in "State Dept. Comments on report on Arming of Salvadoran Rebels," *New York Times*, February 7, 1981.

23. Alexander Haig is quoted in "Excerpts from Haig's Briefing about El Salvador," *New York Times*, February 21, 1981.

24. Ibid.

25. Don Oberdorfer, "Using El Salvador to Battle the Ghosts of Vietnam," *Washington Post* March 1, 1981.

26. Highlights of Walter Cronkite's interview with Ronald Reagan were reprinted in "Excerpts from Reagan Interview," *New York Times*, March 4, 1981.

27. Ibid.

28. Ibid.

29. See, for example, Bernard Gwertzman, "Side Effect of El Salvador," *New York Times*, March 14, 1981.

30. See Judith Miller, "15 U.S. Green berets to Aid Salvadorans," *New York Times*, March 14, 1982.

31. See Raymond Bonner, "Protests on Salvador Are Staged Across U.S.," *New York Times*, March 25, 1981.

32. Caryle Murphy, "23,000 demonstrate Against Role of U.S. in El Salvador," *Washington Post* (March 28, 1981).

33. Judith Miler, "Congress Mail Heavy on El Salvador Issue," *New York Times*, March 26, 1981.

34. Poll conducted by NBC News and the Associated Press, April 13–14, 1981.

35. "No More Vietnams," *National Review*, April 17, 1981, 403–404.

36. Stephen Talbott, "El Salvador: It Is Not Vietnam," *Time*, February 22, 1982, 33–34.

37. Anthony Lewis, "Why the Kid Gloves?" *New York Times*, February 22, 1982.

38. Anthony Lewis, "It's Not Vietnam, But..." *New York Times*, February 25, 1982.

39. Charles Mohr, "Reagan Seems Confused on Vietnam's History," *New York Times*, February 19, 1982.

40. Bernard Gwertzman, "Haig Claims Proof Outsiders Direct Salvadoran Rebels," *New York Times*, March 3, 1982.

41. Adam Clymer, "Public Opinion, Too, Is Running Against the White House," *New York Times*, March 21, 1982.

42. CBS News-New York Times poll conducted March 11–15, 1982.

43. Quoted in "Student Wins War Memorial Contest," *New York Times*, May 7, 1981.

44. Tom Carhart, "Insulting Vietnam Vets," *New York Times*, October 24, 1981.

45. Ibid.

46. Cited in "How to remember Vietnam," *New York Times*, November 11, 1981.

47. Sonja K. Foss, "Ambiguity as Persuasion: The Vietnam Veterans Memorial.," *Communication Quarterly* 34, no. 3 (Summer 1986): 326–340.

48. See Kristin Ann Haas, *Carried to the Wall: American Memory and the Vietnam Veterans Memorial* (Berkeley: University of California Press, 1998).

49. Harry W. Haines, "What Kind of War?" *Critical Studies in Mass Communication* 3, no. 1 (March 1986): 1–20.

50. See, for example, Peter Ehrenhaus, "Silence and Symbolic Expression," *Communication Monographs*, 55, no. 1 (March 1988): 41–57, and Peter Enhrenhaus, "The Vietnam veterans memorial: An Invitation to Argument," *Argumentation & Advocacy*, 25, no. 2 (Fall 1988): 54–64.

51. A. C. Carlson and John E. Hocking, "Strategies of Redemption at the Vietnam Veterans Memorial," *Western Journal of Speech Communication*, 52, no. 3 (Summer 1988): 203–215.

52. See Carole Blair, Marsha Jeppeson, and Enrico Pucci, "Public Memorializing in Postmodernity: The Vietnam Veterans Memorial as Prototype," *Quarterly Journal of Speech*, 77, no. 3 (August 1991): .263–288.

53. M. Beck, "Refighting the Vietnam War," *Newsweek*, October 25, 1982, 30.

54. T. Morgenthau, "Honoring Vietnam Veterans—At Last," *Newsweek*, November 22, 1982, 80–81.

55. Bob Arnebeck, "Monumental Folly," *The Progressive*, July 1982, 46–47.

56. Michael J. Weiss, "Maya Ying Lin's Memorial to the Vietnam War dead Raises Hope—And Anger," *People Weekly*, March 8,1982, 38–39.

57. Arthur C. Danto, "The Vietnam Veterans Memorial" *The Nation*, August 31, 1985, 152–56.

58. John S. Lang, "A Memorial Wall That Healed Our Wounds," *U.S. News & World Report*, November 21, 1983, 68–71.

59. See a discussion of this incident in Donald P. Shaw and Zane E. Finkelstein, "Westmoreland vs. CBS," *Commentary*, August 1984, 31–37.

60. Sally Bodell and Dan Kower, "Anatomy of a Smear: How CBS News Broke the Rules and 'Got' Gen. Westmoreland," *TV Guide*, May 29, 1982, 3–15.

61. *The CBS Benjamin Report*, (Washington, DC: The Media Institute, 1984).

62. Curt Suplee, "Dispatches From the Front: A Blitz of Vietnam Books as the Wounds of War Heal," *Washington Post*, November 13, 1983.

63. An account this can be found in David A. Andelman, "They're Fighting the 'Living-Room War,'" *New York Times*, October 19, 1980).

64. Fox Butterfield, "The New Vietnam Scholarship," *New York Times*, February 13, 1983.

65. Fox Butterfield, "TV Returns to Vietnam to Dissect the War," *New York Times*, October 2, 1983.

66. This figure is cited by the Museum of Broadcast Communications (Chicago).

67. Stanley Karnow, *Vietnam: A History*, New York: Viking Press, 1983.

68. Quoted in Butterfield, "TV Returns to Vietnam to Dissect the War."

69. CBS correspondents Dan Rather and Lesley Stahl are quoted in John Cory, "TV: El Salvador Coverage on the Evening News," *New York Times*, March 22, 1983.

70. Anthony Lewis, "Why Are We in Vietnam?" *New York Times*, March 6, 1983.

71. Howard Baker quoted in "El Salvador and Vietnam," *New York Times*, March 4, 1983.

72. Stephen B. Young, "Salvador Parallels Vietnam; This Time Let's Win," *New York Times*, May 22, 1983.

73. Ronald Steel, "Salvador Isn't Vietnam; Illusions Roll On," *New York Times*, May 22, 1983.

74. John Wheeler, "Shaped by the War in Vietnam," *New York Times*, June 22 1983.

75. Philip Taubman, "Pentagon Seeking a Rise in Advisers in El Salvador to 125," *New York Times*, July 24, 1983.

76. Lindsey Gruson, "Poll Reveals Fear of El Salvador as a New Vietnam," *New York Times*, July 24, 1983.

77. Lesley H. Gelb, "The Boiling Point; White House Puts Central American on a Front Burner," *New York Times*, July 24, 1983.

78. Lydia Chavez, "The Odds in El Salvador," *New York Times Sunday Magazine*, July 24, 1983, p.16.

79. See, for example, Stephen S. McGuirk, "We Have Been Here Before," *New York Times*, November 13, 1983.

Chapter 4

1. "Three Vietnam Veterans Arrested in Burning of a Buddhist Temple," *New York Times*, January 5, 1984.

2. Ibid.

3. Film critics of the time took note of this aspect of the film. See Gary Arnold, "'Blood' All in Vein: Squeezing the Last Drop from Vietnam Movies," *Washington Post*, October 22, 1982.

4. Ibid.

5. David Ansen, "Rebels With a Cause," *Newsweek*, October 25, 1982, 119.

6. Aljean Harmetz, "Autumn at the Movies: Falling Box-Office Receipts," *New York Times*, November 18, 1982.

7. See David L. Sutton and J. Emmett Winn, " 'Do We Get to Win This Time?': POW/MIA Films and the American Monomyth," *Journal of American and Comparative Cultures* 24, nos.1/2 (Spring 2001): 25–33.

8. See Tony Williams, "*Missing in Action*: The Vietnam Construction of the Movie Star," in *From Hanoi to Hollywood: The Vietnam War in American Film*, ed. Linda Dittmar and Gene Michaud (New Brunswick: Rutgers University Press, 1990), 129–144.

9. A useful discussion of ideological aspects of this series is found in G. Marchetti, "Class, Ideology and Commercial Television: An Analysis of *The A Team*," *Journal of Film and Video*, 39, no. 2 (Spring 1987): 19–29.

10. Sally Bedell, "How TV Hit 'The A Team' Was Born," *New York Times*, April 28, 1983. . C22.

11. Elliott Gruner, *Prisoners of Culture: Representing the Vietnam POW* (New Brunswick, NJ: Rutgers University Press, 1993), 18.

12. James Rosenthal, "The Myth of Lost POWs: Real-Life Rambos Have No One to Rescue," *The New Republic*, July 1, 1985, 15–19.

13. Ibid.

14. "U.S. Delegates to Visit Hanoi for MIA Talks," *Boston Globe*, February 19, 1984.

15. "Vietnam Reportedly to Study MIA Cases," *Boston Globe*, April 18, 1984.

16. "Vietnam Returns More Remains," *Boston Globe*, July 18, 1984.

17. "Reagan Says POW Search Goes On," *Boston Globe*, July 21, 1984.

18. Arnold R. Isaacs, *Vietnam Shadows*, 112.

19. Ibid., 113.

20. See H. Bruce Franklin, *M.I.A., or Mythmaking in America*, Rev. ed. (New Brunswick, NJ: Rutgers University Press, 1993).

21. Lawrence L. Altman, "Rare Cancer Seen in 41 Homosexuals," *New York Times*, July 3, 1981.

22. The Vietnam War appeared as a minor issue among the Democratic candidates that year. In March, Gary Hart claimed that Mondale had been slow to call for an end of American troop participation in the Vietnam War as a reason that he did not deserve the Democratic nomination.

23. This appeared in the *NBC Evening News* of January 11, 1984.

24. Carl J. Migdail, "El Salvador Turning Into 'Vietnam West" for U.S.?" *U.S. News and World Report*, February 27, 1984, 29–30.

25. See Bob Schieffer's report as part of the *CBS Evening News* broadcast of June 23, 1984.

26. *Business Week*-Harris, poll conducted July 7–12, 1984.

27. See Peter Jennings's story of this meeting in the *ABC Evening News* broadcast of May 24, 1984.

28. Ronald Reagan, quoted in Lance Morrow, "War and Remembrance: A Bit of Bitterness is Buried Along With an Unknown Soldier," *Time*, June 11, 1984, 29.

29. The cover appeared in *Time*, June 24, 1985.

30. Ronald Reagan, as quoted in Ellen Farley, "The U.S. Has Surrendered: How *Rambo* Is Taking the World by Storm," *Business Week*, August 26, 1985, 109.

31. David Hiltbrand, *"Missing in Action 2—The Beginning," People Weekly*, March 25, 1985, 41.

32. This is noted in Farley, "The U.S. Has Surrendered: How *Rambo* Is Taking the World by Storm," 109.

33. Jack Kroll, "A One-Man Army," *Newsweek*, May 27, 1985, 74.

34. Andrew Kopkind, *"Rambo: First Blood, Part II," The Nation*, June 22, 1985, 776–77.

35. Vincent Canby, "Screen: Sylvester Stallone Returns as Rambo," *New York Times*, May 22, 1985.

36. This promotional effort is described in Farley, "The U.S. Has Surrendered: How *Rambo* Is Taking the World by Storm," 109.

37. Kopkind, *"Rambo: First Blood, Part II,"* 240.

38. John Hellmann suggests the violent revenge fantasy of *Rambo* may have been particularly cathartic for audiences who were steeped in Kennedy-era political philosophy. See Hellmann, "Rambo's Vietnam and Kennedy's New Frontier, 140–152.

39. Among those to phrase it this way was *New York Times* critic Vincent Canby. See Canby, "Screen: Sylvester Stallone Returns as Rambo."

40. Ibid.

41. Scot Haller, *"Rambo: First Blood Part II," People Weekly*, June 2, 1985, 12.

42. Theodore Draper. *A Very Thin Line: The Iran-Contra Affairs*. (New York: Hill and Wang, 1991).

43. Ibid., 13.

44. Ibid., 13–14.

45. See Lou Cannon, *President Reagan: The Role of a Lifetime*, 2d ed., (New York: Public Affairs, 2000), 566.

46. This point, as well as a very informative analysis of the political debate on the issue can be found in Joshua Muravchik, "The Nicaraguan Debate," *Journal of Foreign Affairs*, 65, no. 2 (Winter 1986/87), 366–383.

47. Ibid., 374.

48. Thomas O'Neill, quoted in Ibid., 375.

49. Julia Preston, "Captured American Put On Display by Nicaragua; Crash Survivor, Victim Described as U.S. Advisers," *The Washington Post*, October 8, 1986.

50. This claim was discussed in David Ignatius, "The Contrapreneurs: Skirting Congress and the Law for Years," *The Washington Post*, December 7, 1986.

51. Charles Krauthammer, "Don't Punish the Country," *Washington Post*, November 26, 1986.

52. At this time, the Vietnam War's deep influence in the military was not confined to Oliver North. Instead, it was a widespread phenomenon within the Pentagon.

53. Oliver North, quoted Draper. *A Very Thin Line: The Iran-Contra Affairs*, 56–7.

54. Oliver North, quoted in Draper. *A Very Thin Line: The Iran-Contra Affairs*, 58.

55. Olga Karpushina, "The Military Body: Film Representations of the Chechen and Vietnam Wars," *Studies in Slavic Cultures* 3 (2002): 34.

56. Ibid., 34.

57. Jeremy M. Devine, *Vietnam at 24 Frames a Second* (Austin: University of Texas Press, 1995), 251–52.

58. Vincent Canby, "The Vietnam War in Stone's *Platoon*," *New York Times*, December19, 1986.

59. David Ansen and Peter McAlevey, "A Ferocious Vietnam Elegy," *Newsweek*, January 5, 1987, 57.

60. *"Platoon:* Vietnam As It Really Was," *Time*, January 26, 1987, 56.

61. William M. Welch, "Vietnam Movie, *Platoon*, Draws Criticism, Praise From Vets, *Washington Dateline*,(Associated Press wire report), January 16, 1987.

62. Ibid.

63. Phil McCombs, "Veterans, Reliving the Pain," *The Washington Post*, January 16, 1987.

64. For more on this point, see Marita Sturken, *Tangled Memories: The Vietnam War, the AIDS Epidemic, and the Politics of Remembering* (Berkeley: University of California Press, 1997), 96–111.

65. Two other films from this period worth mentioning were *Good Morning, Vietnam*, a comedic film in which Robin Williams portrays an Army radio disk jockey in Saigon, and the more serious, but only moderately successful, *Gardens of Stone*, a film with a military theme

from director Francis Ford Coppola that takes place within the United States in 1968.

66. See, for example, Susan White, "Male Bonding, Hollywood Orientalism, and the Repression of the Feminine in Kubrick's *Full Metal Jacket*" in *Inventing Vietnam: The War in Film and Television*, ed. Michael Anderegg (Philadelphia: Temple University Press, 1991), 204–230.

Chapter 5

1. Bob Dole, quoted in Bill Peterson, "Quayle's Schedule Cut Short; Senator Leaves Bush in Midwest to Return Here for Coaching," *Washington Post*, August 21, 1988.

2. George H.W. Bush quoted in Stewart Fleming, "Poll Puts Bush in Front Despite Controversy Over Quayle," *Financial Times of London*, August 22, 1988.

3. "Quayle's Schedule Cut Short; Senator Leaves Bush in Midwest to Return Here for Coaching," *Washington Post*, August 22, 1988.

4. "Veterans, resisters challenge Quayle," *Boston Globe*, September 17, 1988.

5. "Political Notebook: Veterans, Resisters Challenge Quayle," *Boston Globe*, September 17, 1988.

6. Ibid.

7. Ibid.

8. George H.W. Bush, quoted in Peter Osterlund "Bush Ship Surges, But It Still Drags Quayle Anchor," *Christian Science Monitor*, August 25, 1988.

9. Phil Gailey, "Quayle defenders point finger at the press," *St. Petersburg Times*, August 23, 1988.

10. Ibid.

11. This document is quoted in William E. Schmidt, "Quayle Receives Standing Ovation," *New York Times*, August 23, 1988.

12. Ibid.

13. I. Brody, " 'Chicken-Hawk' Ambushes the Republican Campaign," *Sunday Mail*, August 28, 1988.

14. Unnamed source, quoted in Ibid.

15. The concept of "Viet guilt" was raised, for example, in E.J. Dionne, Jr., "Reopening an Old Wound," *New York Times*, August 23, 1988.

16. Quoted in Osterlund, "Bush Ship Surges, But It Still Drags Quayle Anchor."

17. Ibid.

18. Cited in Peter Osterlund, "Bush Ship Surges, But It Still Drags Quayle Anchor," *Christian Science Monitor*, August 25, 1988.

19. George H.W. Bush, quoted in Brody, " 'Chicken-Hawk' Ambushes the Republican Campaign."

20. The nature of the younger Bush's career

in the Texas Air National Guard was an issue in the 2004 presidential campaign. See chapter 7.

21. Evidence of the dissonance that this created had been depicted at times on screen, as, for example, in *Apocalpse Now*. One key scene of that film involved a young woman Viet Cong who tossed an explosive into an American helicopter with lethal results. In the film, the response of the Americans is swift, vengeful and results in the use of overwhelming firepower against the young woman. Indeed, Americans seemed never to be able to completely understand or accept this non-traditional female role in the war itself, and depictions frequently show that discomfort.

22. The figures are cited in material compiled by the Vietnam Women's Memorial Foundation (previously known as the Vietnam Women's Memorial Project), Washington, D.C.

23. The founder of the Vietnam Women's Memorial Project outlines the motivations behind seeking a women's monument in Diane Carlson Evans, "Moving a Vision: The Vietnam Women's Memorial" [report] (Washington, D.C.: Vietnam Women's Memorial Foundation, n.d. .)

24. John J. O'Connor, "TV Weekend; The Very Small, Day-to-Day Realities of War," *New York Times*, July 22, 1988.

25. Tom Shales, "*China Beach*; Going Far Beyond Vietnam," *Washington Post*, September 29, 1990.

26. This quotation appears in Elizabeth Norman, "Nurses in Vietnam: Beyond TV's Stereotypes," *New York Times*, May 28, 1989.

27. Ibid.

28. Delany's comments, which originally appeared in *USA Today*, November 10, 1989 are reproduced and cited in "Loss of Spirit," *Nam Vet Newsletter*, January 7, 1990, 68.

29. See Ari L. Goldman, "Ron Kovic Today: Warrior at Peace," *New York Times*, December 17, 1989.

30. Marc Cooper, "Oliver Stone Interview," *Playboy*, February 1988, 59.

31. Vincent Canby, "How an All-American Boy Went to War and Lost His Faith," *New York Times*, December 20, 1989.

32. Vincent Canby, "Film View: At Close Range, the Human Face of War," *New York Times*, January 21, 1990.

33. Bernard E. Trainor, "Washington Talk: Policy; Vietnam Experience Has Made Joint Chiefs Cautious About Using Military Force," *New York Times*, August 17, 1989.

34. David Hoffman and Bob Woodward, " 'It Will Only Get Worse,' Bush Told Aides; Attacks on U.S. Servicemen Were Key factor in Decision," *Washington Post*, December 21, 1989.

35. Diego Ribadeneira, "For Noriega, A Ring

Of Sound and US Fury Loud Music, Tanks Lay Siege To Tony Area," *Boston Globe,* December 30, 1989.

36. Ibid.

37. This poll is discussed in Paul Taylor, "Poll Finds Americans Back U.S. Response, But Warily," *Washington Post,* August 10, 1990.

38. James A. Baker III, quoted in Rick Atkinson and David Hoffman, "Suddenly, a Long, Costly Crisis Looms," *Washington Post,* August 12, 1990.

39. Atkinson and Hoffman, "Suddenly, a Long, Costly Crisis Looms."

40. Todd S. Purdum. *A Time of Our Choosing: America's War with Iraq* (New York: Times Books, 2003), 14.

41. Bill Lambert, "Bush Summons Reserves," *St. Louis Post-Dispatch,* August 23, 1990.

42. Ibid.

43. "Draft Revival Ruled Out," *New York Times,* August 29, 1990.

44. Poll data cited in Lance Morrow, "A New Test of Resolve," *Time,* September 3, 1990, 30–33.

45. Ibid., 30.

46. J. Alter, "The Necessity of Dissent," *Newsweek* September 3, 1990, 40.

47. Ibid.

48. John Murtha, quoted in R.W. Apple, Jr., "Confrontation in the Gulf: Lawmakers Versed in Vietnam," *New York Times,* December 16, 1990.

49. John McCain, quoted in Ibid.

50. Stephen Kurkjian, "Bush Sets Gulf Funds System; Iraqi Warns of a New Vietnam; Crisis in the Middle East," *Boston Globe,* September 26, 1990.

51. See, for example, C. Dickey, "Looking the West 'Right in the Eye,'" *Newsweek,* December 10, 1990, 38.

52. Andy Dabilis, "10,000 March to Prevent Gulf War," *Boston Globe,* December 2, 1990, 26.

53. These and other instances are cited in Ed Siegel, "TV Reflects Rising Fears of a Gulf War," *Boston Globe,* November 20, 1990.

54. Molly Sinclair, "Visitors to Wall Find Specter of New War; Veterans at the Vietnam Memorial Express Mixed Views, But Concern Is Universal," *Washington Post,* November 11, 1990).

55. Ibid.

56. Ibid.

57. Ibid.

58. Ibid.

59. George H.W. Bush, quoted in "Crisis at a Glance," *Boston Globe,* November 16, 1990.

60. This is included in an excellent discussion of this episode that appears in Isaacs, *Vietnam Shadows.* .

61. H. Norman Schwarzkopf, quoted in "Patrick E. Taylor, "Mideast Tension: Vietnam and Gulf Zone: Real Contrasts," *New York Times,* December 1, 1990.

Chapter 6

1. Jim Garrison, *On the Trail of the Assassins: My Investigation and Prosecution of the Murder of President Kennedy,* (New York: Sheridan Square Press, 1988).

2. Jim Marrs, *Crossfire: The Plot That Killed Kennedy,* (New York: Carroll & Graf Publishers (November, 1990

3. "The Week," *National Review,* June 24, 1991, 10–12.

4. John F. Kennedy, quoted in Ronald Steel, "Mr. Smith Goes to the Twilight Zone," *The New Republic* (February 3, 1992), 30.

5. John F. Kennedy, quoted in Ronald Steel, "Mr. Smith Goes to the Twilight Zone," *The New Republic,* February 3, 1992, 30.

6. Quoted in Peter Travers, "Oh What a Tangled Web," *Rolling Stone,* January 23, 1992.

7. Ibid.

8. John Simon, "Reshooting the President," *National Review,* March 2, 1992, 54–57.

9. Bruce Loebs, "Kennedy, Vietnam, and Oliver Stone's Big Lie," *USA Today Magazine,* 121, no. 2576, May 1993, 88–92.

10. Ibid.

11. Ibid.

12. Lance Morrow, "When Artists Distort History," *Time,* December 23, 1991, 84.

13. Ibid.

14. Quoted in Travers, "Oh What a Tangled Web."

15. Oliver Stone, quoted in Gregg Kilday, "Oliver Stoned," *Entertainment Weekly,* January 14, 1994, 28–33.

16. An account of these events, with comments from Kerrey and Harkins, appeared in a wire report, Jill Lawrence, "Clinton Defends Self on Vietnam Draft Issue," Political News, The Associated Press, February 6, 1992. [Archived in the Lexis-Nexis database.]

17. Ibid.

18. Bob Hohler, "N.H. Families Reexamine Front-runner," *Boston Globe,* February 9, 1992.

19. Remarks of Bob Neuman, quoted in "Bruising Blow: Letter Shows Clinton Glad to Avoid Draft," *The Record* [Kitchener-Waterloo, Ontario, February 13, 1992.

20. These and other quotations from Clinton's letter appear in a transcription printed in "A Letter by Clinton on His Draft Deferment," *New York Times,* February 13, 1992.

21. R.W. Apple, Jr., "Clinton and the Draft Issue: Vietnam Era Revisited," *New York Times,* February 14, 1992.

22. Ibid.

23. David E. Rosenbaum, "The Draft: Clinton Could Have Known Draft Was Unlikely for Him," *The New York Times,* February 14, 1992.

24. Michael Kelly, "The Democrats: Clinton readies Answer to Bush on Draft Issue," *New York Times,* September 15, 1992.

25. Lynn Martin, quoted in Walter R. Mears, "Now It's the GOP Trying to Use the Draft Issue," Political News, The Associated Press, August 23, 1992. [Archived in the Lexis-Nexis database.]

26. Ibid.

27. William Jefferson Clinton, quoted in B. Drummond Ayres, Jr., "Issues: Military Record; Clinton Confronts Draft Record in a Frank Address to veterans," *New York Times,* August 26, 1992.

28. Ibid.

29. Robin Toner, "Political Memo: G.O.P. Looks at Clinton Draft Record and Spies Willie Horton," *New York Times,* September 10, 1992.

30. Bob Kerrey, quoted in Steve Gerstel, "Kerrey to Bush: Call Off the Dogs on Clinton Draft Issue," United Press International, September 10, 1992. [Archived in the Lexis-Nexis database.]

31. Dan Quayle, quoted in "The 1992 Campaign: In Their Own Words," *New York Times,* September 20, 1992.

32. An account of this appearance appears in Andrew Rosenthal, "The Republicans: Bush Renews His Attacks About Vietnam and Draft," *New York Times,* October 14, 1992.

33. This appears in Ibid.

34. See, for example, "Report: U.S. Embassies Told to Search Files for Clinton Material," The Associated Press, October 13, 1992. [Archived in the Lexis-Nexis database.]

35. George H.W. Bush, quoted in John King, "Democrats Warn of Overconfidence; Bush Hits Draft Anew," Associated Press, October 17, 1992. [Archived in the Lexis-Nexis database.]

36. "George Bush's Last Chance on Vietnam," *New York Times,* December 18, 1992.

37. Ibid.

38. Steven A. Holmes, "Embargo Is Eased After Hanoi's Help on M.I.A.'s," *New York Times,* December 15, 1992.

39. John F. Kerry, quoted in Ana Puga, "Kerry Presses for Lifting Trade Sanctions Against Vietnam," *New York Times,* April 1, 1993.

40. Bob Smith, quoted in Ibid.

41. See "The Pentagon's New Policy Guidelines on Homosexuals in the Military", *New York Times,* July 20, 1993.

42. Elaine Sciolino, "U.S. to Send General to Vietnam, Hinting a Thaw," *New York Times,* April 10, 1993.

43. Comments of John F. Kerry and Bob Smith quoted in H.D.S. Greenway, "Lifting the Vietnam Embargo Is the Best Way to Unlock POW Secrets," *Boston Globe,* June 17, 1993.

44. "Now Shake Hands with Vietnam," *New York Times,* September 17, 1993.

45. This was reported in many sources, as, for example, in "Michael Kranish and Mary Curtis, "Aspin Quits as Defense Secretary, Says Reasons Are Personal," *Boston Globe,* December 16, 1993.

46. "The Somali Trap," *Boston Globe,* September 11, 1993.

47. Anthony Flint, "U.S. Military Intervention at a Crossroads," *Boston Globe,* October 5, 1993.

48. Burton Yale Pines, quoted in Anthony Flint, "U.S. Military Intervention at a Crossroads," *Boston Globe,* October 5, 1993.

49. William Jefferson Clinton, quoted in John M. Broder, "Clinton Orders 5,300 Troops to Somalia; Vows End in 6 Months," *Los Angeles Times,* October, 8, 1993.

50. Curtis Wilkie, "Beirut Revisited: Somalia Is Being Compared to the 'Quagmire' in Vietnam, But Lebanon Is the More Precise Analogy," *Boston Globe,* 10 October 1993, p. 79.

51. Roger Ebert, "Heaven and Earth," *Chicago Sun-Times,* December 24, 1993.

52. Desson Howe, "Heaven and Earth," *Washington Post,* December 24, 1993.

53. "HoHoHum," *Entertainment Weekly,* January 21, 1994.

54. Randolph Ryan, "Ground Troops for Bosnia," *Boston Globe,* May 8, 1993.

55. This was the view of "many analysts," according to Pamela Constable, "US Seeks Further Talks on Bosnia; Pessimism Voiced on Outside Action," *Boston Globe,* May 18, 1993.

56. Ellen Goodman, "Bosnia: It's Not About repeating History; It's About Making It," *Boston Globe,* May 16, 1993.

57. Ibid.

58. Mar Curtius, "The War Zone," *Boston Globe Magazine,* April 10, 1994, 14.

59. Bob Smith, quoted in Elaine Sciolino, "Clinton Reported to be Ready to End Vietnam Embargo," *New York Times,* February 2, 1994.

60. John F. Kerry, John McCain and Bob Smith, respectively, quoted in Ibid.

61. William Jefferson Clinton, quoted in "Clinton Lifts Vietnam Trade Embargo," United Press International, February 3, 1994. [Archived in Lexis-Nexis database.]

62. See Philip Shenon, "Vietnam Welcomes U.S. Decision on Embargo," *New York Times,* February 5, 1994.

63. See Ibid.

64. Jim Verniere, "Film View: Hanks Is On Target, But Dumbed Down," *Boston Herald,* July 6, 1994.

65. David Sterritt, "The Message Behind the Oscar Nominations," *Christian Science Monitor*, February 17, 1995.

66. Ibid.

67. Ralph Novak, *"The Walking Dead" People Weekly*, March 13, 1995, 17–18.

68. Wallace Terry, ed., *Bloods: An Oral History of the Vietnam War*, (New York: Random, 1984).

69. For a discussion of a similar incident that was originally described in the book *Bloods*, and also of similarities between the written account and the episode in *Dead Presidents*, see Katherine Kinney, *Friendly Fire: American Images of the Vietnam War*, (New York: Oxford University Press, 2000), 101–103, 210.

70. David Sterritt, "A Marine Returns from 'Nam and Goes Back to the 'Hood," *Christian Science Monitor*, October 13, 1995.

71. William Jefferson Clinton quoted in Alison Mitchell, "Opening to Vietnam: The Overview; U.S. Grants Vietnam Full Ties; Time for Healing, Clinton Says," *New York Times*, July 12, 1995.

72. Bob Dole, quoted in Ibid.

73. Pete Peterson, quoted in "U.S. Envoy Arrives in Vietnam, The First Since the Fall of Saigon," *New York Times*, May 10, 1997.

74. Ed Bark, *"A Bright Shining Lie,"* *Dallas Morning News*, May 27, 1998.

75. Eric Schmidtt, "House Approves Renewing Trade Benefits for Vietnam," *New York Times*, August 4, 1999.

76. Douglas K. Bereuter quoted in Ibid.

77. William Jefferson Clinton, quoted in Joseph Kahn, "Vietnam and the U.S. Sign Pact Aimed at Promoting Trade," *New York Times*, July 14, 2000.

78. See Marcella Bombardieri, "Vietnam Visit Hits Nerve, Citing Irony, Many Are Angry at Clinton's Gesture," *Boston Globe*, November 17, 2000.

79. Ibid.

80. Ibid.

Chapter 7

1. This is included as background in Bryan Bender and Michael Kranish, "Vietnam Swift Boat Skipper Comes to Kerry's Defense," *Boston Sunday Globe*, August 22, 2004.

2. The race also included third-party candidate Ralph Nader.

3. Mike Clark, *"Pearl Harbor* Sputters — Until the Japanese Show Up," *USA Today*, June 7, 2001.

4. A.O. Scott, "Film Review: A Porous Underbelly in a Gritty Boot Camp," *New York Times*, October 6, 2000.

5. Edward Guthman, "Boot Camp Misery in Vietnam Era; Rebel Recruit Defends His Soul," *San Francisco Chronicle*, February 9, 2001.

6. Ibid.

7. A.O. Scott, "Film Review: A Porous Underbelly in a Gritty Boot Camp."

8. "Did the Media Force Kerrey's Admission?" *CNN Reliable Sources*, (Television broadcast), April 28, 2001. [Story archived at http://transcripts.cnn.com]

9. Gregory L. Vistica, "One Awful Night in Thanh Phong," *New York Times*, April 25, 2001.

10. Bob Kerrey, quoted in Ibid.

11. Ibid.

12. Ibid.

13. "Kerry Raid in Question," [Press release from CBS News], April 30, 2004.

14. Gerhard Klann, quoted in Ibid.

15. Ibid.

16. News accounts do not agree on the naming of this war. It has often been called the "War on Terrorism," which is the conventional that this chapter adopts. At other times, it has been called the "War on Terror."

17. Jonathan Alter, "The Real Echoes From Vietnam," *Newsweek*, April 14, 2003, 41.

18. John Pilger, "Bush's Vietnam: Once More, We Hear That America Is Being 'Sucked Into a Quagmire,'" *New Statesman*, June 23, 2003, 20–21.

19. John O'Sullivan, "No Quagmire: How to Avoid One This Time," *National Review*, (September 1, 2003), 6–14.

20. Victor Davis Hanson, "Then and Now: There Are Great Differences Between Vietnam and Iraq, and There Are Certain Similarities, and All Must Be Weighed," *National Review*, December 8, 2003, 33.

21. Colman McCarthy, "Chasing Phantoms in Iraq: Today's War on Terror Parallels Failed War on Communism in Vietnam," *National Catholic Reporter*, January 30, 2004, 18.

22. Michael Barone, "The Long shadow of Vietnam," *U.S. News & World Report*, April 12, 2004), 31.

23. Margaret A. McGurk, *"Black Hawk* Gets Down to Detail: High-Tech Tools Bring Horror of Tragic 1993 Somalian Raid Home," *Cincinnati Enquirer*, January 18, 2002.

24. Harold G. Moore and Joseph L. Galloway, *We Were Soldiers Once ... And Young — Ia Drang: The Battle That Changed the War in Vietnam*, (New York: Random, 1992).

25. A brief account of the battle and its significance in the overall war can be found in Stanley Karnow, *Vietnam: A History*, Revised ed., (New York: Penguin Books, 1991), 493–494.

26. This is discussed in Roger Ebert, *"We Were Soldiers,"* *Chicago Sun-Times*, March 1, 2002.

27. David Sterritt, "A Fake Picture of War's Stark Reality," *Christian Science Monitor,* March 1, 2002.

28. A. O. Scott, "Early in the Vietnam War, on Ill-Defined Mission," *New York Times,* March 1, 2002.

29. Peter Travers, "*We Were Soldiers,*" *Rolling Stone,* March 28, 2002.

30. Mick LaSalle, "They Were Heroes; 'We Were Soldiers' Shows the Full Horror of Vietnam and the Full Humanity of Those Who Fought It," *San Francisco Chronicle,* March 1, 2002.

31. Mick LaSalle, "Morris Creates Compelling Story in McNamara Portrait," *San Francisco Chronicle,* January 23, 2004.

32. Mark Thompson and James Carney, "An Absence in Alabama: As Bush's Military Service Re-Emerges as an Issue, Here Is What We Know—and Don't Know," *Time,* February 16, 2004, 36.

33. Ibid.

34. Byron York, "Bush and the National Guard: Case Closed: The Facts About the President's Service," *National Review,* March 8, 2004, 33.

35. Mark Thompson, James Carney and Douglas Waller, "An Absence in Alabama: As Bush's Military Service Re-emerges as an Issue, Here Is What We Know—And What We Don't," *Time,* February 16, 2004, 33.

36. Ibid.

37. McClellan is quoted in Carl Cameron, Teri Schultz and Sharon Kehnemui, "White House Impatient with Bush Service Issue," *FOX News,* February 12, 2004. [Story archived at *http://www.foxnews.com*]

38. See, for example, "Bush Orders Release of Military Records," *FOX News,* February 13, 2004. [Story archived at *http://www.foxnews.com*]

39. Byron York, "Bush and the National Guard: Case Closed: The Facts About the President's Service," *National Review,* March 8, 2004, 33.

40. Beth Lester, "Gaps Remain in Bush Guard Service," *CBS News* (May 4, 2004). [Story archived at http:www.cbsnews.com]

41. Cullen Murphy, "Knock It Off: The Art of the Unreal," *Atlantic Monthly,* December 2004, 187–88.

42. See, for example, reports from several analysts cited in Michael Dobbs and Mike Allen, "Some Question Authenticity of Papers on Bush," *Washington Post,* September 10, 2004.

43. "Marion Carr Knox, Secretary of Lt. Col. Jerry Killian, to Appear on '60 Minutes' Tonight in First Television Interview; CBS News Affirms Its Intention to Continue to Report All Aspects of the Story," [Press release from CBS News], September 15, 2004.

44. Ibid.

45. Carl Cameron, Major Garrett and Liza Porteous, "Kerry Aid Talked to Bush Guard Docs Figure," *FOX News,* September 22, 2004. [Story archived at *http://www.foxnews.com*]

46. Spokesperson John Hastert is quoted in Pamela McClintock and Susan Crabtree, "CBS Stands by Bush Story as GOP Criticism Mounts," *Daily Variety,* September 16, 2004, 2.

47. An unnamed CBS source is quoted in Ibid.

48. Dan Rather, "Statement on Memos," [Press release from CBS News], September 20, 2004.

49. "CBS Ousts Four for Roles in Bush Guard Story," The Associated Press, January 10, 2005. [Archived in Lexis-Nexis database.]

50. "CBS Ousts Four Over Controversy," *CNN News,* January 11, 2005. [Story archived at http://cnn.com]

51. John E. O'Neill and Jerome R. Corsi, *Unfit for Command: Swift Boat Veterans Speak Out Against John Kerry,* (Washington, D.C.: Regnery Publishing, 2004).

52. Michael Karnish, "John Kerry: Candidate in the Making: Part 3: With Anti-War Role, High Visibility," *Boston Globe,* June 16, 2003.

53. Bryan Bender and Michael Kranish, "Vietnam Swift Boat Skipper Comes to Kerry's Defense," *Boston Sunday Globe,* August 22, 2004.

54. Ibid.

55. Douglas Brinkley, *Tour of Duty: John Kerry and the Vietnam War,* (New York: William Morrow, 2004) See also a discussion of this aspect of the campaign in Eleanor Clift, "The Vets Attack," *Newsweek,* November 15, 2004, 90–104.

56. Bush campaign spokesperson Steve Schmidt is quoted in Bender and Kranish, "Vietnam Swift Boat Skipper Comes to Kerry's Defense."

57. Quoted in Wendy Melillo, "Bush Attorney Quits Amid Ad Flap," *Adweek Online,* August 25, 2004.

58. Bender and Kranish, "Vietnam Swift Boat Skipper Comes to Kerry's Defense."

59. Ibid.

60. "Matter of Fact," *The New Republic,* September 6, 2004, 9.

61. Ibid.

62. John Dempsey and Susan Crabtree, "Sinclair to Air Anti-Kerry Doc; Dems Irked," *Daily Variety,* October 12, 2004.

63. Sherwood is quoted in Alessandra Stanley, "An Outpouring of Pain, Channeled Via Politics," *New York Times,* October 21, 2004.

64. "The Best & Worst Managers of 2004: David Smith, Sinclair Broadcast Group," *Businessweek Online,* January 10, 2005.

65. Ibid.

66. Roger Ebert, "Fahrenheit 9/11," *Chicago Sun-Times,* June 24, 2004.

67. Richard Cohen, "The Movie Is So Bad It Could Help Bush," *New York Daily News,* July 1, 2004.

68. See "Poll: USA is losing patience on Iraq," *USA Today,* June 12, 2005.

69. See "Poll: Bush approval ratings hit lowest point of tenure," *USA Today,* July 29, 2005.

70. "Hagel: Iraq growing more like Vietnam," *CNN News,* August 18, 2005. [Story archived at http://cnn.com]

71. Ibid.

72. Phan Van Khai, quoted in Ellen Nakashima, "Vietnam, U.S. to Improve Intelligence, Military Ties," *Washington Post,* June 17, 2005.

73. "Vietnamese Premier Visits Oval Office," *Washington Times,* June 22, 2005.

74. Ibid.

75. See Robert Templer, *Shadows and Wind: A View of Modern Vietnam* (New York: Penguin Books, 1998).

Chapter 8

1. For World War II, the U.S. Department of Defense lists 292,131 combat deaths and 115,185 other fatalities. World War I American military deaths are listed as 53,513 combat and 63,195 other. It lists 47,393 combat deaths and 10,800 other deaths for the Vietnam War.

2. During this time, it was only male Vietnam veteran characters who were emphasized in such productions.

Bibliography

Books, Journals, Periodicals

Addington, Larry H. *America's War in Vietnam: A Short Narrative History*. Bloomington: Indiana University Press, 2000.

Alter, J. "The Necessity of Dissent." *Newsweek*. September 3, 1990, 40.

Alter, Jonathan. "The Real Echoes From Vietnam." *Newsweek*. April 14, 2003, 41.

American Institute for Economic Research. "More Inflation in Our Future, Mr. Greenspan?" *Research Reports* 68, no. 14 (23 July 2001): 78.

Anderegg, Michael, ed. *Inventing Vietnam: The War in Film and Television*. Philadelphia: Temple University Press, 1991.

Ansen, David and Peter McAlevey. "A Ferocious Vietnam Elegy." *Newsweek*. January 5, 1987, 57.

Ansen, David. "Rebels With a Cause." *Newsweek*. October 25, 1982: 119.

Arnebeck, Bob. "Monumental Folly." *The Progressive*, July 1982. 46–47.

Barone, Michael. "The long shadow of Vietnam." *U.S. News & World Report*. April 12, 2004, 31.

Beck, M. "Refighting the Vietnam War." *Newsweek*, October 25, 1982. 30.

Berg, Rick. "Losing Vietnam: Covering the War in an Age of Technology." In *From Hanoi to Hollywood: The Vietnam War in American Film*, edited by Linda Dittmar and Gene Michaud, 41–68. New Brunswick: Rutgers University Press, 1990.

"The Best & Worst Managers of 2004: David Smith, Sinclair Broadcast Group." *Businessweek Online*. January 10, 2005.

Blair, Carole, Marsha Jeppeson, and Enrico Pucci. "Public Memorializing in Postmodernity: The Vietnam Veterans Memorial as Prototype." *Quarterly Journal of Speech*, 77, no. 3 (August 1991): 263–288.

Bodell, Sally and Dan Kower. "Anatomy of a Smear: How CBS News Broke the Rules and 'Got' Gen. Westmoreland." *TV Guide*. May 29, 1982, 3–15.

Brinkley, Douglas. *Tour of Duty: John Kerry and the Vietnam War*. New York: William Morrow, 2004.

Broyles, Willism. "Vietnam: A Television History," *Newsweek*, October 10, 1983, 91–2.

Cannon, James. *Time and Chance: Gerald R. Ford's Appointment with History*. New York: HarperCollins, 1994.

Cannon, Lou. *President Reagan: The Role of a Lifetime.*, 2d ed. New York: Public Affairs, 2000.

Carlson, A. C. and John E. Hocking. "Strategies of Redemption at the Vietnam Veterans Memorial." *Western Journal of Speech Communication,* 52, no. 3 (Summer 1988): 203–215.

Carroll, Peter N. *It Seemed Like Nothing Happened: America in the 1970s.* New Brunswick: Rutgers University Press, 2000.

Carter, Jimmy. *Keeping Faith: Memoirs of a President.* New York: Bantam, 1982.

CBS Benjamin Report. Washington, D.C.: The Media Institute, 1984.

Clift, Eleanor. "The Vets Attack." *Newsweek.* November 15, 2004, 90–104.

Clinton, Hillary Rodham. *Living History.* New York: Simon & Schuster, 2003.

CNN Reliable Sources (television broadcast), April 28, 2001.

Cook, David A. *A History of Narrative Film.* 3rd ed. New York: W. W. Norton, 1996.

Cooper, Marc. "Oliver Stone Interview." *Playboy,* February 1988, 58–9, 112.

Danto, Arthur C. "The Vietnam Veterans Memorial." *The Nation.* August 31, 1985, 152–6.

Devine, Jeremy M. *Vietnam at 24 Frames a Second.* Austin: University of Texas Press, 1995.

Dickey, C. "Looking the West 'Right in the Eye.'" *Newsweek.* December 10, 1990, 38.

Dittmar, Linda and Gene Michaud, eds. *From Hanoi to Hollywood: The Vietnam War in American Film.* New Brunswick: Rutgers University Press, 1990

Draper, Theodore. *A Very Thin Line: The Iran-Contra Affairs.* New York: Hill and Wang, 1991.

Edelman, Murray *The Symbolic Uses of Politics.* Urbana: University of Illinois Press, 1964.

Edelman, Murray. *Constructing the Political Spectacle.* Chicago: University of Chicago Press, 1988.

Ehrenhaus, Peter. "Silence and Symbolic Expression." *Communication Monographs,* 55, no. 1 (March 1988):41–57

Ehrenhaus, Peter. "The Vietnam Veterans Memorial: An Invitation to Argument." *Argumentation & Advocacy,* 25, no. 2 (Fall 1988): 54–64.

Emery, Fred. *Watergate: the Corruption of American Politics and the Fall of Richard Nixon.* New York: Times Books, 1994.

Entman, Robert M. *Projections of Power.* Chicago: University of Chicago Press, 2003.

Farley, Ellen. "The U.S. Has Surrendered: How *Rambo* Is Taking the World by Storm." *Business Week.* August 26, 1985, 109.

Ford, Gerald R. *A Time to Heal.* New York: Harper and Row, 1979.

Foss, Sonja K. "Ambiguity as Persuasion: The Vietnam Veterans Memorial." *Communication Quarterly* 34, no. 3 (Summer 1986): 326–340.

Franklin, H. Bruce, *M.I.A., or Mythmaking in America.* Revised ed. New Brunswick, NJ: Rutgers University Press, 1993.

Fuchs, Cynthia J. "'All the Animals Come Out at Night': Vietnam Meets *Noir* in *Taxi Driver.*" In *Inventing Vietnam: The War in Film and Television, edited by* Michael Anderegg, 33–55. Philadelphia: Temple University Press, 1991.

Gamson, William A. and Andre Modigliani. "The Changing Culture of Affirmative Action." In *Research in Political Sociology,* 3, edited by Richard G. Braungart and Margaret M. Braungart, 137–177. Greenwich, CT: JAI Press, 1987.

Garrison, Jim. *On the Trail of the Assassins: My Investigation and Prosecution of the Murder of President Kennedy.* New York: Sheridan Square Press,1988.

Gaylyn and David Desser. "Never Having to Say You're Sorry: *Rambo*'s Rewriting of the Vietnam War." In *From Hanoi to Hollywood: The Vietnam War in American Film*, edited by Linda Dittmar and Gene Michaud, 101–112. New Brunswick: Rutgers University Press, 1990.

Gerbner, G., L. Gross, M. Morgan, and N. Signorielli. "Growing Up with Television: The Cultivation Perspective." In *Media Effects: Advances in Theory and Research*, edited by J. Bryant and D. Zillman, 17–41. Hillsdale, NJ: Lawrence Erlbaum Associates, 1994.

Goffman, Erving. *Frame Analysis: An Essay on the Organization of Experience.* Boston: Northeastern University Press, 1974.

Gruner, Elliott. *Prisoners of Culture: Representing the Vietnam POW.* New Brunswick, NJ: Rutgers University Press, 1993.

Haas, Kristin Ann. *Carried to the Wall: American memory and the Vietnam Veterans Memorial.* Berkeley, CA: University of California Press, 1998.

Haines, Harry W. "What Kind of War?" *Critical Studies in Mass Communication* 3, no.1 (March 1986): 1–20.

Haller, Scot. *"Rambo: First Blood Part II," People Weekly.* June 2, 1985, 12.

Hellman, John. "Vietnam and the Hollywood Genre Film: Inversions of American Mythology in *The Deer Hunter* and *Apocalypse Now*." *American Quarterly*, 34 (1982): 418–39.

Hellmann, John. "Rambo's Vietnam and Kennedy's New Frontier." In *Inventing Vietnam: The War in Film and Television, edited by* Michael Anderegg, 140–152. Philadelphia: Temple University Press, 1991.

Hiltbrand, David. *"Missing in Action 2—* The Beginning." *People Weekly.* March 25, 1985, 41.

Hunt, Andrew. *The Turning: A History of Vietnam Veterans Against the War.* New York: New York University Press, 1999.

Isaacs, Arnold R. *Vietnam Shadows: The War, Its Ghosts, and Its Legacy.* Baltimore: Johns Hopkins University Press, 1997.

Iyengar, S. *Is Anyone Responsible? How Television Frames Political News.* Chicago: University of Chicago Press, 1991.

Johnson, H. *Divided We Fall: Gambling with History in the Nineties.* New York: Norton, 1994.

Kaagan, Larry. "Assertive America." *Foreign Affairs*, 59, no. 3 (1980). [Special issue title]

Karnow, Stanley. *Vietnam: A History.* New York: Viking Press, 1983.

Karpushina, Olga. "The Military Body: Film Representations of the Chechen and Vietnam Wars." *Studies in Slavic Cultures* 3 (2002): 33–52.

Kilday, Gregg. "Oliver Stoned." *Entertainment Weekly.* January 14, 1994, 28–33.

Kinder, Donald R. and Lynn M. Sanders. *Divided by Color: Racial Politics and Democratic Ideals.* Chicago: University of Chicago Press, 1996.

Kinney, Katherine. *Friendly Fire: American Images of the Vietnam War.* New York: Oxford University Press, 2000.

Kopkind, Andrew. *"Rambo: First Blood, Part II." The Nation.* June 22, 1985, 776–77.

Kroll, Jack. "A One-Man Army." *Newsweek.* May 27, 1985. 74.

Lang, John S. "A Memorial Wall That Healed Our Wounds." *U.S. News & World Report*, November 21, 1983, 68–71.

"Loss of Spirit." *Nam Vet Newsletter* 4, No. 1 (January 7, 1990): 68.

Marchetti, G. "Class, Ideology and Commerical Television: An Analysis of *The A Team." Journal of Film and Video*, 39, no. 2 (Spring 1987): 19–29.

Marrs, Jim. *Crossfire: The Plot That Killed Kennedy.* (New York: Carroll & Graf Publishers, 1990.

"Matter of Fact." *The New Republic.* September 6, 2004, 9.

Maxwell McCombs, Donald L. Shaw, and David Weaver, eds. *Communication and Democracy: Exploring the Intellectual Frontiers in Agenda-Setting Theory.* Mahwah, NJ: Lawrence Erlbaum Associates, 1997.

McGeary, Johanna, Karen Tumulty, and Viveca Novak, "The Fog of War." *Time.* April 7, 2001. pp 24–32

McMahon, R.J. "Rationalizing Defeat: The Vietnam War in American Presidential Discourse." *Rhetoric and Public Affairs* 2, no. 4 (Winter 1999): 529–49.

Melillo, Wendy. "Bush Attorney Quits Amid Ad Flap." *Adweek Online,* August 25, 2004.

Mi Yung Yoon, "Explaining U.S. Intervention in Third World Internal Wars, 1945–1989," *Journal of Conflict Resolution,* 41, no. 4 (August 1997): 580–603.

Migdail, Carl J. "El Salvador Turning Into 'Vietnam West'" for U.S.?" *U.S. News and World Report.* February 27, 1984, 29–30.

Moore, Harold G. and Joseph L. Galloway. *We Were Soldiers Once ... And Young—Ia Drang: The Battle That Changed the War in Vietnam.* New York: Random, 1992.

Morgenthau, T. "Honoring Vietnam Veterans—At Last." *Newsweek,* November 22, 1982. 80–81.

Morrow, L. "A New Test of Resolve." *Time.* September 3, 1990, 30–33.

Morrow, Lance. "War and Remembrance: A Bit of Bitterness is Buried Along With an Unknown Soldier." *Time.* June 11, 1984, 29.

Morrow, Lance. "When Artists Distort History." *Time.* December 23, 1991, 84.

Moyer, D.D. "Editorials and Foreign Affairs in Recent Presidential Campaigns." *Journalism Quarterly* 59, no. 4 (Winter 1982): 541–547.

Muravchik, Joshua. "The Nicaraguan Debate." *Journal of Foreign Affairs* 65, no. 2 (Winter 1986/87): 366–383.

Murphy, Cullen. "Knock It Off: The Art of the Unreal." *Atlantic Monthly.* December 2004, 187–88.

Neuman, W. R., M. R. Just, and A. N. Crigler. *Common Knowledge: News and the Construction of Political Meaning.* Chicago: University of Chicago Press, 1992.

Nixon, Richard M. *No More Vietnams.* New York: Arbor House, 1985.

"No More Vietnams." *National Review.* April 1981, 403–4.

Novak, Ralph. *"The Walking Dead." People Weekly,* March 13, 1995.

O'Neill, John E. and Jerome R. Corsi. *Unfit for Command: Swift Boat Veterans Speak Out Against John Kerry.* Washington, D.C.: Regnery Publishing, 2004.

O'Sullivan, John. "No Quagmire: How to avoid one this time." *National Review.* September 1, 2003, 6–14.

Pilger, John. "Bush's Vietnam: Once More, We Hear That America Is Being 'Sucked Into a Quagmire,.'" *New Statesman.* June 23, 2003, 20–21.

Purdum, Todd S. *A Time of Our Choosing: America's War with Iraq.* New York: Times Books, 2003.

Quart, Leonard. *"The Deer Hunter:* The Superman in Vietnam." In *From Hanoi to Hollywood: The Vietnam War in American Film,* edited by Linda Dittmar and Gene Michaud, 159–68. New Brunswick: Rutgers University Press, 1990.

"*Platoon:* Vietnam was It Really Was," *Time.* January 26, 1987, 56.

Rasmussen, Karen and Sharon D. Downey. "Dialectical Disorientation in Vietnam

War Films: Subversion of the Mythology of War." *Quarterly Journal of Speech*, 77, no.2 (May 1991): 176–195.

Rather, Dan. "Statement on Memos." Press release from CBS News. September 20, 2004.

Rollins, Peter C. "The Vietnam War: Perceptions Through Literature, Film, And Television," *American Quarterly* 36 (1984): 419–432.

Rosenthal, James. "The Myth of Lost POWs: Real-Life Rambos Have No One to Rescue." *The New Republic*. July 1, 1985, 15–19.

Schaller, Michael. *Reckoning with Reagan: America and Its President in the 1980s*. New York: Oxford University Press, 1992.

Schon, Donald A. and Martin Rein. *Frame Reflection: Toward the Resolution of Intractable Policy Controversies*. New York: Basic Books, 1994.

Shaw, Donald P. and Zane E. Finkelstein. "Westmoreland vs. CBS." *Commentary* 78. no. 2 (August 1984): 31–37.

Simon, John. "Reshooting the President," *National Review*. March 2, 1992, 54–57.

Spangler, L.C. "Buddies and Pals: A History of Male Friendships on Primetime Television." In *Men, Masculinity, and the Media*, edited by S. Craig, 93–100. Newbury Park, CA: Sage Publications, 1992.

Steel, Ronald. "Mr. Smith Goes to the Twilight Zone." *The New Republic*. February 3, 1992, 30–32

"Statement by Assistant to the President for Press Relations Fitzwater on the Bill Authorizing Construction of a Women's Vietnam Veterans Memorial," (November 15, 1988) Federal Register Division. National Archives and Records Service. Public Papers of the Presidents of the United States, Ronald Reagan, 1988–1989 (Washington, D.C.: G.P.O., 1956-).

Sturken, Marita . *Tangled Memories: The Vietnam War, the AIDS Epidemic, and the Politics of Remembering*. Berkeley: University of California Press, 1997.

Sutton, David L. and J. Emmett Winn. "'Do We Get to Win This Time?': POW/MIA Films and the American Monomyth." *Journal of American and Comparative Cultures* 24, nos.1/2 (Spring 2001): 25–33.

Talbott, Stephen . "El Salvador: It Is Not Vietnam." *Time*. 22 February 22, 1982. 33–34

Templer, Robert. *Shadows and Wind: A View of Modern Vietnam*. New York: Penguin Books, 1998.

Terry, Wallace, ed. *Bloods: An Oral History of the Vietnam War*. New York: Random, 1984.

"The Week," *National Review*, June 24, 1991, 10–12.

Thompson, Mark and James Carney. "An Absence in Alabama: As Bush's Military Service Re-Emerges as an Issue, Here Is What We Know — and Don't Know." *Time*. February 16, 2004, 36.

Travers, Peter. "Oh What a Tangled Web." *Rolling Stone*. January 23, 1992.

Travers, Peter. "*We Were Soldiers*." *Rolling Stone*. March 28, 2002.

Veterans Administration document, "Attitudes Toward Vietnam Era Veterans Survey," (Washington, D.C.: Veterans Administration, July 1980).

"Vietnam Veterans Memorial: America Remembers." *National Geographic* 167.(May 1985): 552–3.

Weiss, Michael J. "Maya Ying Lin's Memorial to the Vietnam War Dead Raises Hope — And Anger." *People Weekly*, March 8, 1982. 38–39.

Welch, William M. "Vietnam Movie, *Platoon*, Draws Criticism, Praise From Vets." *Washington Dateline*,(The Associated Press), 16 January 16, 1987.

White, Susan. "Male Bonding, Hollywood Orientalism, and the Repression of the Feminine in Kubrick's *Full Metal Jacket*." In *Inventing Vietnam: The War in Film and Television, edited by* Michael Anderegg, 204–230. Philadelphia: Temple University Press, 1991.

Williams, Tony. "*Missing in Action*: The Vietnam Construction of the Movie Star." In *From Hanoi to Hollywood: The Vietnam War in American Film,* edited by Linda Dittmar and Gene Michaud, 129–144. New Brunswick: Rutgers University Press, 1990.

Yoder, A. "The News Media and One World." *Political Communication and Persuasion,* 1, no. 3 (1981): 217–230.

York, Byron. "Bush and the National Guard: Case Closed: The Facts About the President's Service." *National Review.* March 8, 2004, 33.

Zeller, J.R. *The Nature and Origins of Mass Opinion.* New York: Cambridge University Press, 1992.

Newspapers

Various issues of the following newspapers were consulted in the preparation of this book. (Specific information is cited in the text and endnotes.)

Boston Globe
Boston Herald
Chicago Sun-Times
Christian Science Monitor
Cincinnati Enquirer
Daily Variety
Dallas Morning News
Financial Times of London
National Catholic Reporter
New York Daily News

New York Times
San Francisco Chronicle
St. Louis Post-Dispatch
St. Petersburg Times
Sunday Mail
The Los Angeles Times
USA Today
Washington Post
Washington Times

Index